TROUT FISHING

REVISED EDITION

Joe Brooks

Drawings by Tom Beecham
Photographs by R. Valentine Atkinson
Fly Plates by Joseph D. Bates, Jr.

Consulting Editor: Jerry Gibbs,
Fishing Editor, *Outdoor Life* Magazine

OUTDOOR LIFE BOOKS

To Mary

Published by

Outdoor Life Books
Grolier Book Clubs, Inc.
380 Madison Avenue
New York, NY 10017

Distributed to the trade by

Stackpole Books
Cameron and Kelker Sts.
Harrisburg, PA 17105

Library of Congress Cataloging in Publication Data

Brooks, Joe, 1905–1972.
   Trout fishing.

   Includes index.
   1. Trout fishing.   I. Title.
SH687.B833 1985   799.1′755   70-178838
ISBN: 0-943822-44-0

Second Printing, 1987

Manufactured in the United States of America

CONTENTS

FOREWORD

By Jerry Gibbs
Fishing Editor, *Outdoor Life*

Since publication of the first edition of *Trout Fishing*, booming world-wide technology has altered the tackle, and therefore many of the techniques, we use in the sport of angling. Concurrently, a generation of scientifically oriented sport fishermen has reached maturity, garnering in the process invaluable knowledge that has moved us leagues ahead in the understanding of the trouts, their environment and the forage forms upon which they depend for life. Today we are rich in excellent books on specialty trout subjects, from specific water types to individual orders of insects on which trout feed.

From our current vantage point in history, then, one tends to return with certain skepticism to a work that professes to cover the entire discipline of trout fishing as sport, artform, and consuming passion. Any doubts vanish, as you will see, with a near vacuum-like suddeness that draws the reader of *Trout Fishing* irresistibly and so enjoyably from chapter to chapter. The technical fishing instructions for which one major trout fishing school chose this book as their text are still as valid as ever. The novice and intermediate angler will search long to gain as thorough an understanding of the trout fishing game as is presented here. But how fine to report that there is so much for the advanced angler as well—gems that many have long forgotten in commitment to specialization; skills that solve small technical problems that still can nag; clear discussions of fish behavior and subtleties of the sport which, due to their regional nature, only a widely traveled angler will already know. And there is much more.

Besides the facts, the techniques, the insights, one begins to see why the trouts are so much more than merely the target species of a sport. It is to Joe Brooks's lasting credit that the reader comes to understand so much of trout fishing's true meaning through this one work.

The essence of Brooks's *Trout Fishing* was never better stated than in Arnold Gingrich's 1972 review of the work.

"Beginning with the first chapter, a history of trout fishing that has to be the best job of condensation since H.G. Wells wrote *The Outline of History* in one volume, and continuing with the next, "The Trout We Fish For," which is so good it makes you almost start feeling for fins, the master angler puts his reader through the best short course of trout appreciation and understanding that our day affords."

Brooks, the master angler, has indeed told his story well.

History of Trout Fishing

1

While most historians have given credit for the first mention of fishing with a fly to the ancient writer Aelian (circa 250 A.D.), I will go along with the Englishman William Radcliffe. In his book *Fishing from Earliest Times*, published in London in 1921, Radcliffe says: "The kudos for the first mention of an artificial fly belongs, in my opinion, to Martial rather than to Aelian."

Two hundred years before Aelian, the Roman poet Martial wrote:

Who has not seen the scarus rise,
Decoyed and killed by fraudful flies.

Among his early translators there was considerable argument about the correct interpretation of the last word of the verse, whether it was derived from *mosco*, meaning moss, or *musca*, meaning fly. However, in its context, along with the qualifying adjective, I can take it only as does Radcliffe. What else can "fraudful flies" denote but the artificial?

The interesting point also arises that the only "scarus" with which we are familiar today is the family of the parrotfish, which feeds on moss and other growth on coral and rocks. I have spent endless hours casting a fly to parrotfish, both in deep water around Bermuda and on the flats in British Honduras, and have never been able to interest one, either with a fly that looked like an insect or one that might have looked like anything else. And I am convinced that these early anglers did not cast imitations of bits of moss, and that the interpretation of the word "scarus" may be as argumentative as that of the word for flies, and may apply to some other species than the parrotfish as we know it today.

However, to Aelian does indeed go full credit for the first description of the science of using a fly to catch fish. From his words, the fish may very well have been a trout.

I have heard of a Macedonian way of catching fish; between Beroea and Thessalonica runs a river called the Astraeus, and in it there are fish with speckled skins; what the natives of the country call them you had better ask the Macedonians. These fish feed on a fly peculiar to the country, which hovers on the river. It is not like flies found elsewhere, nor does it resemble a wasp in appearance, nor in shape would one justly describe it as a midge or a bee, yet it has something of each of these. In boldness it is like a fly, in size you might call it a midge, it imitates the colour of a wasp, and it hums like a bee. The natives generally call it the *Hippouros*.

These flies seek their food over the river, but do not escape the observation of the fish swimming below. When then the fish observes a fly on the surface, it swims quietly up, afraid to stir the water above, lest it should scare away its prey; then coming up by its shadow, it opens its mouth gently and gulps down the fly, like a wolf carrying off a sheep from the fold or an eagle a goose from the farmyard; having done this it goes below the rippling water.

Now though the fishermen know of this, they do not use these flies at all for bait for fish; for if a man's hand touch them, they lose their natural colour, their wings wither, and they become unfit food for the fish. For this reason they have nothing to do with them, hating them for their bad character; but they have planned a snare for the fish, and get the better of them by their fisherman's craft.

They fasten red (crimson red) wool around a hook, and fix on to the wool two feathers which grow under a cock's wattles, and which in colour are like wax. Their rod is six feet long, and their line is the same length. Then they throw their snare, and the fish, attracted and maddened by the colour, comes straight at it, thinking from the pretty sight to get a dainty mouthful; when, however, it opens its jaws, it is caught by the hook and enjoys a bitter repast, a captive.

After Aelian there is a long hiatus on the subject of fly fishing. Then in 1496 came *The Treatise of Fishing with an Angle*, written, it is believed, by Dame Juliana Berners, who was then Abbess of Sopwell, England. The Treatise was included in a new edition of *The Book of St. Albans*, first published ten years earlier, a book dealing with hunting, hawking and heraldry, and in the new edition, with fishing, in a day when these sports were a part of the training of every young gentleman.

Dame Juliana gave timeless advice on angling and admonitions on stream behavior which are still basic:

> The biting time is early in the morning from four until eight; in the afternoon, from four until eight, but this is not so good as in the morning. And if there is a cold, whistling wind and it be a dark, lowering day, then the fish will usually bite all day. For a dark day is much better than any other clear weather.

Her rules of conduct, if succeeding generations had heeded them, might have saved us many a crisis, and might still do so.

> I charge you, that you break no man's hedges in going about your sports, nor open any man's gates without shutting them again. Also, you must not use this aforesaid artful sport for covetousness, merely for the increasing or saving of your money, but mainly for your enjoyment and to procure the health of your body and more especially, of your soul. For when you intend to go to your amusements in fishing, you will not want very many persons with you, who might hinder you in your pastime. And then you can serve God devoutly by earnestly saying your customary prayers. And in so doing, you will eschew and avoid

many vices, such as idleness, which is the principal cause inciting a man to many other vices, as is right well known. Also, you must not be too greedy in catching your said game (the fish is meant here) as in taking too much at one time, a thing which can easily happen if you do in every point as this present treatise shows you. That could easily be the occasion of destroying your own sport and other men's also. When you have a sufficient mess, you should covet no more at that time. Also you should busy yourself to nourish the game in everything that you can, and to destroy all such things as are devourers of it. And all those that do according to this rule will have the blessing of God and St. Peter. That blessing, may he grant who bought us with his precious blood.

Dame Juliana's complete descriptions of tackle and technique make it clear that fly fishing was highly developed by that era. Sometime between Aelian and Dame Juliana, anglers had discovered that a long, limber rod was helpful both in placing the fly and in absorbing the shock of the lunges of the fish. Rods of the day were often eighteen feet in length and made to demanding specifications, of willow, hazel, aspen, sometimes the middle part of green hazel and the upper section of blackthorn, crabtree, medlar or juniper, and the entire rod carefully tapered.

Horsehair was the material used for lines, according to Dame Juliana's instructions:

> First you must take, from the tail of a white horse, the longest and best hair that you can find; and the rounder it is, the better it is. Divide it into six bunches, and you must colour every part by itself in a different colour, such as yellow, green, brown, tawny, russet and dusky colours.

She even provides the recipes for the dyes, including such exotics as verdigris, ale, essence of walnut leaves and tanner's ooze; and recommends certain hues to match the color of the water or of the growth within the water—surely literature's first description of the camouflaged line.

This, along with her list of the dressings of twelve flies for trout, which twelve, occasionally tied in slightly varied form, are commonly used today, provide evidence indeed that fly fishing has, from earliest times, taken men's hearts and occupied their minds to a degree known in few other sports.

From Dame Juliana's time on, apparently many writers were dealing with the subject of fishing. I have a copy of Leonard Mascall's *A Booke of Fishing with Hook and Line* published in 1590. In 1600 John Taverner came out with *Certaine Experiments Concerning Fish and Fruite,* more of a naturalist's book, with mention of fishing. In 1613 the poet John Dennys published *Secrets of Angling* in verse. And that same year there appeared Gervase Markham's *The English Husbandman.* In this first edition he did not mention fishing, but to the second edition, only the following year, he appended a "Discourse of The General Art of Fishing with the Angle or Otherwise: and of All the Hidden Secrets Belonging Thereunto."

Markham makes what may well be the first mention of artificial flies "moved upon the waters" to attract trout.

From his writings it is also apparent that at this time rods could be purchased in nearly every haberdashery shop.

In 1653 appeared the first edition of *The Compleat Angler* by Izaak Walton. Although regarded as the patron saint of fly fishermen, actually Walton fished with and wrote mostly about bait. Regardless of his approach to the sport, his words express the very spirit of fly fishing:

> No life so happy and so pleasant as the life of a well governed angler, for when the lawyer is swallowed up in business and the statesman is preventing or contriving plots, there we sit on cowslip banks, hear the birds sing, and possess ourselves in as much quietness as these silent silver streams which we now see glide so quietly by us. Indeed, we may say of angling as Dr. Boteler said of strawberries: "Doubtless God could have made a better berry, but doubtless God never did"; and so (if I may be the judge) God never did make a more calm, quiet, innocent recreation than angling.

Walton's writings were so popular that the book went into four editions. Meantime, in 1655, two years after the publication of the first edition, Walton had met Charles Cotton, who lived at Beresford on the Dove River. As a gentleman of the day, he was well-trained in hunting and fishing. He and Walton became fast friends and companions of many a fishing jaunt, to the point that they came to regard each other in a father-and-son relationship. As a result of their many hours of fishing together, Walton asked Cotton to write a section on fly fishing for the fifth edition of the *Compleat Angler*, published in 1676. This appears as Part II, entitled "Instructions How to Angle for a Trout or Grayling in a Clear Stream."

Walton had found the right man for the job. So successful was their joint effort that at one period the fifth edition was touted as the third best seller in the English language, surpassed only by the Bible and *Pilgrim's Progress*.

In 1963 I made a pilgrimage to the Dove to see the Fishing-House that Cotton built there on a bend of the river, and above whose door the initials of the two friends are entwined, in cipher, over the inscription *Piscatoribus sacrum*, 1674. In years past the hut had fallen into some disrepair, but in 1953 the property was purchased and restored by W.H. Collings and his son Norman. When I visited the Dove the scene was much as it must have been in Cotton's and Walton's times, even to the round stone table beside the Fishing-House, in a circle of guardian trees that Cotton planted, to form what he called his "outdoor dining room."

Trout still swim in the Dove, and as I stood by the table I could

Izaak Walton

visualize Cotton sitting there writing, his rod set up and leaning on the far side of the table. Facing the Dove, only seventy-five feet away, he was sure to see a trout rise, and all he had to do was put down his pen and pick up his rod, and go in low, staying well back from the water, and make his cast.

I went down there and caught several trout, brownies all. And later, further downstream, I made a cast over the historic Pike Pool, and there in the shadows, by the glooming pike of rock that gives the pool its name, I seemed to see a long fly rod sweep out over the water ahead of me, and fancied I saw the rise, and the jump as a good trout came clean in an effort to throw the hook. In the soft breeze I thought I could hear an ancient angler murmur, "It takes a fine and far away cast to get them to strike here."

It has been reported that Cotton had only ten days in which to produce his part of the book, yet in it he encompasses practically every

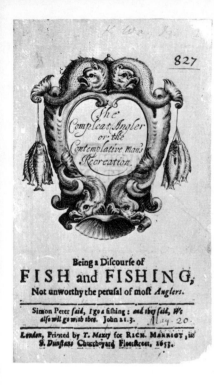

Frontispiece of the first edition of *The Compleat Angler*, from a copy in the British Museum.

Fishing was part of a gentleman's training in Walton's time. The "Angler's Song," reproduced from a copy of *The Compleat Angler*, was double-printed so anglers could stand facing each other and read the score as they sang.

phase of fly fishing of his times. His memories give evidence of long years on the stream, and he was clearly an expert tyer of flies and an accomplished wielder of the rod. His advice, "Fish fine and far off is the principle rule for trout angling," is still the prime recommendation to any trouter today. What more pertinent instruction can you give than that embodied in a conversation between two characters in his writings:

VIATOR: Did you see that, sir?

PISCATOR: Yes, I saw the fish; and he saw you too, which made him turn short. You must fish further off, if you intend to have any sport here.

And again:

PISCATOR: Why now, let me tell you you lost that fish by your own fault, and through your own eagerness and haste; for you are never to offer to strike a good fish, if he do not strike himself, till you first see him turn his head after he has taken your fly, and then you can never strain your tackle in the striking, if you strike with any manner of moderation.

Cotton recommended certain flies for different times of the year, two for January, eight for February, seven for March, seven for April, sixteen for May, twelve for June, seven for July, four for August, two for September—sixty-five in all. For October he suggests that the fly fisherman use the same patterns as for March; for November, the same as for February. And adds a final touch, surely learned only after many years of experimenting, trying and proving on the stream:

In December "few men angle with the fly this month, no more than they do in January. Yet if the weather be warm, then a brown that looks red in the hand and yellowish betwixt your eye and the sun; will both raise and kill in clear water, and free from snow and broth; but at the best 'tis hardly worth a man's labour."

Cotton's rod was sixteen to eighteen feet in length, the line five or six feet longer, and although dry-fly fishing as we know it came much later, he was obviously on its track. "Fly fishing or fishing at the top, is, as I said before, of two sorts; with a natural and living fly, or with an artificial and made fly."

He used a single fly and recommended dropping it as lightly as possible, and with as little line on the water as could be contrived. And of this single fly he says that "on a bright day it must be a little fly, and a very little one, too, that must do your business." Obviously matching a hatch.

While Dame Juliana Berners led him in the description of a camouflaged line, I believe that Cotton was the first to tell how to make a tapered line. The line he describes is what we call a single taper, the heaviest part being at the rod, the finest towards the fish. The leader and tippet as we know it was not used, the line being tied directly to the fly, and therefore the end of line was tapered as finely as the angler dared.

Working from the light end, where the fly was tied, back towards the rod, Cotton advises, "Two of the first lengths nearest the hook should be two hairs (horsehairs) apiece, the next three lengths above them of three, the next three above them of four, and so on through five, six and seven, to the very top. By which means your rod and tackle will in a manner be tapered from your very hand to your hook, your line will fall much better and straighten and cast your fly to any certain place to which the hand and eye shall direct it, with less weight and violence, than would otherwise circle the water, and fright away the fish."

In the present day of strong nylon and such synthetics, it might appear that Cotton is making a strong statement when he writes: "He that cannot kill a trout of twenty inches with two hairs in a river clear of wood and weeds deserves not the name of angler." But a few years ago while considering this apparently light tippet, I decided to make some experiments. I wrote a good fishing friend, Len Kinkie, of Emigrant Peak Ranch, in Pray, Montana, and enlisted his aid.

"Will you ask your son Richard to run down to the pasture and pull

This engraving from the 1900 edition of *The Compleat Angler* shows Walton and a friend, identified as his "scholar," landing a trout on a fly.

a few hairs from the tails of your horses, white hairs would be best," I said, "and round ones. Then I would appreciate it if you will test them on your scales for the breaking strength."

Len's comments were enlightening.

"There's a lot of leeway in horsehair," he said. "We fooled with several double and single strands and found that the average breaking point of the single hair was 2½ pounds. One broke only when we put a 3½-pound pull on it. This same hair stood up to 7 pounds pulled, when doubled. I'd say that the average breaking point of the double hairs we tested was about 5 pounds."

So while horsehair sounds flimsy, Cotton and the anglers of his day were actually using a five-pound-test tippet (with two hairs) which is the equivalent of today's 3X nylon tippet material. Nevertheless, they did very well indeed to land their trout when you consider the short line they were using, and the lack of a reel.

A contemporary of Walton, Colonel Robert Venables, published a book called *The Experienced Angler* in 1662, in which he speaks of mayflies and of fishing both up and downstream. It appears that Venables was quite accustomed to upstream fishing, but preferred to throw a long line downstream, because he thought that an angler casting upstream lined the trout and that it was difficult to control the line coming fast down the current—a situation we are more easily able to overcome, of course, with modern tackle.

Venables's work was incorporated with Cotton's and Walton's in the fifth edition of the *Compleat Angler* in 1676, this being the last edition during Walton's lifetime. After that edition, however, Venables's contribution was dropped as too unlike the writing of the other pair.

There were undoubtedly numerous other authors writing about fishing at the time, and as always, a little professional jealousy shows. In his *Northern Memoirs,* published in 1685, Richard Franck accuses Walton of "scribbling and transcribing other men's notions."

As mentioned earlier, the first fly fishermen did not use a reel. The line, only six feet in length, was tied to the end of the long rod, often eighteen feet, and no doubt the angler merely dapped with this gear. Later anglers went to longer lines, about the length of the rod—in fact, the recommendation was usually "not longer than the rod." With these they had a little more leeway but it was still a game of tug of war, with no means of give and take. A fish undoubtedly had to be heaved out on the bank as best the short-lined angler could manage.

In all my reading of ancient writings on fly fishing I have not been able to put my finger on the angler who first came up with the idea of a contrivance fastened to the rod, and on which line could be stored, fed out and retrieved, as desired. Some writers refer to *The Art of Angling,* published in 1651 by Thomas Barker, in which he claims to have invented a "wind" which he used in trout fishing. And in his *Compleat Angler* Walton says: ". . . some use a wheel about the middle of their rod, or near the hand . . ." but it is probable that this applied to Atlantic salmon fishing, as elsewhere both Walton and Cotton speak of the line connected to the end of the rod in trout fishing.

Certainly by the time Best produced *The Art of Angling*, published in 1787, reels were in general use for various kinds of fishing, and therefore probably for fly fishing. And finally, in *The Complete Angler's Vade Mecum*, published by Williamson in 1808, the author speaks of a reel, or more correctly a winch, capable of winding in line; although not of releasing it as we do when we cast with a modern fly reel.

Alfred Ronalds's *The Fly Fisher's Entomology*, published in 1836, marks the beginning of the scientific spirit among trout anglers. Ronalds did his work so well that his book is still a standard reference.

Not long after, in 1841, there appeared *The Vade-Mecum of Fly-Fishing for Trout*, by G.P.R. Pulman, which was so successful that it was re-written and greatly enlarged. In its third edition in 1850, the author mentions using a fly that is "wet and heavy" and the line "has a certain weight," and observes that they sink below the rising fish. He says, "Let a DRY fly be substituted"—and I believe this is the first mention of a dry fly—"for the wet one, the line switched a few times through the air to throw off its superabundant moisture, a judicious cast made just above a rising fish, then the fly allowed to float towards and over them, and the chances are ten to one that it will be seized as readily as a living insect. This dry fly we would remark should be an imitation of the natural fly on which the fish are feeding because, if widely different, the fish, instead of being allured, would most likely be SUR-PRISED AND STARTLED at the novelty presented, and would suspend feeding until the appearance of their favourite and familiar prey."

Some thirteen years later, in his third edition of another publication, *The Book of the Axe*, Pulman mentions again his "line switching" in the air and describes false casting to dry the fly so it will float down over a trout.

In a book written in 1879, James Ogden claims to have used floating lines some forty years previously, which brings us back to 1839, but there is no mention of false casting to dry the fly.

Among the first advocates of a shorter and lighter rod was W.C. Stewart, whose *Practical Angler*, published in 1857, went into three editions before the year was out. Stewart was convinced that the proper approach to a trout with a fly was by casting upstream, where you would not be seen so easily by the fish. The shorter, lighter rod, he felt, made for better casting and delivery, and he covered the water with his flies in this way, fishing first straight upstream, then moving the fly across the current until it was lighting opposite him.

In *A Book on Angling*, published in 1876, in London, Francis Francis treats various kinds of fishing, and fish; and with regard to trout he speaks of both the wet and the dry fly, stating that the latter is used mostly in the south. He admonishes the fisherman to "not line the fish" in casting; and says "the less force the better." He urges the young angler to practice. He advises that the fly fisher should cast upstream or across stream, and even goes so far as to say that fishing a fly downstream is not fly fishing. And he remarks that fly fishing "is creeping northward" and that more anglers are studying the fly that is "up" and trying for imitations.

One of the greatest contributors to dry-fly fishing lore was Frederick M. Halford (1844-1910). He wrote *Floating Flies* (1886), *Dry Fly Fishing in Theory and Practise* (1889), *Dry Fly Entomology* (1879) and *Making a Fishery* (1902). So complete was his work that William Senior, the renowned "Red Spinner," wrote in 1903: "The Halford series embodies all that can be told for the present of the mysteries of dry fly fishing."

Halford was more than a little dogmatic, holding that the dry fly was the sole way to fish, especially on the chalk streams. And such was his influence that he soon built up a following who would only fish on top. His come-uppance was served him later when G.E.M. Skues published his *Minor Tactics of the Chalk Stream* in 1910, showing that the wet fly or the nymph would take trout from those slick waters even when dries went hitless.

An ad for a 10-foot dry-fly rod made to the specifications of Frederic M. Halford, an English pioneer of the sport. This advertisement appeared in the 1897 edition of Halford's *Dry Fly Entomology*. Hardy Brothers is still manufacturing fly fishing tackle.

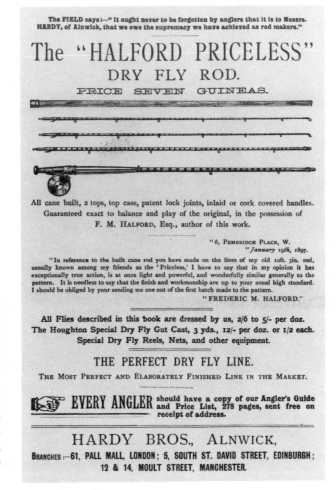

Skues put forth his arguments so vividly that it was not long before he, too, had a following, thoroughly convinced that there are, indeed, other ways to take a trout than on a dry fly. His presentation is so logical that *Minor Tactics*, as well as his later *The Way of a Trout With a Fly, Sidelines, Side Lights and Reflections*, and *Nymph Fishing for Chalk Stream Trout*, all proved to be best sellers and are still guidebooks for the trouter.

Published in 1894, a book called *Walton and Some Earlier Writers on Fish and Fishing*, by R.B. Marston, is full of information about Walton, Cotton, and such early figures as Dame Juliana Berners, Leonard Mascall, John Dennys, Gervase Markham, and also goes deeply into the book, *The Compleat Angler*.

Along the same lines is *A History of Fly Fishing for Trout*, first published in 1921 by John Waller Hills, one of England's fine anglers and fishing writers. Hills mentions that there was some record of fly fishing prior to the good Dame Juliana, but concedes that the true history of the sport started with her. Hills also wrote a book, *William James Lunn, River Keeper*, about the first water keeper for the famous Houghton

Fly fishing for trout became a popular sport in England during the late 19th century; the long rod remained standard equipment.

Club on the Test River; and in 1922 he came out with *A Summer on the Test*, a wonderful book, full of information on chalk stream fishing in England.

Equally well done, and in the same vein, and fascinating to those who like to read trout lore was *Notable Angling Literature*, by James Robb, L.L.D., covering fishing writers up until 1900.

Also early in the 1900s, there appeared two books by an English writer-photographer. In his *Marvels of Fish Life, as Revealed by the Camera*, published in 1911, Francis Ward writes of various fishes, and his words on trout and their environment are worthy of any angler's perusal. The book was published by Cassell and Company, Ltd. of London; and the same company came out with his *Animal Life Under Water* in 1919. In his chapter "The Angler and His Lures," he brings up many fine points about how a trout sees the fly and the angler, how the fly appears as it nears and then comes into its "window" (*see* DRY FLY) and reasons that, while the trout might not see an angler when he is beyond this circular window, he could, and often does, see him as he comes up into the wind to take the fly. This is a very well-written and lucid bit of trout fishing lore, well illustrated with views from beneath the surface.

Another English writer of the early 1900 era was Eric Taverner, author of *Trout Fishing from All Angles*, published in 1929, which to my mind is just about the most all-encompassing writing on trout fishing. He also wrote other books about trout fishing, one notable one being *Divers Ways to Tackle Trout*.

Of especial interest to those of us who have ever had the sport of going for that great adversary the European sea trout, *Salmo trutta*, is a book which was written by G. Herbert Nall, and published in 1930 in London, by Seeley, Service & Co. Ltd. under the title *The Life of the Sea Trout*. As Nall was of a scientific turn of mind, his research is detailed, and he has turned out a complete and authentic study of this fish.

Of much later date is John Goddard's *Trout Fly Recognition*, published in 1966 in London by A. & C. Black, Ltd. It is full of fine color pictures of the nymphs, duns and spinners of the different orders; along with suggested artificials to match; and with an Appendix of Artificial Flies by John Veniard.

And yet another English book I have much enjoyed is A. Courtney Williams's *A Dictionary of Trout Flies*, which includes patterns for sea trout and grayling. This book has 149 flies illustrated in color, and lists some 400 dressings of flies. The book was first published in 1949 as *Trout Flies: a Discussion and a Dictionary;* and has gone through several editions, the fourth appearing in 1965 under the current title.

Still another prolific English writer was C.F. Walker, who lived in Sussex, England, and whose works included the editing of G.E.M. Skues's *Angling Letters;* as well as his own *Brown Trout and the Dry Fly, Riverside Reflections, Chalk Stream Flies,* and *The Art of Chalk Stream Fish-*

In this 1879 Currier & Ives print, two American fly fishermen are depicted in a comical situation. In those days before creel limits and stocking, anglers caught incredible numbers of native trout.

ing. This last was published in the United States, in 1968, by Stackpole Books, Harrisburg, Pennsylvania.

Meantime, fly fishermen had begun to drop their flies on North American waters and it was only a matter of time until the New World would produce its own literature on the sport of fly fishing. In the *American Angler's Guide*, published by D. Appleton in 1849, John J. Brown comments, "The artificial fly, so much used in England, finds but little favor in this country, not because it is not as good a bait, but because more skill is required in using it."

He goes on to say, ". . . while the more experienced sportsman from foreign parts will astonish the native by his dexterity in throwing the fly and killing an almost incredible number of fish, where the unbeliever regards the fly as a useless article of tackle . . . but the skill necessary to success in this branch of the subject, is not so great as the novice imagines."

He further adds that "there are hundreds of good fly anglers, and many that can throw a fly with the most experienced in Europe."

Brown reports that ". . . the short one-handed rod, from ten to twelve feet in length, is most common in use. Attached to the rod should be a reel, containing thirty to fifty yards of hair, grass, silk, or silk and hair line, the latter description should be used if it can be procured, tapering from the tenth of an inch almost to a point; to this should be attached a leader of from one to two yards in length; and finally your fly, on a light length of gut; if you wish to use two or three flies, place them on your leader or short gut, about twenty-four inches apart."

In *Fish and Fishing,* written by Henry William Herbert, under the pen name Frank Forrester, and published in 1850 by Stringer and Townsend of New York, it is obvious that early anglers were keenly interested in the species of trout they found in the New World. The brown trout had not yet been imported, but Herbert mentions the various other trouts, and also mentions the Arctic grayling, which he calls Back's grayling, and typifies as native to the waters flowing into Great Slave Lake. (He seemed to think that there were no grayling within the confines of the United States.) Herbert's identification of the Arctic grayling by Back's name intrigued me, because in G. Brown Goode's *American Fishing* (1887) Back is described as the first man to catch one of these fish on an artificial fly. I first encountered information about Back when studying the history of Great Slave Lake, and while there in 1970 I caught many of the grayling named for him.

Herbert also mentions the salmon trout and gives the other names of sea trout and white trout, plus the correct scientific name of *Salmo trutta*—the sea trout of Europe. He says that they are found nowhere on the continent of America except on the eastern side of the Province of New Brunswick and the Gulf of St. Lawrence.

That trout fishing with a fly was of increasing interest to North Americans was shown by the continued appearance of new books on the subject. *The American Angler's Book,* by Thaddeus Norris, first published in 1864, gives a fine account of trout fishing, including instructions on how to cast a fly and how to handle a fly on the water. ". . . the angler should not cast at random over the water, but each portion of it should be carefully fished, the nearest first."

Another writer of the middle 1800s was Genio C. Scott, whose book *Fishing in American Waters* was published in 1869 by Harper & Brothers. In Part II of his book he writes: "To cast a fly gracefully, so that it will fall in the right place like a snow flake, or light like a winged insect, requires practice. So soon as the angler learns to lay out thirty feet of line straight, without a bend from the tip of his rod, he may count himself a fly-fisher!"—a point a lot of us might remember today as we try to heave out extra-long casts.

Scott does not actually mention a dry fly, although he does speak often of trout rising and says, "And as a floating lure is better than a sinking one, the fly-tyers prefer such floating hairs as those from hog's ears, seals, bears, the South American fox, otter, etc." While he does not actually call a dry fly by that name, he describes what must have been dry-fly fishing on the Rapid River, half a mile below Middle Dam

American fly fisherman lands a ''double'' on a brace of wet flies in this 1883 print. Wet flies were preferred by Americans until the 1890s, when Theodore Gordon helped to popularize the English style of dry-fly fishing.

Camp, in Maine. He tried and failed to take trout there with his flies, much to the amusement of some other anglers. Then he sat down on the dam and saw "a trout rise gracefully and swallow an ash-colored midge which had floated down from the dam." He saw a cloud of drab ephemera swarming over the dam, and ". . . ever and anon, as one fell on the water, a trout rose very gracefully and swallowed it."

Scott searched for an ash midge. He soon found one and the first cast he made with it he hooked and landed a 3-pound trout. He landed five in all and played two more that came off the hook. His final comment, in the face of those formerly scoffing onlookers: "I felt satisfied."

In his book *Fishing with the Fly*, published in 1883, Charles F. Orvis includes contributions by a large cast of angler-writers. The book includes such now-famous names as Charles Hallock, Henry P. Wells, Seth Green, W.C. Prime, R.B. Roosevelt, Dr. James Henshall, and Dr. C.J. Kenworthy.

In 1892 another such book was published by Rand, McNally & Company, with an introduction by A.M. Cheney. It includes chapters on The Brook Trout, Trouting in Nipigon, The Rocky Mountain Trout, The Grayling. In the last chapter, William C. Harris, editor of *The American Angler*, speaks of fishing the Gallatin, Madison and Jefferson rivers in Montana for grayling, using a Brown Hackle and a Coachman, and having such good fishing that at the end of half an hour he was "sated."

Meantime, in the late 1800s, Theodore Gordon had appeared on the angling scene. Throughout most of his life Gordon was a sick man and had retreated to the mountains of New York State for his health. There he discovered the charms of the Neversink River, and of fly fishing. He was in correspondence with both Halford and Skues in England, and in 1890 Halford sent him some sample English dry flies. Gordon studied them and went on to design his own patterns to match the aquatic hatches of the Neversink, and his Quill Gordon dry fly is still used and always will be.

While Gordon was primarily a dry-fly man, he also fished other types of flies. His Bumblepuppy was described as "breathing" as it was retrieved in short jerks, just as we handle our bucktails and streamers today.

When Gordon died in 1915 he left behind him the basis for many of the developments which have followed on the American scene, and he has taken his place as the father of American fly fishing. Unfortunately the manuscript of a book he had been writing was lost, so we have no record of this kind of his work.

One of the first North American books to deal with fly fishing in a technical way was written by Emlyn M. Gill, and published by Charles Scribner's Sons in 1912. In his *Practical Dry-Fly Fishing*, Gill takes the reader through the English dry fly to the American, and states that up to that time no fly-fishing entomology had been developed here.

He describes upstream fishing with a dry fly, and tells how to overcome drag, stalk a trout from behind, and all in all, gives a very complete work on dry-fly fishing. He speaks often of George M.L. LaBranche, whom he knew well.

"I should be lacking in all ordinary instincts of courtesy if I did not mention my friend, Mr. George M.L. LaBranche, in the author's opinion one of the very best all-around American anglers, and the most expert of American dry-fly fishermen. I have been on streams with him, and when watching his work have seen by far the most skillful handling of the fly that has ever come under my observation in an experience of thirty-eight years as an enthusiastic fly-fisherman."

George M.L. LaBranche himself published *The Dry Fly in Fast Water* in 1914, very clear evidence of the truth of Gill's claims for him. It was my good fortune to meet LaBranche in the later years of his life, when I lived at Islamorada on the Florida Keys and LaBranche had a winter home nearby. I was with him on the day when he went out to make his first try for a bonefish on a fly, and at the age of eighty he proved himself still the expert caster Gill had known. When the guide put him in position to cast to the bonefish, that elusive, unpredictable, highly nervous swimmer of the shallow salt flats, LaBranche made one false cast, and dropped his fly right on the spot, a couple of inches from the fish's nose, and had him.

In the early 1930s, Edward R. Hewitt, another angler who did his research on the Neversink, produced much fine writing on the technique of fly fishing for trout, including two outstanding books, *Better Trout Streams* and *Telling on the Trout*. In 1935 he wrote an article for *Spur* magazine called "*Butterfly Fishing,*" which gave dry-fly anglers a new way of getting hits from big trout (*see* DRY-FLY FISHING). Hewitt also did a lot of work on nymphs and how to fish them, and came up with the flat-bodied nymph patterns which have been so successful. And he invented the bivisible flies, tied so that he, as well as the fish, could see them.

The late Eugene V. Connett III, in his writings, shows the trend of the American angler-writer towards a scientific approach to how to fool the trout. In his introduction to *My Friend the Trout*, published by Van Nostrand Co., Princeton, New Jersey, in 1961, one of the greatest books on trout that I have ever read, he says, "I am satisfied that nothing can take the place of a real knowledge of the trout we fish for—how they live, how they see, what makes them do what they do when they do it."

This book and his earlier ones, *Any Luck?*, published by Windward House in 1933, and *Random Casts*, a Derrydale Press publication, dated 1939, the latter a collector's item, are packed with his great knowledge of trout and how to fish for them. He gives the best description I have ever found of the "window" through which the trout looks at things floating on the surface, and the mirror effect of the underwater surface outside that window, and the blind spots in the trout's vision.

Like all good writers who take the scientific approach to the game, Connett had been in touch with the English writers of his day. One time when I was browsing through a rare-book store in England, I spotted a copy of *Random Casts*, the Derrydale Press book mentioned above, which is long out of print, and very difficult to obtain. I opened it, and there on the fly leaf, in Connett's own writing, I read:

To G.E.M. Skues
> In appreciation for the many valuable lessons I have learned from his delightful writings.
>
> Sincerely,
> *Eugene V. Connett*

Needless to say, I added it to my own library.

One book that I have also found very worth reading is *An Angler's Entomology*, by J.R. Harris, published in this country by the Countryman Press of Woodstock, Vermont, which, however, is one of those irritating publications with no date. It provides good material for the angler-naturalist in his approach to the insect life of the stream.

Of special interest to those who fish the eastern parts of the United States is *A Book of Trout Flies*, by Preston J. Jennings, published in 1935 by Crown Press. It is mostly concerned with the naturals and matching artificials of the East. Full of good information, it is obviously derived from years of study and is illustrated with fine color plates.

Outstanding from the early 1930s to 1959 was the work of Ray Bergman, Fishing Editor of *Outdoor Life* magazine for twenty-six years. He covered the trout fishing scene from coast to coast, always watching for new things to aid the novice fisherman. His book *Just Fishing*, published in 1932, and *Trout*, published in 1939, have been best sellers ever since they first appeared. The latter, now in its seventh printing, has seldom been surpassed for the information contained and for the fine illustrations of flies.

It was on American streams that fly casting as an art in itself began to assume a place of special importance. Perhaps this was because North American rivers usually ran through wilder country than did those of Europe. Getting into position to place the fly, moving upstream where banks were not passable, and the speed and force of the current all put more demands on the caster's skill in handling the rod and line. While Europeans continued to sweep the streams with long rods and a comparatively short length of line, American anglers began to move towards shorter rods and fly presentation based on increased casting skill. The ultimate outcome of this is seen today. Lee Wulff, one of our great modern fly casters, pioneered the short fly rod, 6 to 6½ feet, and popularized it to the point that today hundreds of anglers go for trout and have great fun with the tiny fly rod. Wulff's famous hairwing flies, the Royal Wulff, the Brown Wulff, the Grizzly Wulff, the White Wulff, and the Gray Wulff have also become an integral part of the trout fishing scene wherever the flyman goes.

Another great fly caster and author, John Alden Knight, inventor of the Solunar Tables, published *The Modern Angler* in 1936, and later his *Theory and Technique of Fresh Water Angling*, in which he expounds the principle of free wrist movement in modern casting, and in other ways added to our knowledge of trout and how to take them.

Just as the bulk of fishing literature dealing with trout came from the chalk stream area of England, so the bulk of modern writing about trout fishing in the Western Hemisphere and about the design of flies has come from a part of the United States in which there are waters uniquely suitable for trout. The State of Pennsylvania has produced probably more outstanding fly fishermen and more writers about fly fishing for trout than any other part of North America. Surely tops among these works is *A Modern Dry Fly Code*, by Vince Marinaro, first published in 1950, and republished in 1969 (*see* FLIES). This book, describing the experiences and inventions of the author and his friend Charles K. Fox, as they fished the Letort River near Carlisle, is certainly the single greatest addition to American trout fishing writing that has ever been made.

Charles Fox, himself, has also produced two fine books, *The Wonderful World of Trout*, published in 1953; and *Rising Trout*, published in 1967.

The trend among these Pennsylvania fly fishermen was towards the tying of flies, and among the great naturalists who worked on them was Charles M. Wetzel, often called The American Halford. Wetzel authored *Practical Fly Fishing, The Art of Fly Tying*, and *American Fishing Books*. The results of many years of scientific study and artful fishing of flies is given in his *Trout Flies, Naturals and Imitations*, published by Stackpole Co., of Harrisburg, in 1955.

In 1951 the same company issued *The Lure and Lore of Trout Fishing*, by Alvin Grove, Jr., Professor of Botany at Pennsylvania State College. Along with his friend, George Harvey, an expert fly caster, tyer and angler, he has fished almost every stream in Pennsylvania, and the book is crammed with information on his fishing.

Meantime, in other eastern areas, the same era had produced a number of outstanding anglers and writers on the subject of trout and trout flies. In 1947, Art Flick of West Kill, New York, came out with his *Streamside Guide to Naturals and Their Imitations*, published by G.P. Putnam's Sons of New York. This is a bible for eastern tyers and anglers, and in 1969 the book was revised and republished by Crown Publishing Co., with additional information and fine color photos. Flick includes a chart of Natural and Artificial Flies, showing the common name and the scientific name, a description of the natural, the emergence time, the nymph imitation and the hook size, a great aid to newcomers to the scene.

The year 1947 was also marked by the publication by Charles Scribner's Sons of *The Complete Fly Fisherman*, by Fortune Editor John

McDonald of New York. The book presents a masterful compilation of the notes and letters of Theodore Gordon, including much material that might easily have been lost. In 1968, McDonald made a present of the rights to *The Complete Fly Fisherman* to the Theodore Gordon Fly Fishers of New York, and it has been revised and reprinted by that organization with a preface by the late Arnold Gingrich.

Gingrich—founding publisher of *Esquire* magazine—was the author of a fine book, *The Well Tempered Angler*, published by Alfred A. Knopf in 1965. He contributed the ''Literature of Angling'' for McClane's *Standard Fishing Encyclopedia* and edited and wrote an introduction for the *Gordon Garland*, published by the Theodore Gordon Fly Fishers.

A midwesterner came on the scene in 1951 when Stackpole and Heck, Inc., of Harrisburg, Pennsylvania, published *Fishing Flies and Fly Tying*, by William F. Blades, certainly one of the best books dealing with American insects and their imitations. And Ernest Schwiebert of Princeton, New Jersey, made a big contribution with his *Matching the Hatch*, published by Macmillan in 1955, a fine book of great importance to everyone interested in aquatic insects. It was followed in 1973 by *Nymphs*, published by Winchester Press, one of the more comprehensive works on the subject.

In 1960, A.S. Barnes of New York published *The Fisherman's Handbook of Trout Flies*, by Donald DuBois, an information-packed book that lists six thousand patterns and gives a simplified system for identification. He also provides instructions on tying the patterns.

Fishing from Top to Bottom, by Sid Gordon, a trout fishing technologist in Wisconsin and Michigan reputed to be able to catch fish when no one else could, was published by the Stackpole Company in 1955. It presents information on trout, their waters, their food, how they take it, as well as abundant data on flies and their uses. It is a very informative volume from which both beginner and expert can pick up valuable tips.

Many others, whose interests have varied from the study of the natural insects we imitate, to the development of fine trouting techniques, to the writing of books about these arts, are all too casually glossed over here, in the interest of getting the past down. Joseph D. Bates, Jr. of Longmeadow, Massachusetts, deserves full recognition for his writings about the modern fly scene. Bates's book *Streamer Fly Fishing* was first published in 1950, including information on how to fish streamers and bucktails, and providing details of the tackle required for casting these flies. In 1966 the book was revised and republished under the title *Streamer Fly Tying and Fishing*, with an enlarged list of flies and directions on how to tie them; the whole providing probably the greatest collection of patterns for streamers and bucktails ever assembled.

Al McClane, of Palm Beach, Florida, one of the best fishing writers in the United States, produced his *Practical Fly Fishing* in 1953, published by Prentice-Hall. And in 1965 he came out with the monumental *McClane's Standard Fishing Encyclopedia*, which contains within its covers a world of information on all the trouts and how to fly fish for them.

An important book, especially for beginners in the fly-fishing field, is *Simplified Fly Fishing*, by Sam Slaymaker II, published by Harper & Row in 1969. This is a valuable book for anyone learning to cast, removing, as it does, a lot of the old mysteries from the art, and making it possible to learn to lay out a respectable cast within a short time, with a little practice.

An historic American trout stream in the Midwest was the scene of research for the theories expounded in the latest addition, as of this writing, to the art of fly tying. Dr. Carl Richards, a dentist, and Douglas Swisher, a plastic salesman, both of Rockford, Illinois, did all of their initial work and experimentation on Michigan's Ausable River, once one of the truly great trout streams of North America; and they have come up with the no-hackle dry fly, an important and purely American invention (*see* FLIES). Besides the fascinating story of their development of the no-hackle fly pattern, these angler-entomologists tell about many other patterns and describe many interesting and scarcely known hatches and suggest flies to match them. This book outlines the most significant advance in dry-fly and nymph fishing for trout in many years.

I cannot close a discussion of trout fishing literature without mention of a few of the writers whose works have appeared "down under," in Australia, where trout were introduced many years ago. One of the most interesting books I have read about this part of the world is *Trout and Fly in Tasmania*, published in 1938 by Angus & Robertson, Ltd., Sydney, Australia. The book was written by R.H. Wigram, one of the earliest flymen and writers in Tasmania, and his chapter on the fantastic "Shannon Rise" brings sadness to the trout fisherman's heart. This was a rise of the snowflake caddis, which when the time is right hatches on the surface in such quantity that the far bank is obscured. The female, Wigram says, seldom even makes it into the air; as she emerges she is set upon by hordes of males and forced down into the stream, living only long enough to release the fertile eggs before she is eaten by the trout or drowned. The female is bigger than the male and when she does float on top, the trout will often pass up a male and wait for the egg-ripe female. Wigram's favorite fly for this hatch was a moth tied with flat wings lying back over the body, and a very little short hackle.

In 1968 Angus & Robertson also published *A Fly on the Stream*, another good book on Australian fishing, and trout fishing in general, written by John Turnbull.

Another excellent book about trout fishing in Tasmania is *Fly Fisher in Tasmania*, written by David Scholes, of Launceston, and published in 1961 by Melbourne University Press in Parkville, Australia. The book deals mostly with Tasmanian waters, but the information on flies and trout can be applied anywhere in the world.

In 1963 Scholes came out with another book, *The Way of an Angler*, describing his early fishing days in Tasmania, New South Wales, and some parts of Great Britain and North America, a fine book to browse through, and full of information.

Editor's Note: The 1970s saw the publication of many angling titles, some new, others reissues. Some of these are among our finest works on trout fishing. A selection follows. From Winchester Press, 220 Old New Brunswick Road, CN 1332, Piscataway, NJ 08854: *The Trout and the Stream; Nymph Fishing for Larger Trout* by Charles Brooks; *The Trout and the Fly* by Brian Clarke and John Goddard; *Caddisflies* by Gary LaFontaine; *Stoneflies* by Carl Richards, Doug Swisher, and Fred Arbona, Jr.; *Guide to Aquatic Trout Foods* by Dave Whitlock; *Mayflies, the Angler and the Trout* by Fred Arbona, Jr.; *In the Ring of the Rise* by Vincent Marinaro. From other publishers: *Stillwater Trout* edited by John Merwin, Box 765, Dorset, VT 05251; *Tying and Fishing Terrestrials* by Gerald Almy, Stackpole Books, PO Box 1831, Harrisburg, PA 17105; and the fine little booklet *Techniques of Fly Tying and Trout Fishing* by George W. Harvey, The Pennsylvania Fish Commission, Box 1673, Harrisburg, PA 17120.

2

THE TROUT
WE FISH FOR

All the trouts are believed to be of Arctic marine origin, apparently having spread over a wide northern area in prehistoric times as they retreated southward during glacial periods. Authorities believe that the rainbow and cutthroat came south through the Bering Straits to the Pacific coast of the United States, while the brown trout migrated down between Norway and Greenland and spread along the European coast as far south as Spain. The first browns were brought to America in 1885 from Germany and were called German brown or Von Behr trout, after the member of the German Fisheries Society who sent them over. At about the same time browns were stocked in North America from Loch Leven, Scotland.

As the trouts ran before the extreme cold of the glacial era, seeking warmer water, they sometimes moved into rivers and on up to head-water lakes, and in both lakes and rivers they adapted themselves to freshwater living. Many of them stayed permanently in the fresh water but others, perhaps finding a shortage of food or perhaps stirred by some primeval memory of the ocean, traveled back down the rivers and out to sea. Yet when spawning time came, they returned to their river.

BROWN TROUT

The European brown trout that stays at home is still called *Salmo fario* by some ichthyologists, while the migratory or sea-run brown is called *Salmo trutta*. There is some variation in the coloring and markings of the brown trouts that occur in various water locations. In Loch Leven, Scotland, the fish have a somewhat silver coat as compared to the dark hues of the small burn trout found in the runs and becks and lochs of the Scottish Highlands. But if you take such a burn trout and put him in Loch Leven he will soon put on length and girth and blossom out in the same silvery sheen, all no doubt as a result of the increased food supply, plus, perhaps, some difference in mineral content in the water he is living in.

Similarly, in the Rocky Mountain states I have heard anglers insist that there are two definite kinds of brown trout, the German brown and the Loch Leven or Lochie. These anglers have pointed out that one is heavier than the other, or darker, or wears different spots. In my own fishing I have not been able to differentiate enough to say whether the brown trout I have caught is a Loch Leven or came from the German stock. I have found much difference in coloration between one river and another and one lake and another. I have taken browns on which the spots were round, while on others they were more like stars. I've seen them with red dots and black ones, and with basic color ranging from light tan to dark brown. I've even fished for browns with apparant physiological differences, but which I believe are nevertheless simply members of the brown trout family. Such is the gillaroo, or "gizzard trout," I encountered while fishing the Drowse River between Lough Melvin and Donegal Bay on Ireland's west coast. While this trout wears the same outward dress as other browns, the gillaroo has a different stomach. Evidently at some time in its history the supply of aquatic insects, freshwater shrimp and minnows fell off and the trout were forced to feed on the small snails that abound in the river and lough, and on which the trout still feed, in addition to the current standard food. The sharp points of the snails irritated and punctured the lining of the stomach, so nature took over and gradually the gillaroo built its defense. The walls of the stomach hardened so that it has the appearance of the gizzard of a fowl. If you press in on the stomach between the pectorals and the vent you can feel this hard place.

From a strictly scientific point of view I would like to discover if all these markings and other idiosyncrasies of the brown trout are indications of different ancient ancestors or merely mutations due to food and mineral content of the water they live in. But actually, as far as fishing goes, it does not concern the angler because the brownie is the same challenge in whatever guise you find him, spotted or starred, bright or dark.

I long ago lost my heart to the trouts as my favorite species to fish for, and of all the trouts I put the brown at the top of the list. The greatest single mistake made in the stocking of fish in the United States has been the insistence on rainbows over browns. Millions of small rainbows are dumped into streams every year, many of them dead before they even hit the water. So-called anglers follow the trucks and catch their limit fast, because hatchery-reared fish are easy to catch after such a dumping. And these fish reproduce so slightly that the program of stocking must go on year after year, with no possibility of increasing returns, to maintain even a few fish in the river for anglers to fish for. If the same time and effort and money, or even half of it, had gone into stocking brown trout we would have a basis of self-perpetuating fish that could survive even in some of our polluted waters and in waters that have become too warm for the more-demanding rainbow.

The brown is the most adaptable of trouts, being able to withstand a wide range of temperatures, more pollution, and able, in general, to take care of itself as far as reproduction is concerned. There was

A husky brown trout from Montana waters. The brown is most adaptable of the trouts and has taken hold nationwide.

ample proof of that for anyone who was in Montana during the earthquake of August 17, 1959, which dammed the Madison River for a few days and bared wide sections of the river bottom. As the water level lowered the fish were concentrated in pools where they could readily be checked. In this, one of North America's most famous "rainbow streams," which is heavily stocked with rainbows every year, by far the greatest number of trout were browns. Big, fat and healthy. They still are.

But the brown trout is more difficult to raise in captivity, and costs more, so to keep the politicians happy, and let them announce how many millions of tiny fish they have fed into the rivers, we go on dumping rainbows and downgrading the brown as "too expensive to raise," and "cannibalistic." And the final argument is that the brown is too hard to catch.

To demolish each argument in turn: (1) if browns were stocked the cost would diminish in time, as the fish perpetuated themselves, which rainbows cannot do; (2) all fish are cannibalistic, but even so, I have never taken a brown whose stomach held a member of its own family; (3) the difficulty of getting a wily brown trout to take a fly is what keeps fly fishermen going to the river; while the bait and spin fishermen come into their own everywhere they find browns, which hit spinners and spoons with vigor. Every year the biggest trout taken in any given stream or lake will nearly always have fallen to the bait fisherman's worm or minnow.

Another argument I occasionally hear about browns is "they don't jump." Granted that, like the salmon, the rainbow is a fabulous aerial performer; but anyone who has caught browns in clean, fresh water, on flies, knows that they do indeed jump! More browns I have caught have jumped than have not jumped. In fact I could go to the superlative and say that *most* browns I have caught have jumped. A 14½-pounder I hooked in the Chimehuin River in Argentina jumped six times, straight up two feet into the air each time. My biggest, an 18½-pounder from the same river, jumped three times. All over the Rocky Mountains, wherever I have fished, the browns make spectacular jumps. I think that perhaps the mistaken belief about their lack of jumping ability originates with those who fish for the species in warm water or who use big, heavy spoons with weights, to get down deep.

Those big browns of the Chimehuin River in Argentina are an example of the adaptability of the brown trout. The original brown trout stock was sent down there from the United States in 1903. Now spread over twenty-five hundred miles of the Andes, they provide some of the world's greatest fishing for the species.

In 1935 a fine angler named John Lovell, who lived at Estancia Viamonte on Tierra del Fuego, at the southern tip of Argentina, had some trout eggs shipped from England. He planted them in several streams which empty into the south Atlantic. A few years later anglers were taking brown trout in all those rivers; and not much later the special bonus arrived. They began to catch big, fat, silvery brown trout that had obviously been out in the salt, putting on weight in the tremendous larder of the ocean. They were sea-run browns. Apparently that shipment of eggs had contained some of the European sea trout, as well as the river resident breed.

When I first fished the Rio Grande in the early 1950s, one of the streams which had been stocked on Tierra del Fuego, seven of us fishing one day in a big pool on the Estancia Maria Behety took two hundred trout, including both browns and rainbows. All the fish that appeared to be residents of the river were long and slim, and had big heads, the typical conformation of trout that are not getting enough food. Obviously there was not enough food in the river for the numbers of fish. But those that were marked by the salt were plump, silvery and strong.

We suggested to the owners of the Estancia that they net the pools and remove some of the fish. They did this, and with the addition of increased angling pressure the situation leveled off. The next time I fished there, three years later, every resident fish we took, both brown and rainbow, was fat and fit, and they ranged in weight from four to eight pounds.

Sea-run browns do not stay for a long time in the salt, and they often move in and out of a tidal pool before they make their spawning run up the river. It is believed that after spawning a few stay in the stream over the winter but most seem to drop down that autumn and head out to sea again. In Europe the runs of the sea trout are as popular with anglers as the salmon runs, with which they sometimes coincide. Often the sea trout are harder to catch than the salmon. On the Oykel River in northern Scotland I found that even in mid-August when the salmon were what the gillie termed "dour," unwilling to take a fly, we could catch one or two each day. But not until evening put a pall over things and did away with shadows or any glint of light to betray our presence could we get a sea trout to come to a fly. Most of the British Isles sea trout are taken after dark.

If I ever had any doubts about the extreme awareness of danger that sparks the sea trout, I was put straight one day on the Dovey River in Wales. I had crawled in to the side of the pool, and kneeling there I slowly raised my arm to make a cast. Ten feet out from me a school of about twenty trout flushed like a busted covey of quail and disappeared in a trice, looking like the shadows of a flight of bluewing teal. I managed to get a couple of those Dovey sea trout before the day was out, but only by calling on every trick in the book. I crouched, crept and crawled, and used a side-arm cast, and a very long, light leader. And even then, many more of them saw me than rose to my fly.

The same situation holds true elsewhere. At the Laerdal River in Norway the sea trout arrive on a split-second timetable, on August 1, each year. Although the anglers know they are there, they never go out in the daytime but wait for dusk, the only "night" at that time of year in the land of the midnight sun. Then, around 7:30 or 8 o'clock, they start to have a chance at presenting a fly in safety to the wily sea-run browns.

All over Europe fishing for sea trout has become so popular that today it is almost as difficult and almost as expensive to get a beat for sea trout as it is for Atlantic salmon. Sea-trout populations, like those of the Atlantic salmon, have declined markedly, making things even more difficult. At some of the more famous lakes in the British Isles, which are frequented by sea trout, as for instance, Loch Maree, it is necessary to book years in advance.

In Scotland I had the pleasure of meeting Charles C. McLaren, former long-distance fly-casting champion of England and Scotland, and a great fisher for sea trout. He had started at it very young. On October 24, 1928, when he was only thirteen years old, he had caught a sea trout in Loch Maree in the Scottish Highlands that weighed twelve and a half pounds and that, by scale count, was nineteen years old, and is believed to be the oldest sea trout on record. Then on October

12, 1929, McLaren caught another sea trout, this one in the Kinlochewe River at the head of Loch Maree, that weighed fourteen pounds.

It was a good start in a fishing life, and he has never got away from those sea trout. Today he operates an angler's hotel at Altnaharra in Northern Scotland, close to Loch Hope and the Naver River, both of which furnish good sea-trout fishing. His book *The Art of Sea Trout Fishing*, published in 1963 by Oliver & Boyd in Edinburgh, is a must for anyone going for these fish in Scotland.

THE SONAGHAN

The European sea trout has his variations, too. In Lough Melvin, in northern Ireland, I encountered the sonaghan, a brown trout that is believed to go to sea only once in his lifetime, then return to his home lake or river. In the lakes they usually go to considerable depth, twenty feet of water, seldom if ever moving into the shallows. Yet they will rise in that twenty feet of water and take a dry. On a visit to Lough Melvin my wife Mary and I caught many of the sonaghan on dries, and were astonished by this lengthy rush for the floating fly, in my experience the longest rise of any fish to a fly. We would cast the fly out and wait patiently, the fly sitting on the surface, and then, splash, he had it, and the fight was on. Those fish averaged about twelve to fourteen inches and each fought very hard for his size, a nice little battler in a family of many mysteries.

Brown trout that make their homes in big, deep, freshwater lakes sometimes take on the same coloring as sea-run trout, probably because of the abundance of food, to better blend into the big, wide spaces, or because of certain minerals in the water. In Lago Huechalaufquen, out of which the Chimehuin River flows, the spawning brownies come out of the lake as bright silver slabs and only after some time in the river do they revert to their true brown trout hues.

RAINBOW TROUT

The natural home of the rainbow trout extends from Alaska southward to the mountains of Mexico. While most rainbows found east of the Rocky Mountain Divide are transplants, there is some possibility that those of the Yellowstone drainage are an exception and that they came to these waters of the eastern slope by ascending Pacific Creek on the west side of the Continental Divide, crossing Two Ocean Plateau above Yellowstone Park, and moving into and running down Atlantic Creek, whose waters eventually reach the Atlantic Ocean.

The first rainbows transported to the more easterly part of the United States were sent from California to Michigan in 1873; and a couple of years later rainbow eggs were also shipped to New York State. Within a few years the Michigan stock was going strong, and later these fish began to show in the Great Lakes. In 1898 further fish were stocked in the St. Mary's River between Lake Superior and Lake Huron. The famous Soo Rapids were soon furnishing some of the greatest rainbow fishing in the country.

Like the brown, the rainbow includes many variations, but these are mainly based on scale count or some slight difference in appearance and do not necessarily indicate a different fish. The Kamloops is an example. The Kamloops is so named for a lake in British Columbia where the rainbows were found to be especially robust and fast-growing and which consequently made a very desirable strain for stocking in other waters. Similarly, rainbows found in a few big lakes, which make annual runs into available rivers, are called steelhead in some places. For instance, the fish stocked in the Great Lakes showed a strong migratory urge and roamed far and wide, and were often called steelhead. But I think the name steelhead should be reserved for the true sea-going rainbow, the great sporting fish of the Pacific coast, which runs out to sea to feed and returns to his native river to spawn. Regardless of local names, of course, they are all rainbows, bearing the scientific name *Salmo gairdneri*.

The rainbow trout is a fish of fast water. The strength he builds up in this environment gives him the power to make startling jumps when hooked.

Very little authoritative material has been available on the Kamloops, but in early 1971 a very complete book appeared on the fish, written by Steve Raymond. It does a great deal to clear up the differences between the steelhead and the resident rainbow and the Kamloops. It also gives the best flies for the last.

The rainbows of some of the big western rivers of the United States cross with the native cutthroat, and while the crossbred fish cannot reproduce the combination develops a big, healthy, extra-bright-colored and extra-hard-fighting fish. This has been true of nearly every rainbow I have taken that displayed the red slash under each gill plate and the distinctive markings that revealed his hybridization. A large proportion of the rainbows weighing four pounds or better that I have taken in our western rivers have been such hybrids. In my experience the standard rainbow does not grow to such large size in most rivers, with the exception of Alaska.

When the rainbow makes his home in a big lake or goes to sea where he can find extra food, he can grow to sensational size. Wherever you find these big rainbows you find an exceptional food supply. In Lake Pend Oreille, Idaho, which was stocked with fingerlings of the Kamloops trout from British Columbia, this food supply consisted of millions of landlocked kokanee (Pacific sockeye salmon). Those small Kamloops rainbows maintained their normal growth for two years. Then they were big enough to feed on the kokanee, and suddenly in the next two years they practically blew up, sometimes into thirty-pounders.

The rainbow is a fish of the fast waters. He likes plenty of oxygen and is often found up in the heavy water that pours into the top of a pool, reveling in the force of the current. The strength he builds up in this strenuous life gives him the power to make the startling leaps for which he is famous. And when found in his favorite milieu of bright, clear, rushing water he is one of the most beautiful trout on the books, his silvery sides slashed with scarlet and a brilliant greenish cast to the top of his back. Because he is generally a fish of the fast water, the finer points of fishing are not always as critical as with a brown trout, but when you find a rainbow in calmer water, it takes all your skill to get him to hit.

When a rainbow goes to sea, he really builds up size and vigor and the result on the West Coast of North America is the steelhead, probably the strongest fish that swims. Steelhead travel great distances in their oceanic visits, and I have heard of one case where a tagged steelhead was traced on a twenty-five-hundred-mile trip from tidal water of his home river. Even within the river they make prodigious journeys, often following the main stem for many miles, then forking off into a feeder stream, and months later finding their spawning beds and perpetuating their kind.

The steelhead of the Babine River in British Columbia come up the Skeena River waterway to the Babine, and we catch them there two hundred miles from the sea. By this time they have begun to lose the bright silver look of the sea-traveler and are beginning to show their rainbow parentage. There are big buttons of vivid red on the cheeks and the rainbow down each side is aglow. They seem to set the water on fire, and they certainly light the hearts of fishermen.

The time when a steelhead run enters a river differs widely throughout their range. The angler must know the dates of the run into any particular river he plans to fish. Some rivers host a "summer run" in September and October, often called "half-pounders" although this is a misnomer, since the fish range from half a pound to ten or twelve pounds; and a winter run of much bigger fish, in January, February or March—cold fishing indeed. Of late, many northwestern U.S. rivers are experiencing excellent summer runs in June and July.

Strictly speaking, the steelhead we take in the Babine River are a summer-run fish, and they are certainly not half-pounders. While the fish we lose are always bigger than those we land, I am convinced that one steelhead I lost in the Babine in early October of 1970 was an all-time record. I knew from the moment he hit that I would never stop him. But I tried. I followed him quite a way downstream, but suddenly felt a slack line. I expected to find that he had cut me off on a big rock he went around, but when I reached the spot where the end of the line lay in the water I found that he had merely dropped the fly. That fish had to be at least forty pounds.

The steelhead of the entire Skeena River watershed are a race apart, especially big and strong. The rivers of this drainage, including the renowned Kispiox, produce our biggest steelhead.

Steelheading isn't the contemplative trout fishing of spring creek or limestone stream, or even a big western river. The steelhead follows the Pacific salmon into most of his home rivers, feeding on their spawn. On many of the streams where you fish steelhead you see the salmons—sockeye, humpback, chinook, chum and coho—all bound upstream to perform the last act of their lives, as the Pacific salmons die after spawning. They are covered with whitish blotches of fungus, gaunt and sunken-eyed, many of them already half dead as they dig out spawning beds and deposit the eggs. The sockeyes in particular are brilliant red along the body with contrasting greenish head and tail, the mouths like beaks, studded with sharp teeth, and the males show a decided hump, another manifestation of the spawning phenomenon. Sometimes anglers catch these salmon while steelheading and they give a terrific fight.

The steelhead river is usually running high, sometimes murky, the weather wet and cold. Casts of eighty to a hundred feet are often needed to reach the eddies and broken water on the far side, where the fish often lie. On many of the steelhead rivers such as the Klamath in northern California, the Eel, the Rogue in Oregon, and the Kalama in Washington, you have to throw a fly a long way to consistently take the migrating steelhead.

While the steelhead will take a dry fly when you find him in shallow, clear water, most fishing for the species is done with sinking lines, and the flies are almost universally tied to represent salmon eggs either in color or shape or both. Still, nymph patterns in more somber colors produce their share of fish.

CUTTHROAT TROUT

Another dweller of the west-coast waters of the United States is the cutthroat trout, *Salmo clarki*. This fish, in many species and subspecies, is found all the way along the Rocky Mountain chain from Alaska to California. When you hear a westerner speak of the "native" it is the cutthroat. And while there are many color variations, and they bear local names in various rivers and lakes, they are all readily identifiable as *Salmo clarki* by the red slash under each jaw, which slash gives the trout his common name.

Because the cutthroat is a wilderness trout rather than an urban dweller, he is one of the easier members of the family to catch, and his numbers have been decimated by heavy fishing wherever he can be reached. Today the Yellowstone River is probably the only stream outside of primitive areas which supports a good population of cutthroat trout.

As mentioned earlier, the cutthroat crosses readily with the rainbow, producing strong, healthy fish with the good qualities of each. The hybrid is more difficult to fool than the full-blooded cutthroat, bigger in size, usually, and extremely beautiful with the brilliant red throat slashes added to the flashing rainbow on his sides.

In Pacific coastal rivers flowing directly to the sea, the cutthroat acts like the other trouts. He goes to sea, on occasion, and can be caught in coastal water in some places. On this sea voyage they seem to stay closer to the influence of the home river than do the rainbow and brown, moving in and out and hanging around offshore islands. Like the other trouts, the cutthroat that has been to sea is stronger, spunkier, and gives the angler on his beat a great deal of sporty fishing. He is also much harder to catch.

GOLDEN TROUT

The cutthroat has been known to hybridize with another trout, the golden, but because of the limited waters in which the cutthroat occurs, and the rarity of the golden, this is a cross that not many anglers ever see. The golden trout, *Salmo aguabonita*, originated in the headwaters of the Kern River in California, and prefers high altitudes almost exclusively, either high mountain streams or high lakes at the headwaters of mountain streams. From California, goldens have been carried to high lakes in Wyoming, Montana and Idaho.

The golden has launched more high-country pack trips than any other fish, for anglers seek them for trophies and also for food, as this is one of the finest tasting trout. In most cases the catch will be small in size and limited in numbers, although in some few lakes goldens grow to large size, and a few double-figure fish have been taken.

Perhaps with further stocking the golden will adapt to changing environmental conditions, as other trouts have done on occasion. My wife, Mary, is convinced that a fish she took on a dry fly in the Big Hole River in the summer of 1970 was a golden or a golden hybrid with some other trout. It was neither rainbow, brown or cutthroat, nor Dolly Varden, as she has caught and can identify all those. It had brilliant orange-red sides in a widespread pattern, black-dotted fins, but no white edging that would suggest brook trout or cutthroat, and no throat slashes. She returned the fish to the water quickly, and only after she had done so realized that she could not identify it.

In another instance I know of, an angler brought a golden back alive from the high country and put it in the aquarium at Dan Bailey's Fly Shop in Livingston, Montana, where the altitude is only four thousand feet. The fish survived in fine health for fifteen months. Finally compassionate Dan carried him out to the river in an aerated bucket and released him in one of the sloughs of the Yellowstone.

BROOK TROUT

The brook trout, *Salvelinus fontinalis*—fish "of the springs"—is well named. He must have clear, fresh, sparkling water. This was the native trout of the eastern part of the United States. Those of us who are old enough to have fished the small streams of the Appalachians and the Adirondacks before dams and pollution destroyed the habitat remember them as the first trout we caught, with a stick, a piece of line, a hook and a worm. I can still see the first one I took, the trout flying through the air to land on the ground behind me as I heaved back when he hit, my own lightning pounce on him, my awe at the beauty of his red and black dots all circled in halos, and how I carried him home, a six-inch bragging fish, and next morning tasted him, crisp from the pan, the best fish I have ever eaten.

In the eastern states, the brook trout as a native has now been pushed back to smaller streams, upper river reaches, and backwoods ponds, often at high elevations. With the limited food supply the trout often become stunted, 6 or 7 inches being the full adult size in most instances except in beaver ponds and backcountry lakes. Nevertheless, they still provide good fly-fishing sport. In shallow water they are alert, knowing themselves susceptible to attack on all sides. But they still can't resist a fly. They zip up from their shelter beside or under a rock, hit, and if you don't hook them, turn and dash back, all in a second, a fleeting flash of wild trout.

That obliging willingness to hit a fly, be it dry, nymph, wet, streamer or bucktail, is a hallmark of the species. Once when Walt Weber,

National Geographic Wildlife Artist, and his wife, Grace, went to fish the famous Kennebago Pool in Maine, they found that the popular spot was overcrowded that day, all the best places already taken by hard-casting anglers. Walt anchored off to one side, and suggested to Grace that since they were not going to get into the good fishing, this might be the time for her to practice her casting. The big pool lay out in front of them, a ten-foot patch of lily pads behind them. Walt tied on a Royal Coachman dry fly and told Grace to fire away. Out there over the best part of the pool five boatloads of anglers cast, retrieved, picked their flies off the water and cast again, methodically, and with perfect form—and no strikes.

Suddenly the sanctified air was rent by a piercing scream. Walt looked up from tying a tippet on his own leader in time to see a seven-inch trout come hurtling at him from behind.

"I've got one!" screamed Grace.

"On your backcast," said Walt with disgust.

He tossed the trout back.

On her next cast Grace again managed to put her backcast right on top of a hungry seven-incher. He, too, came hurtling through the air towards Walt. Again the screams, and the snort of disgust from Walt. Eleven brook trout from seven to nine inches fell before Grace's accurate backcasting.

It became too much for the stern-visaged purists who were keeping their backcasts well in the air where a properly executed cast should put it. One by one they up-anchored and departed.

Walt pulled anchor, too, and rowed out and settled in the best spot in the pool. On his first cast with a size 10 Brown Hackle dry, a great brook trout rolled up and took. It weighed 2½ pounds.

In the United States the few spots where you can still find good fishing for fair-sized brook trout are those that are difficult to get to. Anglers ambitious enough to walk in three miles to catch them find fourteen-inchers in some of the mountain waters of Virginia, West Virginia and North Carolina. In Quebec, which has always been one of the great habitats for the species, you can find some really big ones in places which have not been fished too hard. In some of the rivers and lakes of Quebec it is not unusual for fly fishermen to take two- and three-pounders, a few four-pounders, and an occasional one that goes to five pounds. A few fast rivers and fly-in lakes in Maine also produce such fish.

God's River and others that flow to Hudson's Bay in northern Ontario and Manitoba also host big, strong brook trout; and again they are remote, fly-in spots. The more accessible Nipigon Lake and River, in northwestern Ontario, once produced many big brook trout, and for decades held the world record for the species, with a 14½-pound fish taken in 1916 by Dr. W.J. Cook. These waters still produce some big fish but not the consistent numbers and size of old. Trophy and fly-only regulations continue to preserve Labrador's Minipi river-lake chain as one of the last strongholds of truly large brook trout. Fish in the 6- to 8-pound class can be taken to this day.

Some of the lost eastern brook trout fishing is being restored through a program of stocking, and now, in a few rivers from Georgia up through the Middle Atlantic area, Maine and the Canadian Maritime Provinces, fair-sized brook trout of this origin can be taken from these stocked streams. They have also been planted in the Rocky Mountain states and have thrived there, especially in lakes. I have taken brook trout up to fourteen inches in the upper waters of the Big Hole River in Montana, in a series of beaver ponds at eleven thousand feet altitude, above Gunnison, Colorado, and in similar high-country lakes in the Big Beartooth Mountains of Montana.

My best fishing for brook trout in either lake or stream has been in Argentina. The brook trout was stocked there from U.S. sources, and in that cold, unpolluted water teeming with food they have grown to the utmost in size for the species. I believe it is only a matter of time until one of these Argentine fish, or one from the Argentine-Chilean border lakes, will take over top billing for the species.

When I fished the Senguerr River and Lago Fontana on the eastern slope of the Andes, far down in Patagonia, in 1957, those brookies came to our dries as if they had been on a hunger strike, and we took a four-pounder on nearly every cast. There were so many fish that probably the food supply has now become somewhat limited and holds them at about this weight, but with more fishing this situation will change and then there will be some really big fish.

In 1963 I went with an ABC-TV crew to Lago General Paz on the Argentine-Chilean border, to film a fishing contest for the Wide World of Sports program. The Argentine team was composed of Tito Hosman of Buenos Aires and Erik Gornik of Futalaufquen, Patagonia. TV announcer Curt Gowdy and I represented the United States. We won the contest in the last minute of time, but that is not the story. What stood out was the fish we caught. We fished for three days, using both fly and spinning gear. But because of the remote spot where we were camped we had to run two hours down the lake to the best fishing grounds each day, and back again before dark, thus missing the best fishing times, early and late. After dark, travel on that forty-five-mile-long lake was out.

In spite of this loss of the prime times, we landed 54 fish that totaled 256 pounds, an average of 4.47 pounds. The largest, taken on spinning gear, was 8 pounds, the largest on a fly only one pound less. In a few hours on the Corcovado River, which flows out of the lake, a beautiful, clear stream where we could see tiny pebbles on the bottom in twenty feet of water, we took brookies to five pounds on our flies. It was a wonderful place, with high, snow-capped alps at the northern end, the kind of spot where *fontinalis* was meant to live.

In many places the brook trout, just like other trouts, goes to sea; and when he returns he indeed surpasses his inland brothers for size and strength. Newfoundland's resident brook trout of some of the inland lakes is called mud trout and doesn't attract too many anglers. But the brook trout that comes into Newfoundland's rivers as a sea-run fish is something else again. Twenty years ago (1952) when I fished salmon there it was common to see them in droves in the salmon pools, blackening the bottom, so thick they were. The average weight was four to five pounds, and some went as high as ten pounds. And how they would hit a size 12 Royal Wulff fly!

The Labrador coastal rivers also play host to these sea-run brook trout, as do some coastal rivers on Prince Edward Island.

DOLLY VARDEN TROUT

The Dolly Varden, *Salvelinus malma*, named for a reigning English beauty, is a western form of the eastern brook trout. The Dolly takes flies fairly well when found in suitable water, but he really prefers meat and is inclined to lie deep rather than near the surface. Hence the fly fisherman will do better when he goes for this species if he uses a sinking line.

Once on the South Fork of the Flathead River in Montana, I was fishing for the cutthroat trout for which the river is famous. Martin Bovey, angler and photographer, was along and had brought his movie camera.

"I'd like to get some footage of you catching a cutthroat," he said.

I eased into position, and when he had the camera focused on a spot about thirty-five feet upstream from me, I made my cast, dropping the Royal Wulff dry fly out in the current. I saw the cutthroat coming, but instead of taking the fly he continued on into the air. There was a tremendous splash and right behind him out came a Dolly Varden that must have weighed twenty pounds. It missed the cutthroat, but Martin got the pictures and later I saw the film of that hungry Dolly on the trail of a substantial meal.

We did catch a few small Dolly Vardens later on flies, but none on a dry, and none of such size.

GRAYLING

The American grayling, *Thymallus arcticus*, is the only grayling in the Western Hemisphere, though subspecies occur in isolated areas. The only other form is the European grayling, *Thymallus thymallus*, widely distributed from continental Europe to the USSR, but limited to specific clearwater habitat throughout this range. The grayling is found in many of the same waters as the trout and is fished in much the same way. The fish is readily identifiable by the high dorsal, almost sail-like fin, and the small mouth which seems to open into a square O, quite different from the mouth of a trout. The latin name *Thymallus* is derived from the slight odor of thyme which can sometimes be discerned in the fish. Various other tags have been added throughout its range.

The Montana grayling, which is called *Thymallus montanus*, was native only to the Missouri River above Great Falls, but has been stocked in many other rivers and high lakes in Montana, and in Wyoming. The waters chosen for planting are selected with a view to the preference of the species for pure, cold, fresh water. The Montana grayling wear a dull silver coat with faint overwash of purple, and black dots on the shoulders. They do not grow to much size, usually from nine to twelve inches, with an occasional fourteen-incher showing.

The Upper Big Hole River holds more Montana grayling than most rivers of the Rockies. They seem to like the cold water up there in the wild hay country near Wisdom and Jackson in the Valley of 10,000 Stacks. Only the odd one used to come to my flies further down in the Big Hole, but since the dam went out at Divide more and more are showing around Melrose and Glen. The last time I fished this area, in the lower Big Hole, I caught four grayling in one day, my biggest take of them ever.

The Arctic grayling encountered in Alaskan rivers is more brilliant than the Montana grayling and is, indeed, one of the most beautiful of all freshwater fishes.

My own first encounter with the grayling, in August 1947, was with the Arctic branch of the family. Frank Dufresne, then Chief of the Alaska Game and Fish Commission, had organized a fishing and hunting trip to Alaska for a group of Outdoor Writers. When we convened at Whitehorse, we were offered a choice.

"Joe, do you want to go to Admiralty Island for giant Alaska brown bear?" Frank asked me. "Or would you like to try the Lewes River for grayling?"

As far as I was concerned, it was no choice. I had never caught an Arctic grayling, and I had been hoping to since reading of its beauty and fly-taking qualities.

"It was grayling that brought me here," I said. "I'll take the Lewes."

Where I hit the Lewes, only five miles out of Whitehorse, the river moves right along, yet the surface was slick and unruffled. All over it I could see the markings of rising fish. I tied on a Black Gnat, size 12, dry, and cast to the nearest feeder. Bang! I had a hit. I struck and missed.

"You gotta be fast," called my fishing companion, Gene Letourneau, of Waterville, Maine, who had waded out into the stream not far from me. "They hit and then they're gone before you know it."

I cast again, and bang again, another fish piled into the Black Gnat so hard I saw his dorsal and knew for sure, then, that these were grayling I was working over. He looped out, waved that angel-wing at me, and slipped back into the water. But I had this one securely hooked and fought him safely through a couple more jumps and finally brought him in.

He must have weighed about two pounds, a fish that was almost cigar-shaped, his back wearing a silver-gray sheen and flaring above it the sail that makes him so sensational, a dorsal fin that stood two and a half inches high and seemed to have been brushed with all the colors of the borealis.

"He should be called the Northern Lights Fish," I said, holding him up for Gene to see.

His mouth opened in an O as I removed the hook, and his pear-shaped eyes opened, too, then seemed to blink in gratitude as I slipped him back into the water.

Arctic grayling of two pounds are fairly common throughout their range, and you can expect an occasional one of three pounds.

These bigger members of the grayling family like the same flies that take the Montana grayling. In the Fond du Lac River and Black Lake, near Stony Rapids in Saskatchewan, we took them on small nymphs and dry flies tied on number 12 and 14 hooks, only slightly larger than those used in small streams.

Many of the lakes and streams in the Northwest Territories produce extra-large grayling. Bud Williams, then owner of Arctic Star Lodge on Great Slave Lake, took one that weighed four pounds, and three-pounders are fairly common in this lake. In 1969 one was taken which went a little over five pounds. The world-record grayling came from the Northwest Territories, too, a beautiful five-pound fifteen-ounce fish taken in the Katseyedie River on August 16, 1967, by Jeanne P. Branson. This fish hit a Mepps lure cast with a spinning outfit.

On a recent trip to the Northwest Territories I traced some of the history of the Arctic grayling. It was in 1819 that a young English midshipman named George Bach saw fish rising one summer evening on the glassy surface of Great Slave Lake in what is now Canada's Northwest Territories. Bach had brought a fly rod with him from England—undoubtedly the fourteen-footer typical of English usage of the day—and he wasted no time in putting it together and dropping a fly over those rising fish. One of the risers took and, at least as far as historical records tell, Bach became the first man to catch an Arctic grayling on a fly.

George Bach was a member of Sir John Richardson's staff, on the Franklin expedition to the North Pole, and his catch was made as the party camped at the site of Fort Reliance, on the eastern end of Great Slave Lake. I like to think of Sir John and his young midshipman standing there in the bright Arctic evening admiring this beautiful fish with its flaring dorsal fin that glimmered with rose and gold, hints of yellow, shots of green like an early aspen leaf, and was liberally dotted with purple and blue, some of the dots further enhanced with circles of green and gold and rose.

Both men knew the grayling species in England, but this was a new member of the family to them.

"We'll name it for you," Sir John said. "Bach's grayling." (Sometimes spelled "Back," as is also the river named for him.)

To the scientific generic name of *Thymallus*, which applies to all graylings, Sir John also added *signifer*, meaning standard bearer, both as a comment on the beautiful, extra-large sail flaunted by the fish, and as a compliment to the young seaman's calling.

When early settlers fishing the Ausable River in Michigan came up with a catch they could not identify, they sent a couple of the fish to Washington. There the authorities named it a member of the grayling family, a fish highly regarded in Europe for both sporting and food qualities. When the news of the presence of large numbers of these fish got around, there followed a spree of uninhibited fishing, so widely publicized that the citizens of one of the towns central to the grayling streams changed its name from Crawford to Grayling.

Unfortunately, in that era of belief that nature's bounty knows no limits, the grayling was practically wiped out in Michigan waters within a few years. In an article written by Kendrick Kimball in the *Detroit News* of December 15, 1929, we can read the story of what happened to the Michigan grayling. He quotes Rube Babbit, of Grayling, an old man in 1929:

> From 1875 to 1881 my father and I shipped our catches of grayling to a Chicago restaurant, which paid the unheard of price of 25 cents a pound. I'd take fishermen down the Ausable for more than 200 miles in a houseboat. When we reached Lake Huron I'd sell or leave the boat and go back to Grayling and build another one. Those houseboats were equipped with wells, so we could keep our catch alive. Later we built camps on shore, to which we constructed our own roads through the timber. The grayling was the greatest game fish in Michigan and was the only native of the trout family in the waters below the northern tip of the Lower Peninsula. The biggest one I saw weighed around one pound 10 ounces. They averaged a bit smaller.

> An Englishman came from his homeland every year to catch grayling. Artists came from the east to paint their beauty. One in particular put up his easel beside the live well in one of my houseboats and took fish after fish from the water, exposing them for a few seconds then throwing them back, so he could catch the exact shades. The loggers were responsible for the loss of the grayling. When the pines went, the streams became impure through erosion. Soil was washed into them by the rains, and the grayling could not live in muddy, dirty waters. No longer shaded by trees, the rivers rose in temperature, which also hurt as the grayling needed water almost as cold as ice. When the logs came down the rivers they raked the spawning beds, destroying the eggs or the young fish. In the jams the bark was ground off the Norway pines, filling the water with fine particles that sifted into the grayling gills. I found innumerable dead with festering gills, and in every case the fine particles of bark were the cause. The State has endeavored to plant them below the straits in recent years, but they also died. No, the grayling is gone forever, gone with the pines and the pigeons and the Michigan that used to be.

What happened to the Michigan grayling, then, was well known and should have been a lesson. But all over the country we still allow money-mad people to pour poisons into the rivers. And then we dig into our pockets to pay more taxes to raise fish to plant in the streams those poisons have destroyed, to live for a day, a week, or perhaps a month, in the waters we are still polluting. It's an expensive way to maintain our sport.

In England, particularly in the chalk streams such as the Test and the Itchen, there was a period when grayling were sometimes regarded as pests, competing with the more desirable trout for food. Many a grayling was ignominiously heaved out on the bank to die. But this school of thought rapidly disappeared; the grayling continues to be highly regarded wherever he is found, as a fly-taking, sporting fish, and has earned such fancy terms of admiration as "The Flower of Fishes" and "Queen of the Waters."

The renowned Charles Ritz, Europe's most famous fly fisherman, has stated that he prefers the grayling to the trouts. I cannot go along with him on that, but I do think that the grayling can be very difficult to fool at times, hard to tempt to come to your best-chosen and most discreetly offered fly. One of Ritz's favorite fishing streams for grayling was the Traun River in Austria. Indeed, in this clear, lovely river the grayling is at his best, feeding constantly, and is a particular challenge to the fly fisherman.

It was while fishing the Traun that I had a good opportunity to study the peculiarity of the grayling's rise as compared to that of a trout. The grayling will often let your fly go by, so you think he is going to ignore it. Then he turns and drifts downstream under it, and cork-screws up to take, a nerve-shattering procedure that always seems to catch you unready and accounts for many missed strikes. So it always pays to let the fly float well through, when you are putting your offering over grayling, and watch it carefully throughout a long float.

I have often heard anglers say that grayling are hard to hook because they have a tender mouth. I believe, however, that we lose a few grayling because the point of the small hooks usually employed either bend or are straightened out under the pressure. Or the hook goes through a bit of flesh over the lip of the fish and pulls out.

The English and the Austrian grayling are a little less brilliant in coloring than their North American counterparts. They are smaller than the Arctic grayling, but average larger than the Montana. And the grayling I found in the beautiful, crystal-clear waters of the Sava and other rivers in Yugoslavia was slightly different again, sometimes almost transparent looking, so you seemed to see through the fish in the water; and was generally a little more brown in overall coloring and the dorsal fin not quite so gay. But, in numbers and response to the fly, they provided some of the best grayling fishing I have found.

3 TROUT TACKLE

TROUT RODS

The first trout rods of which we have record were long and of very slow action. Dame Juliana Berners (*see* HISTORY), recommended that the butt be of willow, hazel or aspen, the middle section of green hazel and the upper section of blackthorn, crabtree, medlar or juniper, the parts being attached and tapered. These rods were of such considerable length—up to eighteen feet—because casting as we know it was not done in those days, the fly being presented only by a short line attached to the end of the long rod.

From the recommendations of Juliana Berners of various woods, solely or combined, rod makers gradually moved towards bamboo. From such reports as I have been able to locate, Samuel Phillipi of Easton, Pennsylvania, was reputed to have been the first rod maker to produce a bamboo rod. In 1845 he created one of which the tip and second joints were made of three splits of bamboo and the butt of ash. The first completely split-bamboo fly rod seems to have been made by E.A. Green of Newark, New Jersey, in 1860. All three joints of this rod were made of four split sections.

Apparently the first split-bamboo rods for the trade were made by Charles E. Murphy of Newark, New Jersey, in 1863. These were also four-section rods and were sold through Andrew Clerk & Company of New York City, by L.H. Abbey, later of the firm of Abbey and Inbrie, organized in 1867. In 1870, Hiram L. Leonard of Bangor, Maine, put the first six-section split-bamboo fly rods on the market; and the first cork grips appeared on fly rods in 1888.

On the North American fishing scene, several rod manufacturers of the early 1900s produced outstanding split-cane fly rods: The Orvis Company, of Manchester, Vermont; the Paul Young Company, first of Detroit, then of Traverse City, Michigan; and the Leonard Company, whose rods were made by William Mills & Sons, of New York.

Tubular steel was also used and Hardy of London made a cane rod with a steel center. In the United States, Everett Horton made a telescopic steel rod that he could stick down his pants leg when he went fishing on Sunday so he would not be discovered by those who disapproved of the sport on the Sabbath.

The first glass rods began to appear just as we turned the corner into the 1950s—only a short time ago as fishing years go. Early glass rods were solid and a far cry in delicacy from fine bamboo. But they needed far less care than cane. Today's tubular glass rods are lighter than corresponding cane, more delicate, and designed for effective casting.

Fiberglass rodmaking technology was near perfection when over-shadowed in the mid-1970s by a new material gleaned from the aerospace industry. Tough, carbon filaments (graphite) of higher mod-ulus than glass or bamboo, permitted rods to be manufactured with less material. The result was lighter, smaller-diameter rods than ever. Rodmakers continue to experiment with other modern materials. Bo-ron, another aerospace product, has its supporters, and a second gen-eration graphite makes possible increased performance with less weight than ever.

The modern trout rod is also much shorter than long ago. Undoubt-edly the very long rods (approaching 20 feet) originally employed by English trouters (and still in use on many English and European streams) came about because the anglers fished with short lines; and they fished salmon and trout with the same rods. Many of the salmon rivers were either heavy by nature or were in spate when the angler fished them, and therefore were not wadable. The long rod was needed to put the fly out where he wanted it, from his position on the bank, and always with the wind in back of him. These early anglers fished always with the wind behind them, to get the line out. The development of heavier lines brought a corresponding development in the technique of casting. Trout rods became shorter because of the greater ease of handling. The very long stick continued to have its place, for fishing some of the very large, heavy-flowing rivers in Norway for European sea trout and for trout in lakes. But trout fishermen have increasingly gone to shorter rods.

In the U.S., rod length passed through two extremes in recent his-tory. Increasingly shorter rods became the vogue through the 1950s and early 60s. The so-called midge rod of 6–6½ feet—which is an ef-fective tool on small streams—saw use in ever larger waters. In the hands of skillful anglers short rods proved sporty and effective even on lakes. Anglers used them in large rivers for steelhead and salmon. Short rods demand precision timing, however, and many anglers found this plus the lost ability to raise much line from the water during a drift reason to return to a longer rod.

The most popular, general-purpose length for fly rods again seemed to hover around 8–8½ feet. Then came graphite. With the new material, two factors resulted in rods again being built in increasing length. First, graphite fibers are stiffer and manufacturers had not refined tapers and building methods. The result was that shorter graphite rods were stiff to a fault. Second, with reduced material weight it was

The trout rod was developed in America to suit the variety of our waters and the importance of casting skill to native anglers. *Above*, an angler casts with a fairly short rod on small stream; *right*, and adherent of the long rod throws a line on a big river.

possible to produce a longer rod that weighed about the same as shorter models. Soon 9–9½-foot rods became the standard and many anglers were singing the praises of 10–11-foot models.

As technology improved, delicate 9½-foot rods built to handle light lines were designed. In the past, rods of such length were matched only with heavier lines. Ease of casting (including brush-clearing back-casts), fly control on the water, greater distance, smooth, slower action were some of the advantages enjoyed by those fishing the longer fly rods.

Eventually, the cycle came 'round again; the 10–11-foot rods became available only from a few builders. The 14-footers available only on special order. Such ultralong equipment (by U.S. standards) has its use in specialized situations, but for the most part we are again back to mid-length rods. However, though some argue that the 8½-footer is

the most popular on trout streams, it is evident that more 9½-foot fly rods for different line weights are in use than ever before.

The trout rod has been developed to its greatest variety in North America, where the pleasure of executing a skillful cast holds almost as much importance as does the catching of the fish. Accordingly, the rod has been adjusted to be the most capable of casting in the circumstances in which we fish. An angler perfectly equipped to fish for all species of trout dealt within this book would need a minimum of six rods: a midge for the smaller streams, a 7- or 7½-foot stick for slightly larger brooks and creeks, an 8-foot rod for wet and dry flies and nymphs on medium rivers, an 8½-footer for the same waters when using a bucktail or streamer, a 9-footer for really large streams and lakes, and a 9½-footer for some of the big steelhead rivers. The selection may be somewhat reduced if the rods are of space age materials. Modern synthetics result in rods capable of handling generally at least three different line weights.

The choice of a rod is often a difficult one for the novice trouter, and indeed, even for experienced anglers, because of the variation of action in rods of the same weight and length, as produced by different manufacturers. This, plus the fact that far too much emphasis has been put on a rod style suitable for tournament casting, as compared to practical fishing.

The tournament casting rod, made to throw a heavy line a long distance, is just the antithesis of what a good trout rod should be. You can adjust to some of the mechanics of this powerhouse through your leader and tippet, but not enough to take care of the effect of dropping a too-heavy line on the surface. A heavy line is bound to create some disturbance, and thus scare the fish. I have seen fishermen using a 9½-foot stiff-action rod with the heavy WF-11-F line that it demanded, and trying to fish a stream only 60 feet wide. They have not caught many fish that way. And these big, powerful rods do not give the feel and fun to a caster that a smaller, lighter outfit does.

When you buy your rod you may find two excellent rods of equivalent length and weight, each marked by its manufacturer for a recommended line. One may carry the recommendation for a WF-6-F while the other suggests a DT-4-F. How do you make your choice? You must make it according to how you plan to use the rod. In the above instance, WF-6-F, according to standards established by the American Fishing Tackle Manufacturers' Association, means a weight-forward line whose basic weight in grains meets the 6 category, and which floats. Weight forward indicates that when you cast, the weight of your line, the big part, which causes the most commotion, is going to be out near your leader. Conversely, the DT-4-F means a double-taper line, with a basic weight of 4, which floats. However, the heavy part is in the middle, that is, it tapers from light to heavy and back to light. Now, when you cast, you have lighter line up front, near the fish, then the heavy part, far enough forward to help you to cast, then more light running line to follow.

While nothing in trout tackle is quite this simple, it could be boiled down to the following: You could use the first line, with its heavy belly, where you must cast a fairly long distance and therefore need that weight; or where you will cast a large, wind-resistant fly such as a spider, big dry fly, bucktail or streamer. You would use the lighter outfit where you need greater delicacy of casting, in the way the line hits the water, and where you will use small flies. With a big, stout rod and a heavy line you lose the finesse of casting and the delicacy of presentation which are an intrinsic part of trout fishing. Therefore, in making a choice of a trout rod, no matter what the material, I always urge the angler to look for a rod that is not too stiff and this is doubly important in rods which will be used on small streams. I have seen 7½-foot rods which are capable of throwing a #8 or even a #9 line. But this will not add to the trouter's fishing success. Even on an 8½-foot rod, the trout fisherman should never use heavier than a #7 line. On the other hand, a too-light line on a stiff, heavy rod is equally difficult to throw. The rod needs more weight to bring out the action. Today, many experienced anglers feel the best way to choose a rod is to begin

Unidirectional graphite fibers come in an inert epoxy resin on paper backing in a strip 12 inches wide, on a roll 100 feet long. Here a rod-length strip will be cut for wrapping on a tapered mandrel under controlled heat and pressure.

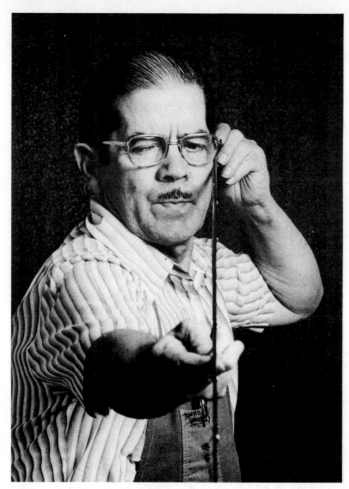

Rod sections in a quality manufacturing plant are hand checked for straightness before being released. *Photos courtesy of Orvis Company.*

with the size flies you need to cast. The flies determine the line weight needed to cast them. The final step is to choose a rod designed to handle the required weight line in a length suitable for your purposes. See the table under Fly Lines.

The "midge" or "flea" rods, as they are often called, measuring only 6 to $6\frac{1}{2}$ feet in length, are great fun to use if they are properly lined, and even with the light line they require it is possible to cast far enough, 60 or 70 feet, for such streams as the Letort In Pennsylvania and the spring creeks of the Rocky Mountain area. Small mountain streams are also best fished with the short rod because of the woods and brush that overhang them.

On bigger streams, the eight-footer is better. In fact, if I were limited to only one rod for all my trout fishing, I would choose an eight-foot stick. It is entirely usable on the smaller streams just mentioned, and is the ideal size for fishing larger streams with dry flies, wet flies, nymphs, and even small streamers and bucktails tied on a number 10 or 12 hook. You can get an even bigger fly out but it takes some effort. I never like to force a rod, not because it will hurt it, but because it spoils the pleasure of casting. You lose the feel of the outfit.

When you want to go to bigger flies, go to a bigger rod, too. An $8\frac{1}{2}$- to $9\frac{1}{2}$-foot rod is perfect for throwing big, fluffy dry flies on big water, and for the average streamer or bucktail or heavy nymph used for trout. It is also powerful enough to get out into the wind that you often encounter when fishing.

More powerful trout rods are necessary mostly when using a sinking line, because of the added weight of the line and the distance you must cast, plus the weight of some of the big streamers and bucktails used on sinking lines. In such fishing, delicacy of delivery is not as important as in shallower and probably more placid water, and these powerhouses have plenty of backbone to put the line out, then handle it in the water.

FLY LINES

Each rod calls for its own special line. The first fly lines described in English literature were made of horsehair, and Dame Juliana Berners speaks of using a line of a single hair for minnows, three hairs for dace and roach, nine hairs for trout and fifteen hairs for Atlantic salmon. In her day, apparently, the entire line was formed of the same number of hairs. Charles Cotton (*see* HISTORY), knowingly or not, described the first tapered fly line. During a trip to Wales in 1958, I found some few Welsh anglers still using horsehair tippets, usually a single hair for trout.

That same year, in England, I stopped in at the Foster Brothers Tackle Shop in Ashburton, near the famed Dove. The shop is owned by the grandsons of David Foster, who compiled *The Scientific Angler*, published in 1882 (*see* HISTORY), from columns he wrote under the title "Notes on Angling." David Foster was a keen angler and a noted naturalist, and he made many contributions to the improvement of fly-fishing tackle. He came up with a steel-center fly rod; and he advocated shorter rods than were then in use. Another of his findings was a waterproof silk line, which superseded the old hair and the hair and silk lines.

The Foster Brothers to whom I spoke said that they had still sold some horsehair lines, however, up until 1939. I asked for one, but was too late.

"We had a few up until three years ago," they said. "But now no one knows what happened to them."

From horsehair anglers progressed for line material through silk (still highly regarded by some) to the synthetics. Today's lines are almost entirely made of some form of synthetic. The taper is built up by means of thinner-thicker coatings around a braided core, to provide the weight wherever in the line it is wanted. Today's lines may also be floating or sinking, or may combine the two capabilities. A floating line allows the angler to manipulate the line easily and quietly, so that the fly will continue to float without drag much longer than it would otherwise. With the combination floating/sinking line, he can mend the floating part which is nearest to him, on the surface, to maintain the position of the sinking portion and keep the fly out in the deep water current where the fish lie.

Many line manufacturers have experimented with color in their lines, and you can purchase them in many hues, from white through blue, green, orange, to mahogany. I almost always use a white line. I like white for several reasons. One is that I can follow the line all the way to the end, with my eyes, and then, knowing the length of the leader, I can just tell where the fly should be, and even if I can't spot it at the moment, I'll still have a good idea of where it is. I've had guides—particularly in other countries—tell me that they believe a white line scares the fish. But more times than not, especially if you use a sufficiently long leader, the fish never sees the line. If you overcast and line the fish, it will bolt regardless of the color of the line.

The American Fishing Tackle Manufacturers Association has done a great job in recent years in standardizing lines in order to help the angler find the right one for his rod and for the fishing he plans to do. The listing below gives the comparative weights of lines according to their number designation, the weight being based on the first thirty feet of the line. The No. 3 line is the lightest line for which rods are normally made. The lighter formulas see use as running lines. How-

Electron microscope photo of a cross section of a floating line. Many modern synthetic floating lines achieve their floatability through tiny glass microspheres clearly visible here in the coating material. The denser pattern at the center is braided Dacron, which forms the core of today's flylines. *Photo courtesy of Cortland Line Company.*

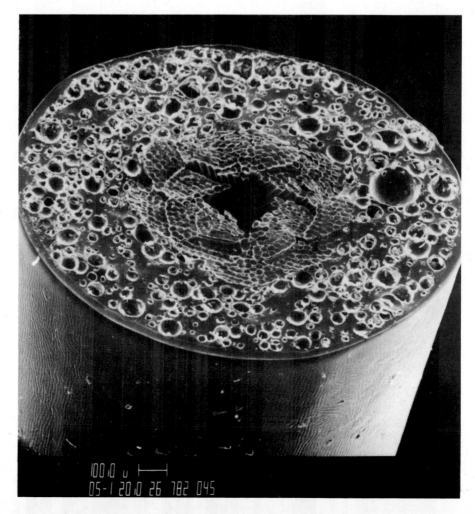

ever, The Orvis Co., of Manchester, Vermont, has introduced a No. 2-weight rod, and supplies the proper line for it. The rod is well designed and excels at presenting small flies. Other manufacturers are likely to experiment with such ultralight models of their own.

Line #	Weight (Grains/30')	Tolerance
1	60	Plus or minus 6 grains
2	80	6
3	100	6
4	120	6
5	140	6
6	160	8
7	185	8
8	210	8
9	240	10
10	280	10
11	330	12
12	380	12

While the weight of any fly line is based on the first thirty feet, whether it is a double taper or a forward taper, the somewhat smaller diameter of the double taper will fall to the water more quietly. It is better for fishing small, slick pools, or, for that matter, for almost any type of dry-fly fishing where you are making casts of from thirty to fifty feet. A properly tapered leader should be used, with a heavy butt section and progressively lighter strands down to the tippet. This allows you to drop the fly lightly and it allows more lifelike action in the fly.

The light line, the short throw usually results in more trout. A heavy line on a short rod, seven or eight feet, is too heavy. Some anglers use a seven-foot rod with a line as heavy as an F-8 or even 9. But much of our trout fishing is practiced in small streams and rivers where such an outfit is too heavy. You don't need the weight of the heavier line to make casts of thirty-five, fifty or even sixty feet, and such a line on slick water is often going to chase the trout away. The light line allows you to get to the fish quietly and lightly and results in more strikes.

Because of the varying action of rods, it is not possible to give an absolute line recommendation for any specific length fly rod. Only recently the rule of thumb was: the longer the rod, the heavier the line needed. With today's modern materials it's possible to obtain a longer rod to handle light lines—a 9-footer for a No. 4 line, for example. The advantages of long and shorter rods for your particular fishing assignments must be carefully considered. Though not etched in stainless steel, the following table is a general guide to matching flies with line weight. One then chooses a rod in suitable length, that will handle the required line.

Fly Size	Fly Type	Line Weight
18-28	Weighted nymph, wet	3
16-28	Dry, wet, nymph	3
16-28	Weighted nymph, wet, streamer	4
14-26	Dry, wet, nymph	4
14-26	Weighted nymph, wet, streamer	5
12-24	Dry, wet, nymph, streamer	5
12-24	Weighted nymph, wet, streamer	6
10-22	Dry, wet, nymph, streamer	6
8-20	Weighted nymph, wet, streamer	7
6-18	Dry, wet, nymph, streamer	7
4-16	Weighted nymph, wet, streamer	8
1-14	Dry, wet, nymph, streamer	8
1/0-14	Weighted nymph, wet, streamer	9
2/0-12	Dry, wet, nymph, streamer	9
4/0-12	Weighted nymph, wet, streamer	10
4/0-10	Dry, wet, nymph, streamer	10
5/0-10	Weighted nymph, wet, streamer	11
5/0-8	Dry, wet, streamer	11

Because a sinking line "feels" heavier on the rod than does a floater, possibly because of reduced air resistance when casting, and also to avoid overloading a small rod, a sinking line will sometimes be a few grains lighter than its corresponding number floating line. For instance, if you planned to use a sinking line on anything as light as a rod which called for a #5 floating line, then the corresponding sinking line, also wearing the #5 designation will weigh only 135 grains as compared to the 146-grain floater—thus taking advantage of the tolerance provided for in AFTMA Specifications.

LINE TAPERS

Many beginners purchase a level line, and this is fine to get started with. You can make casts long enough to take trout, and you can learn timing and the basics of casting. And, of course, the level line is the cheapest.

If you are going to fish a lot, and want to get into the fine points of casting, a tapered line is a great help. And actually the most economical line you can buy is a double taper, because the line is reversible. In the double taper the front end is light, tapers up to a heavier middle section, then tapers down again to a smaller diameter. The middle section provides the weight for casting, while the thinner forward end falls more lightly on the surface than would a line of the same overall dimensions as the belly. When the front end of the line begins to show wear, you simply reverse it, and it is like getting two for one. The belly of a line seldom shows any wear.

The double-tapered fly line is for almost all dry-fly fishing, for fishing small nymphs near the surface, and for very small—say #12—streamers or bucktails. If you go to the larger flies on this small-diameter line and the matching small, light rod, it makes for difficult casting and a poor presentation. But with the flies mentioned above, and the matching double-tapered line, you are well equipped for the delicate line work often required on the waters where you fish such a small outfit.

Some anglers who fish light lines prefer the weight forward, rather than the double taper. They find that with the weight-forward line they can get out a longer cast, get it out faster, and cast better into the wind. They take plenty of fish and I doubt that the little bit of weight at the end of a #5, #4, or #3, the lightest weight-forward taper made commercially, makes that much difference to an angler capable of handling a long, light leader under these circumstances. But I stay with double-tapered line because I think that on the average, when used on small, slick pools, or even on bigger pools and streams, the double taper delivers the fly more gently, more accurately, and permits more delicacy of line work, such as mending the line.

To me, the weight-forward line comes into its own when you are using a rod measuring 8 to 9 feet, or perhaps 9½ feet, and fishing big water where you have to make long casts and are using either a big spider or floater, or big bucktails, streamers, wet flies or nymphs. The heavy weight-forward line shoots out like a bullet, even in a strong wind, and that's what you need, rather than finesse, in such fishing.

There is another new taper worth consideration for trout fishing. The so-called Triangle Taper developed by Lee and Joan Wulff of Lewbeach, New York, and marketed by them, incorporates a continuous

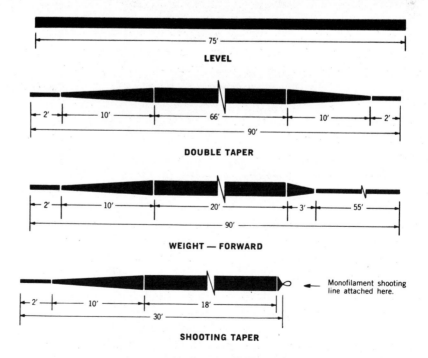

Taper configurations of modern fly lines.

taper in the first 40 feet of the line. By comparison, the normal double-taper line typically has an 8-foot taper length before the body; the front taper of the weight-forward line is generally 10 to 12 feet. The long, continual taper of the Triangle results in heavier line constantly turning over lighter line for power efficiency, easy roll casts and mending. Additionally, the finest diameter is always closest to the fish. When the full 40 feet of taper is past the rod tip, the line works like a weight-forward line for easy, long casts.

SINKING LINES

The situation is different when you get into sinking lines. Sinking lines are formulated according to the same AFTMA weight standards as floating lines. They are available in three styles: floating/sinking (FS); full sinking (S); and shooting tapers or heads (30 feet of sinking line backed by small diameter running/shooting line, and designated ST).

The floating-sinking lines allow good fly control in that the floating section (nearest the angler) can be mended, thus keeping the fly swimming correctly longer. They also are easier to pick up for the next cast compared to full sinkers which must be retrieved almost entirely before casting. The F/S lines are available with a 10-foot sinking section, 20-foot sinking section, and 30-foot sinking section. These lines are generally called wet tip, wet belly or wet head, respectively. The wet-tip formulations can be obtained in double-taper or weight-forward design, while the other two come as weight forwards only.

Some anglers prefer full sinking lines for several reasons. Where longer casts are required, the feeling is that because of the different densities of the floating and sinking coatings, the F/S lines give a somewhat unbalanced sensation during the cast. The full sinkers are smoother for the longer shoots, and, of course, all the line descends, thus keeping the fly down over the full length of the retrieve. The full sinking lines are available in slow-sinking through ultra-fast sinking densities.

Where extreme distance and fast sink rates are needed, the shooting taper or shooting head is popular. These heads are formed of 30 feet of sinking taper to which the angler attaches a 100-foot running/shooting line of either monofilament or very fine-coated fly line. The running/shooting section being of fine diameter has less water (as well as air) resistance, thus making it less affected by strong river currents. It has come to be a very popular steelhead line in some areas.

The full sinking lines are also used in large rivers or in lakes, while the various style F/S lines are finding increased use in a variety of rivers and lakes for all the trout.

There are some steelhead rivers where at certain times of the year you can take fish on floating lines and even on dry flies, but the majority of streams which play host to the rainbow returning from the sea are high and turgid when we fish for them. And even in the Babine River in British Columbia, my own favorite steelhead stream, which is sparkling clear, the fish do not come up to a high-riding fly. It takes a sinking line to put the fly down where they want it. I like to use a 30-foot, high-density sinking shooting head that weighs 330 grains, to which I add 100 feet of floating fly line, .029 in diameter, for the running/shooting line.

The first time my friend Moses Nunnally of Richmond, Virginia, fished there with me, he had never used a sinking line.

"Couldn't I do just as well with a floater?" he asked.

"These fish are holding deep in the riffles and pools," I said. "They don't want to come up to take. Now and then they move up a foot or two, but most of the time they nose down and pick up a fly as it slides along the rocks on the bottom."

Moses's first cast was good. He threw the sinking head eighty-five feet. But as soon as the fly and line hit, the current grabbed the line and pushed a big belly in it; I knew that consequently the fly was rushing down the pool headfirst, far too fast.

"Mend your line! Mend your line!" I said hastily. "Flip the floating part upstream so the water will not be pulling on it and dragging the fly out of the lie of the fish. In any steelhead river where there is a fairly stiff current, the heavy push of the water will belly the line and pull the leader and fly out of the lies of the fish in a hurry," I said. "What you want to do is throw a slack line, a serpentine cast, then mend the floating line. That lets the fly continue to float freely for a longer distance, straight down the current, out where the fish are."

Moses brought his line in and made another cast, a good serpentine throw, and this time he mended his line neatly and kept mending it, so the fly floated freely out where he wanted it.

Some fishermen make the cast and feed the shooting line out of their hands, or let it run out of the shooting basket if they are using one, so the fly gets down and works along the bottom.

"After the fly has finished the downstream float and the current starts to pull it across the pool," I went on, "you should let it go, keeping the rod tip high, and not imparting any action to the fly. It will work across the pool and come to a stop immediately below you. A steelhead may hit at any part of this float, sometimes as soon as the fly lands, sometimes out in the current, or he may follow it across and hit on the swing. Most of them do hit on the last part of the swing, and often just as the fly stops moving and hangs in the current."

"That's just what he did!" said Moses, who had been following my instructions religiously. "I've got one!"

He raised his rod tip and out there thirty feet from us a steelie took to the air. He was a good, deep fish and he fought a great fight. Moses finally slipped him up on a sloping gravel bar. He weighed fourteen pounds even.

As earlier mentioned, sinking lines, like floaters, are adapted to the types of water in which they will be fished. Thirty-foot coils of high-density line, called shooting heads—great for long throws and for getting down deep—are available in the following line specifications:

Line Designation	Weight in Grains
ST-6-S (Sinking taper, sinker)	160
ST-7-S	185
ST-8-S	220
ST-9-S	250
ST-10-S	300
ST-11-S	350
ST-12-S	400
ST-13-S	450
ST-14-S	500
ST-15-S	550

Fly-line manufacturers have developed ultrafast-sinking shooting heads with lead particles in the coating. These lines are designed for extremely high water in rivers, or for salmon fishing out of the rivers in salt water. An example is Scientific Anglers' Deep Water Express lines. There are three in the series 550, 700, and 850 grains in weight. The 700- and 850-grain lines demand extremely powerful rods.

Some anglers find they can get greater distance if they use monofilament line as backing to the shooting head, in place of the level floating fly line I prefer.

In either case, the shooting head is attached to the backing by either a splice, loop, or a knot. Some of the shooting heads come with a loop to which the backing can be tied with a clinch knot.

You have to be very careful when casting the big shooting heads. If you get the knot or joining down into your guides and make a cast, sometimes that point of larger diameter will come up against the tip guide and refuse to go through, and it jolts you practically off your feet. The best way is to false cast all the shooting head out until the joining is about a foot past the tip guide. Let the shooting head fall to the grass, or water, or skiff bottom, according to where you are fishing. Strip additional monofilament or shooting line off, thirty or forty feet for a start. Pick up the shooting taper on the backcast, pulling part of it into the guides, if necessary, and again false cast until the loop is a foot or two past the guide tip. Make a forward cast, and as the line goes out release the shooting line. At all times, a sinking line should be retrieved until most of the heavy section is in close before you attempt to pick up for the next cast. If you try to lift forty or fifty feet of a full sinking line from the water, or the shooting head when it is far out or deep, it scares the fish, ruins your casting rhythm, and puts too heavy a load on the rod tip. Monofilament will be less likely to tangle if it is well soaked and stretched before you start to fish.

The shooting line is held in loops in the left hand. When using monofilament, some anglers hold the loops in their lips, and release them as the line starts to shoot out.

Whenever you use backing behind a fly line, the spool should not be loaded to the extent that the line will rub against or come up tight against the crossbars. If the line jams in such a way it may cost you a good fish.

In order to get the best drift through with a sinking line you have to judge the depth of the water and its force. Sometimes the current is so great and the water so deep that even with a sinking line you must cast upstream so the line has time to sink before it reaches the place where you know or believe the fish to be lying. On the other hand, the fish may be in such shallow water that if you drop the line upstream or even straight across it will sink too quickly and probably become snagged on something. In this case, you drop fly and line a bit downstream and use the S-cast (see CASTING) which allows it to float down the current as those curves straighten out; and thus you keep the fly from moving too slowly and the line from sinking too deep.

I had a perfect illustration of the importance of the right sinking line for the purpose when I fished the Tongariro River in New Zealand in 1969. We had come a long way to try for the big rainbows of the Tongariro. My wife, Mary, and I had flown Pan American World Airways jet from New York to Honolulu, and then to Auckland on the North Island of New Zealand, and then we took a car and drove to Turangi, where we met our guide, Tony Jensen.

The first morning he took us to the Island Pool, which lies almost within the town limits. Tony told me to wade across the small run on the near side of the island that gives the pool its name, and cast into the heavier water on the far side of the island.

"Fish lie on both branches of the river," he said. "But the main run is up that far side."

I waded over and started to fish the same way I would in one of our larger American rainbow streams, using a 9-foot fly rod, a #8 weight-forward floating line, and a size 4 red setter fly, a local pattern from Dick Sanderson's Fly Shop at Turangi. In order to cover all the water I started carefully, dropping the fly out only twenty feet, fishing it through, then throwing the next cast two or three feet farther, and so on, until I had reached out within a foot of the far bank. Nothing happened. I moved downstream twenty-five feet and started the casting series again, fishing hard, concentrating all the time. I went down the entire length of the pool that way, hitting every bit of water. I didn't get the first pull.

I turned and waded in towards Tony, who was standing on the island.

"I know what's wrong," I said. "I'm going to have to change to a sinking line. I have one with me. But I'll need a shooting basket."

"I've heard of shooting baskets," Tony said. "But I've never seen one in use here and I know there aren't any in the tackle stores. Why do you need one?"

A shooting basket is worn strapped around your waist. When you are using a shooting head, or any line with which you want to make extra-long casts, you can strip off all the shooting line and lay it evenly in coils in the shooting basket. When you make the forward throw, that line comes zipping up after the heavy forward taper and goes on out, easily. To retrieve, you strip the line back into the basket with your left hand, instead of holding it in loops or coils, which might become entangled by the wind and then bunch up in the guides on your forward throw. Or if you want to bring the line in very quickly, after your fly has had the desired float, you simply tuck the rod under your arm and strip the line back into the basket hand over hand.

"If I can't buy one, I'll manufacture one," I said. "Let's go to the nearest grocery store and pick out a few cardboard cartons."

It didn't take us long to drive to Tony's favorite grocery store. The manager led us into a storeroom piled high with cartons.

"I need something about sixteen inches wide and twelve inches from front to back," I explained.

"Help yourself," he said.

The boxes were variously printed with food names: beans, tomatoes, peas, and so on. I chose one marked beet root for myself, and one with Felix Cat Food for Mary. At the river again, we cut off the tops of the boxes and made two four-inch slits about twelve inches apart in the backs. Through these slits we threaded the belts that we always wear around the waist of our waders, and then, when the belts were buckled on, the baskets were held firmly at waist height in front of us.

"Presto," I said. "A shooting basket."

I changed over my tackle to a 330-grain hi-density sinking head, 30 feet long, plus 150 feet of .029 level floating line, this attached to 200 yards of 18-pound-test nylon squidding line for backing. I used a 6-foot leader because with a long leader and a sinking head, you defeat your whole purpose. The line goes down and stays down but the fast current washes the long leader up, pulling fly with it, out of bounds of bottom-holding fish.

"This is the outfit we use back home for steelhead," I said to Tony, when I was rigging up. "And I believe it will work here. These fish seem to be lying deep."

"You're right," Tony said. "They are on the bottom and they don't want to rise very much. You have to put the fly down to them."

"This sinking head will do it," I said. "The heavy part will take the fly down, but I can mend the level floating line to keep the heavy part out there in the current. With a line that sinks in its entirety, the heavy flow of water would push the line out of the current and often into dead water right in front of me. You sometimes have time to mend the floating part of the line two or three times during a float."

I waded out to the head of the pool and started casting. I made my throw, let the fly float through, mending the line when necessary, and then when the float was complete I tucked the rod between my right arm and my body, and stripped in fast, like a milker at a State Fair contest, using both hands to drop the line into the basket. When I made the next throw, it would come up and out of there free and easy, with no wind twists or water friction to hamper it. I fished the width of the pool this way until the lengthened casts finally dropped the fly about a foot from the far bank.

On that last throw I had made an S-cast so the fly would float free in the current, then let some fifty feet of shooting line slip over the edge of the basket, controlling it lightly between my thumb and forefinger, allowing the heavy shooting line and the short leader and the fly to work along the bottom. I could feel the fly hitting the gravel, digging in a bit, coming free, surely a teaser for a rainbow.

About halfway through the float something latched onto the fly with a vicious pull. The rod tip bent down and I struck. I felt the weight and the power, and then he busted out into the sunlight, a beautiful fish, deep and thick, crimson-sided, a prime rainbow that knew how to fight. He settled for a moment, then rushed for the surface again, flung himself out in an arching leap, fell back, got a tailhold and bolted up the thread of the current, racing, and got slack. I reeled fast to get right to him and before I did he jumped right in front of me, ten feet out, a bigger fish than I had thought. Luckily the hook was well set. We had it hot and heavy for another ten minutes, then I began to gain line. I finally walked slowly towards the shore, held my rod back a bit downstream from me, and parallel to the shore, and skidded that beauty up on the sloping, gravelly beach.

"He'll go a good six pounds," said Tony.

From then on we had no trouble because our sinking lines were putting the flies down where they needed to be, where those Tongariro rainbows like to swim and lie, along the bottom.

LEADERS

A properly tapered leader is just as important as any part of your equipment in trout fishing. You can adjust to a rod that isn't quite right. You can struggle along with a line that is a little too light or too heavy. But a badly tapered leader, or even a level leader, can really do you in. A level leader of light diameter doesn't have the backbone to turn over and to deposit the fly gently on the surface; and while a heavy level leader might cast the fly well enough, it will be seen by the trout, and if you are using small flies will not permit them a light, buoyant action.

Many beginners at fly fishing are afraid they can't cast a long leader—a needless fear. Almost anyone who can cast the line can cast a well-tapered leader because such a leader is so constructed that it becomes a continuance of the fly line. The butt section of the leader, which is fastened to the fly line, is only a bit less in diameter than that line. The next section is a little lighter, and so on down to the very delicate tippet. That heavy butt section furnishes weight and backbone to turn over the leader, and the final, light section is designed to fall quietly on the water with a minimum of disturbance and a minimum of visibility.

Nowadays there is a variety of nylon leader material available in various formulations from very stiff to quite limp. Some anglers combine the two. Dan Bailey of Bailey's Fly Shop, at Livingston, Montana, makes the top half of hard nylon, which will turn the leader over forcefully, and the bottom part of soft nylon.

Commercially tied leaders are obtainable in knotless form, in lengths of $7\frac{1}{2}$ to 12 feet; or you can buy the same lengths in knotted leaders. It has been my experience that I always end up with a knotted leader, anyway, because I am always tying on a new tippet, or if somehow the leader becomes broken above the tippet, I add more material there. So actually whether you start with a knotted leader or a straight one, is of minor importance. Some anglers feel that the trout may see the knots, and certainly I have had very small trout and whitefish hit at the knots, or perhaps at the little bubble of air that seems to form around them. But I do not believe the use of a knotted leader has really affected the number of strikes that have come to my flies. In weedy water the fewer knots the better because moss or other vegetation can collect around the tiny knobs of the knots.

Similarly, I do not believe that color in a leader or tippet is of much concern to the trout. For many years, back in the days of gut leaders, I always used Ray Bergman's black leaders and tippets. But now and again I would try a regular gut leader without color, and it seemed to me that strikes came just as often as with the others. I believe that it is the diameter of the tippet, rather than the color, that really matters.

Many anglers, doubtful of their own ability to play and land a fish, go to a heavy leader in hopes that they will be able to hold and even "horse" their fish in. They work to their own defeat and never even have a chance to play and lose the fish because their tippet is too heavy. The trout takes one look and shies away from it. It is far better to go light and get your strike and lose the trout, if you must, than never to hook him at all.

In a big pool with lots of swimming room and few obstructions you can land a good trout, and I mean a four- or five-pounder, on a 5X tippet. Keep a tight line but let him run when he wants to. Drop your rod tip when he jumps. Follow him down or up the pool, as you need to, or into the next pool, and eventually you'll get him. When you consider that most trout you hook will be from eight to fourteen inches, you really don't need a heavy tippet as far as the fish itself is concerned.

Your peril comes from striking too hard and breaking a fine tippet. If the fish heads for a brush pile or beaver dam or into heavy grasses, it is difficult to stop him on a very light tippet. If he reaches his haven he has a good chance of breaking off. But that's the luck of the game. At least you have hooked him.

It is often the big fish, lying in the most difficult spot, that requires the finest tippet. In many of the small spring creeks and the eastern limestone streams with super-slick water, you need a 6X or 7X tippet to get strikes, both because of the slick water and because the small size of the fly requires a small diameter tippet to go through the eye and to allow the fly to float right. With such a tippet it is very hard indeed to avoid striking too hard, especially if you have been watching the fish rise, and are all tensed up. I remember one day when I took a nice brown that had six Light Cahills, size 18, besides mine sticking out of the side of his mouth, the evidence of the previous defeat of six other anglers. Or perhaps not so many, as a couple of those flies could well have been my own. I had been broken off a couple times earlier in the week in that same pool.

With such small flies, the thing is not to strike at all. The points of the small hooks are needle sharp and will easily penetrate the mouth of the trout if you just lift the rod tip gently.

Yet when you see a big trout rise, or spot him lying in the river, your first inclination is to take off that light tippet and tie on a heavier one, 2X or 3X. If it is a clear day the chances are he'll refuse your offering on that heavier tippet. He may come up and look, and drop down. Go to a 4X and expect a hit. Go to 5X and your chances are still better. The lighter the tippet, the better your chances for that strike. The X designation relates to diameter in thousandths of an inch. To determine diameter of the leader material, subtract the X number from .011. Thus, 3X = .008, 4X = .007, and so on.

Tippet designations. Nylon leader and tippet materials of different manufacturers may vary in strength, but generally test out about as follows:

Tippet Size	Pound Test
0X	9.0
1X	7.2
2X	6.3
3X	5.2
4X	4.3
5X	3.3
6X	2.1
7X	1.2

While the 5X, 6X and 7X tippets are often necessary when using small flies in the delicate situations of slick water, you can go to 4X when you come to the bigger, heavier streams and are using nymphs and the smaller streamers and bucktails. And you can move up to 2X and 3X when you fish fast rapids and use large streamers and bucktails. The 2X would also be the tippet when you are skating a spider. If you use a smaller diameter with the big, fluffy spider, the leader and tippet will twist, sometimes well up into the line, and you cannot cast well. But this is one of those exceptions. Apparently the trout is so intent on that big, alluring spider he sees dancing across the surface that he has eyes only for it and doesn't even notice the large 2X tippet.

Another time you can use a 2X tippet is towards dusk and at night, when you are fishing a big river or lake for big trout. If you think you may tie into a double-figure fish, you can even go as high as nine-pound breaking strength, the 0X. For steelhead, well, those sea-going rainbows don't seem to notice the leader tippet, and although you can readily land a twenty-five-pounder or ten- or twelve-pound-test tippet, many anglers go even higher and catch lots of fish.

There's a considerable difference of opinion as to whether or not a leader tippet should sink or ride the surface, particularly when you are using a dry fly. I used to take great pains to try to sink the leader, either all of it or just the final half, or at least the tippet. I used one after another of the leader sink materials manufactured commercially. Failing that I would use what nature supplies, some slime rubbed from the body of a trout, or mud picked up at streamside. The trouble with all of them is that after a couple of casts the water washes the leader clean again and there it is, sitting up high and obvious. And since many hits have come to my files as they rode along on such a high-floating leader tippet, I am not sure, even after all these years, that it is important if the leader is visible from the air, so long as the float of the fly is right. I believe it is the *diameter* of the leader under or on top of the water that may put the fish off.

I do think that a leader that lights on the surface in curls upsets the fish, partly through water commotion and partly through visibility. I always carry a small piece of inner tube, and if my leader starts to coil, I pull it through the rubber, pinched between my fingers. Leather or chamois would probably serve the same purpose. We all think we have discovered something new, but in my reading of early books on trout I found in Salter's *Angling Guide*, on page 349, a mention of straightening coiled gut and hair leaders with India rubber.

SHORT LEADERS   The one instance when the long, tapered leader is not important—in fact, is a disadvantage—is when you are using a sinking line to fish big streamers and bucktails. When you use a sinking line the leader should not be more than six feet in length. A long leader—ten or twelve feet or more—as used with the floating line, would only defeat your purpose. The heavy, sinking line would go down all right, but the current would force the long, light leader upward, carrying the fly up too, towards the surface, out of bounds for deep-lying fish. The shorter leader keeps the fly down where you want it, only inches from the bottom.

When I am using these short leaders for my sinking fly lines, I do away with the usual heavy butt section of the leader, and instead taper the 6-foot leader from a butt section of 3 feet of 15-pound-test nylon to 1½ feet of twelve-pound-test and then 1½ feet of 10- or 8-pound test. If I want to fish with a 12-pound-test tippet, I use 3 feet of 15-pound test and 3 feet of 12-pound test. The smaller diameter of the butt section offers less water resistance and helps get the fly down. In the extreme, some Western anglers are now using leaders of 2 feet, 18 inches, and even 6 inches for nymph and streamer fishing in situations where the impact of the line hitting the water near the fly won't spook fish.

REELS

The basic purpose of the reel is to give the angler extra line with which to reach the fish on the cast, and then to play him through his runs and lunges. Early handline fishermen used a notched piece of wood to store their line on, and perhaps from this evolved the winch or "wheele" mentioned in early fishing writings (*see* HISTORY). The original purpose was simply to hold the line. Today's fly reels have reached a considerable degree of sophistication in the addition of drag mechanisms. But the trout reel does not call for a great deal of drag, that is, the capability of the reel itself to apply pressure on the line to prevent a fish from running. Drag is important in big-game fishing and saltwater fishing in general, and when you go after big steelhead; but in most trout fishing where the tackle is delicate, the less drag you have the safer you are from breaking a fish off. If the reel has a strong drag and it is set down tight, and you raise your rod tip to strike just as the trout starts away, something has to give, and it will be the tippet. There are many good trout reels without any drag at all, merely a click mechanism with just enough pressure to keep the reel from overspinning. You can add drag when you want to simply by pressing the fingers on the inside of the revolving spool. Some anglers "palm" the reel, but this can be a dangerous procedure because it is easy to exert too much pressure.

On those occasions when I do need a reel that has a strong drag and has plenty of capacity for backing, I use a Fin-Nor #2 fly reel; a design based on the very successful saltwater fly reels used for big tarpon and long-running bonefish. It has the spool capacity to hold the fly line and two hundred yards of twenty-seven-pound-test dacron as backing, which is often needed for a long-running fish. Today there are many new makes offering ultrasmooth, strong drag systems.

The automatic reel was a long-time favorite with many trouters because its spring mechanism enabled you to quickly pick up a lot of loose line and get tight to the fish. Automatics were widely used by

Selection of single-action reels which retrieve one turn of line for each crank of the handle (*from left*): Marryat, Orvis CFO, Scientific Anglers, Hardy.

Single-action reels for big fish (*from left*): old Scientific Anglers No. 10 is simplest; it uses a pawl for click drag. Fenwick reel uses metal-to-metal drag; Fin-Nor #2 reel has a cork drag. Drags on these two reels are extremely strong and smooth.

those who fished with a fairly heavy tippet. The danger, of course, is that when you press the lever to retrieve the line, you may jerk up tight to the fish, and if you are using a light leader you may break him off. But this can be overcome with practice in using the reel. The major drawback of the automatics comes when you need backing to your line, as when you get into a big trout or steelhead. The automatic does not have the capacity to hold both backing and line. And if you have only a hundred feet of fly line on your reel and you hook a big trout and he runs, the chances are that he will take out all the line, and when it comes tight against the reel core it will snap your tippet.

Even in small streams and with light tippets you often need backing, as I found out to my sorrow last summer. I was using a small Scientific Anglers System 4 outfit: the rod seven feet two inches, a small matching reel (not an automatic), a DT-4-F line and a 7X tippet, as I fished Armstrong's Spring Creek near Livingston. I nearly always use backing, but on this particular day I didn't have any on that small reel. There are plenty of good-sized trout in that creek but you can usually handle them on the line. But this one was extra big. He hit and took off, and started downstream and he never did stop. If I had had some backing I might have had a chance to let him run into the slough below, then follow and fight him down there. But he took all the line. I heard it come tight to the reel core and away out there the big fish simply snapped my gossamer 7X tippet.

Some anglers prefer multiplier reels because they facilitate picking up more line with each crank or rotation of the spool. Overall the single action reel remains the favorite of trout fishermen.

BACKING

Depending on the size of your reel, the backing may be from a hundred feet to two hundred yards. For day-to-day fishing, new fine-diameter braided Dacron such as Cortland's Micron is best.

The backing may be attached to the fly line either by a splice, a nail knot, or interlocking loops. In either case, the joining must be as small and smooth as possible, in order not to catch in the guides and prevent a smooth cast or lose a fish during the fight because one of those too-big knots catches and holds tight against a guide on the rod. A big knot or splice will also give you trouble as you reel in. If you use the nail knot, the end fibers of the fly line, where you have clipped it off after tying the knot, can be broken down by using the point of a tapered nail or the clippers to cut through and soften the protruding end.

4 CASTING TECHNIQUES

Trout fishing is the most demanding of all types of fly fishing in that if you are to take fish from difficult lies or under difficult circumstances you must be able to handle your equipment efficiently. Trout fishing does not call for extra-long casts; in fact, usually an extra-long cast will work against the proper presentation of the fly. You sometimes see a fisherman walk to the edge of a pool, wind up and throw the fly a country mile. Then he retrieves and makes the next cast even longer. What he is overlooking is that there could be, and often are, trout right under his rod tip. Just like a golfer who likes to hit a long, powerful drive down the fairway, so it is with a fisherman. We all want to make the long throw. It always strikes me as funny when fly casters gather and the first thing they do is strip all the fly line off the reel and strive to cast it all out. To be able to do so may give some idea of how the rod and line are matched and how far we can throw it, and that is fine for those competing in long-distance championships. But it isn't necessary in order to take trout.

If you would take more fish you should work the near water first, extending your casts gradually, so that finally you cover all the available water. Sixty feet is plenty of distance for any trout cast with very rare exceptions such as fishing a big river with streamers and bucktails, or when steelheading. In day-to-day trout fishing you do not have adequate control of fly or line for delicate presentation when you get beyond sixty feet. It is surprising how short the cast may be to make a consistent catch. You can take trout within twenty feet of you and, if they are feeding on a hatch, even closer. Instead of working for distance, the beginner should aim at perfecting his cast.

THE GRIP

Comfort and ease in the way you hold the rod is of major importance in executing a good cast. The more tightly you grab the rod, the tighter your hand and arm muscles become, and the less dexterity you will have in your cast. The rod should be held loosely in the palm of the hand and the fingers closed easily around it, not clenched. There are three grips commonly used. In the free wrist grip advocated by the late John Alden Knight, the rod is held in the four fingers of the casting hand, the thumb coming over the tip and down on the left side of the rod, forming a V at the base of the first finger and the thumb. This does give great freedom of the wrist, and I started my fly fishing with this grip. However, in more recent times I have found that it is possible to obtain greater accuracy and put more power into the cast by placing the thumb along the top of the rod grip. The third way of holding the rod features the forefinger lying along the top of the grip, as if pointing down the rod.

The Grip

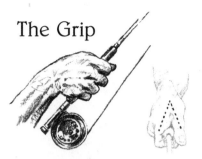

Free-wrist grip, with thumb along side of rod grip, forming a V at base of first finger and thumb.

Thumb along the top of rod grip, gives better accuracy and more power.

Forefinger along top of rod grip, favored by some anglers.

GETTING LINE OUT The first thing you have to do to be able to cast is to get line out. In spin or plug casting the angler has only to flick the rod and the flex of its taper is sufficient to snap the weight of the lure out, pulling the line after it. But in fly casting the fly is light, insufficient in weight to be cast of itself. It is the weight of the line which the fly caster throws, and the line pulls the fly out after it. The aim of every cast is to make that line flip over and drop the fly at the end of the leader.

In order to get started, then, the caster must have some line on the water or in the air, and for the beginner the simplest way is to strip about fifteen or twenty feet of line out by hand and let it fall to the ground or water in front of him. Now hold the fly in your left hand by the bend of the hook (to avoid it sinking into your hand if you should inadvertently give it a sudden yank). Raise the rod in front of you to about a forty-five-degree angle, then continue on up and with a quick flip of the wrist snap the line up into the air, and back. Stop the rod at a position of about one o'clock, behind you, then with easy movements of arm and wrist, bring it forward, still in the air. Keep false casting this way until you get the feel of the line working on the rod, using only this small amount of line which you have lifted on that first upward flip. Then, with the line in the air, use the left hand to pull another foot or so of line from your reel, and on the forward throw let that go out. Keep false casting and working line out until you have all that line which you originally stripped from the reel out. Then make your forward cast.

As you practice keeping that line in the air, try never to let your wrist go back too far. The rod should never be allowed to drop beyond the two o'clock position. On the forward cast it should not point lower than the ten o'clock position. In one case the line will hit the surface behind you and in the other it will hit the water in front of you. In either event, your timing will be thrown off.

Basic Cast

To make the basic forward cast, with the line on the surface in front of you, raise the rod tip to start that line moving towards you, using your wrist, not your arm, until the rod points at about the ten o'clock position. Bring the line slowly your way across the surface (1). At this point the wrist should be held on a slight down-slant, cocked, ready for an upward flip. This position, with the elbows bent a bit, the rod pointing at ten o'clock and the wrist firm but bent a little downward, is the perfect position from which to lift line and fly. It is also a good position from which to strike if a fish should hit the fly as you get ready to pick up. All that is needed is a flip of the wrist and the line and fly move towards you, and the fly comes off the water, or the barb sinks in, as the case may be.

Once you have picked the line off the water and sent it back (2) as you have been doing in your practice false-casting, let it straighten out behind you, then drop the elbow about six inches and at the same time snap the wrist forward (3). Think of hammering a nail into a wall at head height in front of you. This is the level at which you want to start the cast, so that your throw will go out a bit above the parallel to the water. A cast driven directly at the surface will splash the line into the water and scare the trout. It will also cut down on your distance. So aim to have the line go out above the parallel to the water and at the end of the forward impulse drop lightly down.

Once the forward throw is underway, the rod can be allowed to follow through to about the ten o'clock position and held there as the line falls to the surface.

Basic to a good cast is a strong backcast, firm, and with a flip of the wrist, then sufficient wait at the top to allow the line to straighten out behind, but not enough to allow it to fall to the water. If you bring your tip in too quickly, the line near the rod starts forward before the end has straightened out, and comes through in such a tight bow that the fly often catches on the leader or line, or on the rod itself. If you allow the backcast to drift down, on the other hand, and give too slow a snap to the forward cast, the sudden speed imparted to the line will make it crack like a whip and probably snap your fly off.

False casting for practice is the best way to achieve the feel of the line in the air, but in actual fishing, false casts should be limited in number to absolute necessity. In the first place, the more false casts you make, the greater are the chances for the fish to see your arm waving, or the line in the air. And the greater are your chances to make a mistake in the cast and lose your timing. Most anglers, especially tyros, false cast far too often. Three false casts should be sufficient for any throw, and two are better. One is perfect.

Raising the elbow during the back-cast helps in getting line in air.

Do not break the wrist during the backcast and allow the rod to fall beyond two o'clock.

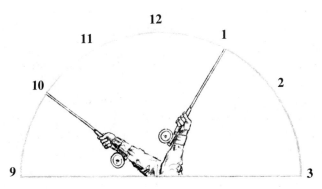

All references to clock positions in text and captions are from the viewpoint of a righthanded angler looking at his own casting arm, or an angler viewed from his *left* side. The instruction to stop the backcast at one o'clock, for example, assumes that the angler's relationship to a clock is as shown in the diagram. For maximum clarity, however, the drawings of the different casts throughout this chapter show the angler's right side and casting arm.

Drop elbow about six inches during the forward cast, and snap the wrist forward, much like hammering a nail into a wall at head height.

Do not allow rod to come down parallel to the water on the forward cast. This will splash the line on the water.

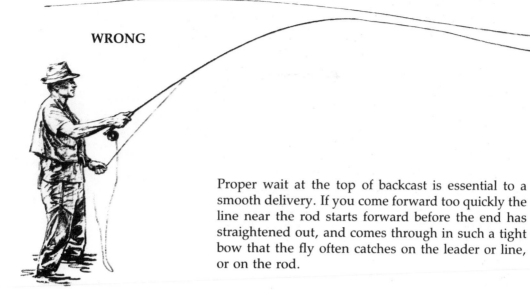

WRONG

Proper wait at the top of backcast is essential to a smooth delivery. If you come forward too quickly the line near the rod starts forward before the end has straightened out, and comes through in such a tight bow that the fly often catches on the leader or line, or on the rod.

WRONG

Too long a wait at the top of backcast allows line to drift down, and when you start the forward cast, the sudden speed imparted to the line will make it crack like a whip and snap off the fly.

1

2

Shooting the Line

To be able to make a fairly long throw with only one backcast, the angler must learn to shoot the line. This means being able to throw a longer line than the amount you have picked off the surface and than you have been handling on the backcast. To be able to shoot the line saves your arm if you are fishing all day and also lets you get the fly out quickly if you spot a fish rising or cruising somewhat beyond the distance you had originally planned to drop your cast.

(1) Line is stripped from the reel and held in loops in the left hand, the cast made as usual, and as soon as the forward thrust is begun one or more, or all, of the loops are released from the left hand. (2) The momentum of the forward cast will pull that line out through the guides and let you achieve that much more distance. You can also shoot the backcast by releasing one or more loops of line as you make the backcast. In this way you add two or three feet to the length of line you have in the air very quickly. Then shoot the forward cast as well, and you get considerable extra distance in one cast. Once the angler has started the shoot, and the line is running out through the guides, the fingers of the left hand should be held in a sort of circle, around the line, but not touching it. As the rod is brought down to just above the parallel to the water, on the finish of the cast, the left hand drifts up to rod level and lets the line go on its way.

This procedure serves several purposes. It keeps the line up on a level with the guides on the rod, and therefore makes for less friction. It allows you to close down with your fingers on the running line and stop the forward impulse, if you think the cast is going to take the fly too far out. It gives you all-around better control of the fly line. And when your fly has lighted in the water, your left hand is then in the proper position to start the strip retrieve.

1

2

S-Cast

Once the fly caster can make a good forward throw with consistency, the next thing is to master the serpentine or S-cast. This throw is more essential than any other in dry-fly fishing. Its purpose is to overcome drag, that unnatural movement of your imitation fly on the surface of the water when it floats faster or slower than the current, or across current. Drag is sometimes scarcely noticeable to the angler but is readily discovered by a suspicious trout, who will pass it up and take a natural floating within half an inch of it.

(1) To achieve the S-cast the line is thrown harder than is needed for the distance you want to reach, and the rod is stopped and pulled back very slightly, only an inch or two, at the end of the forward movement. The speeding line, thus stopped, hits the reel spool and bounces back and falls to the surface in a series of serpentine curves. Before the current has straightened those curves and begun to pull the line downstream, the fly achieves several feet of free float.

As this snake of line floats down, you retrieve just fast enough to keep the near line from being caught in the current in front of you, which, of course, would add to the pull and straighten out the curves that much faster. You also thus keep a tight line so that when you are ready to pick up the line for the next cast all you need to do is bring the rod slowly back and up.

Serpentine curves in the line can also be obtained by making the conventional forward cast, and then as the line goes out and the fly is nearing the place you wish to drop it, imparting a side-to-side movement to the rod **(2)**, sending the line into a series of curves that drop to the surface.

Whichever method is used, the curves should be kept within reasonable limits. If the loops of line on the water are exaggerated, it is hard to control the line and the curves themselves add to the drag. Such a hard-thrown and sloppy presentation is also bound to hit the surface hard and scare nearby trout.

The serpentine cast can also be used across stream, and downstream (*see* Dry-Fly Fishing). On such a throw it is possible to achieve additional free float by pushing the rod hand out as far as possible in the direction of the floating line and fly. It sometimes gives you a couple more feet and often brings a strike that otherwise would not have come.

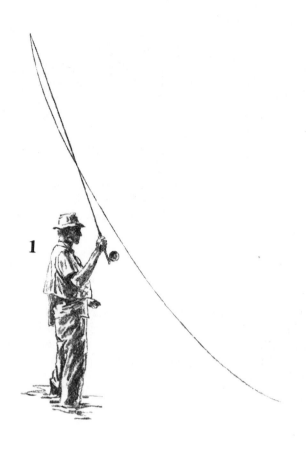

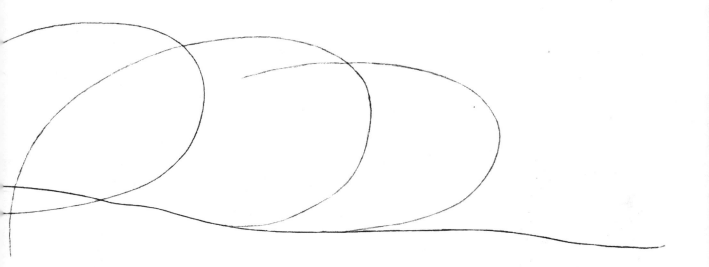

The Roll Cast

The roll cast can add immeasurably to the success of your trout fishing where trees or a high bank behind you prevent a backcast; and again, when a smooth pickup of line is necessary in order not to disturb the water. To start the roll cast the line should be out on the water in front of you. (1) Bring the rod back and up, slowly, until it is at about the two o'clock position, pulling the line across the surface until you have only fifteen to thirty feet on the water. The near line forms a downward arc in front of you, or right beside you, from rod tip to surface. (2) Now bring the rod forward, hard but smoothly, and at the same time snap your wrist and follow through with the rod. The line of that arc comes up off the water right beside you and, following the point of the rod, it rolls out, taking the fly with it and depositing it out there on the surface.

Carefully executed, this cast can also pick your fly off the surface with a minimum of disturbance, as line, leader and fly slip out of the water on an angle, rather than being lifted straight up. The roll cast is most effective within limits of twenty to sixty feet. It can prove a great boon on windy days when the wind knocks down your backcast and prevents a good forward throw.

The roll cast not only eliminates the backcast but if you can manage to take up a position so you are fishing downwind, it can help the throw. The strong gusts will often carry your fly out even farther on the forward roll. In this circumstance, the rod should be stopped quite high, to allow the wind to pick up the line on its outward movement.

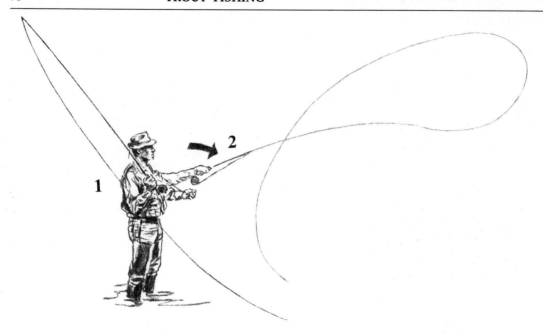

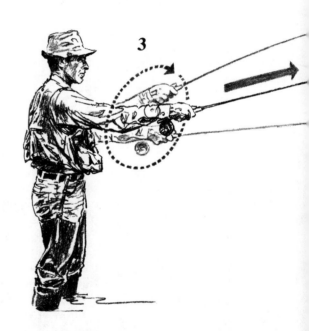

Aerial Roll Cast

Sometimes a fly fisherman finds himself in a spot where trees in back of and on both sides of him prevent him from making any backcast at all. In such a position he can achieve at least a short cast by using the roll cast pickup to get the fly off the water. Then, instead of continuing with the backcast in the normal way and going into the forward throw, when he gets the line into the air he repeats the forward movement, keeping the line rolling in air by the forward-circling movement of the wrist, a sort of oval loop, so it is like

a wheel rolling in front of him. When he is ready to cast, he simply drives forward with his wrist on the forward roll and sends the fly out. It does not produce much distance but will often get the fly out far enough to take a fish in a very difficult spot.

The same aerial roll cast often saves the day when you have to fish from a high bank. In this position, it is important to follow through hard and downwards.

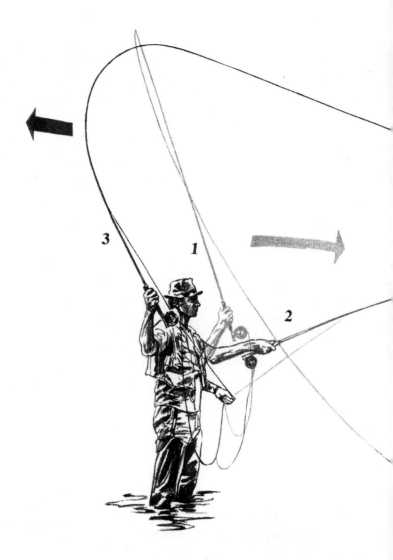

Roll Cast Pickup

The roll cast is useful to pick up a fly any time you cannot do so with the normal float and retrieve. Often when a trouter is fishing a dry fly upstream in very fast water he finds that the fly comes down at him at such a fast pace that he cannot keep up with it as he retrieves his line. He ends up with line or leader or both wrapped around the rod, or his arm, and often the line entangled in his legs.

In such fast water the trouter should limit himself to short casts, thirty or thirty-five feet, then strip line fast and when the fly is within ten feet of him, make the roll cast to snatch the fly off the water and go into the backcast, ready for the next throw. This is a very effective way to fish fast water.

The roll cast pickup is also useful on slick surfaces where you want a minimum of disturbance as you pick up the fly. To lift even a few feet of line and leader leaves a track on the surface and makes noises sufficient to scare a nearby trout. But if you retrieve the line and leader very carefully to within twenty-five or thirty feet, then make a roll cast pickup, line, leader and fly come out of the water smoothly and slickly, and you can go right into another backcast and forward throw and deposit the fly on the water without any commotion.

Horizontal Pickup

The horizontal pickup is really a variation of the roll cast pickup. It brings the line off the water in corkscrew form, and is of great use to trout fishermen on small meadow streams or placid creeks or the eastern limestone streams. On such water there are many times when it is almost impossible to retrieve the fly without disturbing the water, either through pulling the line across the surface so it leaves a track, or because the fly threatens to hook up on floating weeds or cress. Sometimes, to get to a fish feeding right beyond or even beside a floating weed patch, you must allow your line to drop on the weeds, in order to get the fly to float over him. Then if he doesn't take, there you are, with no way to pull the fly back without disturbing him.

    In such a situation the horizontal pickup will allow you to lift the fly straight

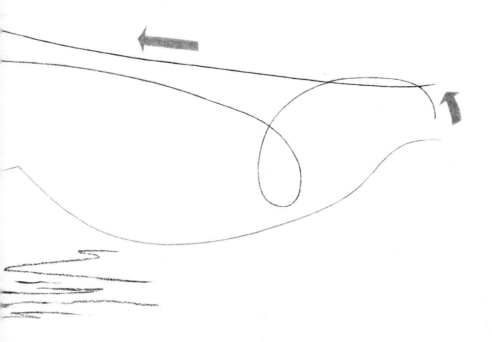

up off the water without excessive commotion or the danger of getting caught in the weeds. It looks like the natural takeoff of a fly. When it is in the air you simply go into your backcast and you are ready for another try at that wily feeder.

To perform this cast, turn the rod until the back of the hand is horizontal to the water, reel facing up (**1**). The left hand holds the line so it will not slip. Holding the rod this way, parallel to the water, give a quick forward and upward roll of the wrist, a corkscrew motion that is translated by the upward and forward movement of the rod to the line (**2**). The line rolls forward about a foot, then line, leader and fly all come off the water in a spiral, up to five feet or more. Once again you go into the backcast (**3**).

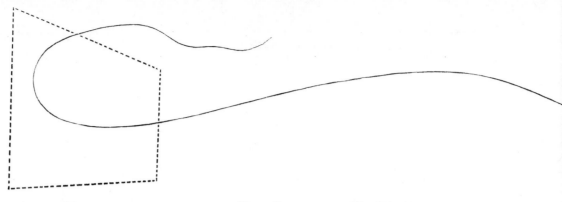

Reverse or Galway Cast

This is the traditional cast when you find yourself in a spot where trees crowd you from behind and you need to get out more line than you can with a roll cast. Many a time in such a situation, if you look carefully you can find some opening in the brush or trees behind you. To put a backcast into that opening accurately would be well nigh impossible. So you turn halfway around and make your *forward* cast into that safe spot amid the branches (1). Just as line

Change-of-Direction Cast

You can beat streamside obstructions by using a change-of-direction cast. To get this throw away you false cast straight up and down stream, just as if you were going to drop the fly straight up-current above you (1). When you

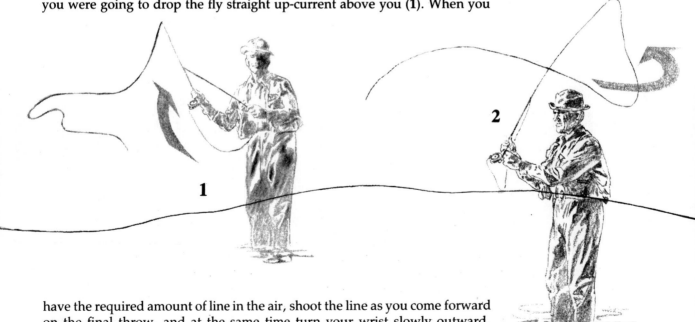

have the required amount of line in the air, shoot the line as you come forward on the final throw, and at the same time turn your wrist slowly outward, aiming the fly at the point you wish to reach (2,3). The false cast should be made very deliberately, slower than in an ordinary cast, to be sure that the line rolls out fully behind you, so that when you turn your wrist and the line follows around it will not tangle in itself. With this cast you can reach out as much as sixty feet and drop the fly at any angle, to right or left, from only a few degrees up to ninety degrees. The same thing can be done with a back-hand cast but the throw must be limited to a shorter line.

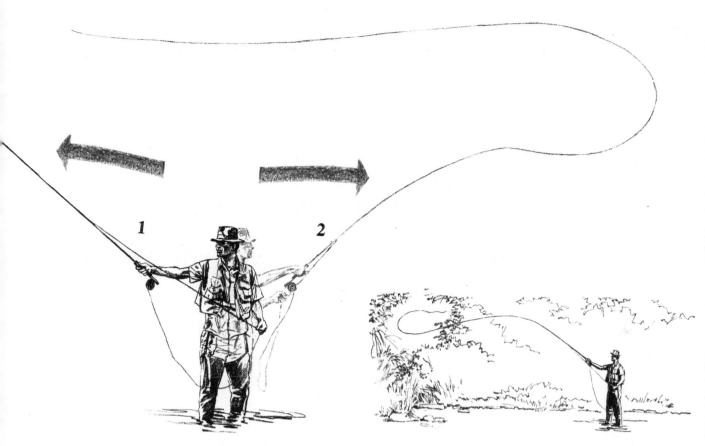

and leader are ready to roll over up there, turn to face the stream and at the same moment bring your rod forward and make the usual forward cast to drop the fly on the water (**2**).

The same thing can be achieved by using a backhand cast to put line, leader and fly into a hole amid the trees. But it's harder to get accuracy with a backhand than with a forward throw.

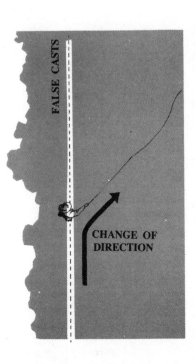

FALSE CASTS

CHANGE OF
DIRECTION

Curve to the Right

When you are fishing a dry fly upstream, the fly often lands upstream of the tippet, in a straight line with it. A trout that rises to that fly will often bump his nose on the tippet as he attempts to take. I have seen many a frustrated fisherman miss strike after strike and go away convinced that the trout are striking short or merely nosing the fly. Actually, he is casting too straight a line; the fly zips out and lights above the tippet so the fish, rising from a downstream position, has to hit the leader tippet first with his nose as he comes up to take. The S-cast will often solve this problem, but sometimes the position of the fish amid conflicting currents and eddies calls for a curve to the right.

   The curve to the right is delivered so that at the end of the cast the fly flips around to your right, ahead of the tippet. When the trout rises there is nothing to impede his take and you can hook him.

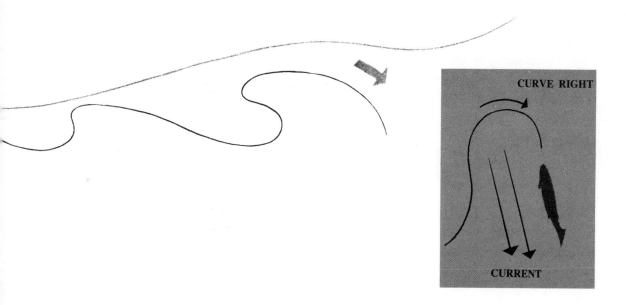

One way to throw this curve is to use only the middle of the rod. Avoid putting the tip into it as you come forward (1), and since the force of that last thrust is missing, the line goes out under the rod, without much juice (2), in a sloppy curve to the right (3). The fly is deposited ahead of the tippet and comes over the fish first and with enough slack line for a free float of several feet.

You can also throw a curve to the right by casting up and downstream, then, as the forward throw is started, turn the wrist towards the spot where you want the fly to land, just as you would in the change-of-direction cast described earlier. As the end of line and leader start to roll over, shoot a couple feet of line and drop the rod tip slightly. The end of line and leader will go into a curve to the right, and usually the throw will put the fly down-current ahead of leader and line.

Curve to the Left

The opposite curve, to the left, is often useful to get around obstructions. It is easy to execute and you can become quite accurate, with a little practice, and find that it gets you to many spots you used to have to pass up. To make a curve to the left, hold the rod at about a forty-degree angle to the side (1), aimed a little to the right of the spot you want the fly to land. As with the S-cast, make the throw with more drive than required for the distance. At the end of the throw halt the rod abruptly, and even pull back a little (2). The sudden stoppage at this forty-degree angle will cause the end of the line to flip the fly around to your left. This cast allows you to drop your fly above a feeder close to your bank.

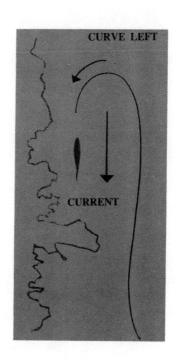

Backhand Casts

There are many times when a backhand cast is the simplest way to fish a difficult lie, as for example, when you are working upstream with a bank on your right, and it is too obstructed to allow room for a backcast in that direction.

To perform a backhand cast the rod is held in the usual manner, then the casting hand is raised across the body toward the left shoulder, palm facing out. From this position the false casts are made back and forth over the left shoulder where the fly has room to move without hanging up on anything. After you have mastered the basic position it soon becomes easy to raise or lower the rod slightly as the need may arise, so that you can execute a backhand cast from shoulder height or at waist height. The main point to keep in mind is that the back of the hand must always be towards the body, and that you must maintain a free-moving wrist.

You can also make a backhand roll cast in this way, to avoid branches which may hang over the bank above you, and where there may be fish feeding right at the edge of these branches. Again, with line, leader and fly on the water in front of you, bring arm and wrist across to the left so the hand comes more or less across your face, with the back of the hand towards you. From this position bring the rod forward and out with good power, and the line will pull in towards you on the water, then roll up and forward and flip the fly over as in the regular roll cast. This is necessarily limited to short distances, but will help you to get to plenty of close-in fish that are hard to reach in any other way.

Cast into the Wind

You often hear a fly fisherman say he can't cast because it's too windy, so he stays home. To be beaten by the wind is going to limit his days astream severely because there are very few days when there is not some degree of breeze. There are plenty of casts to beat the wind; unless it's an absolute howler you can get off your throw with some success. The simplest way is to adjust your position to the wind, so you can cast across wind or downwind. But even if you are using a dry fly, you can often get it up into the wind, at least for a reasonable distance, by using a low cast into the wind.

To make this important throw, all you do is make the usual forward cast but come through hard at the end, bringing the rod down so the tip almost

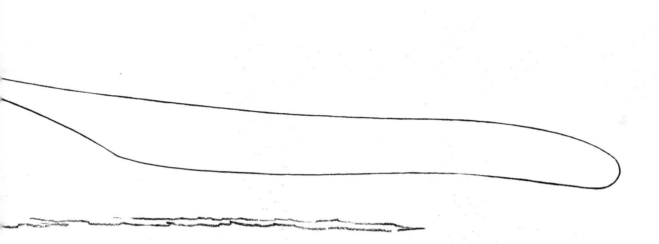

touches the water. This hard, low push sends line and leader out in a tight, flat bow and the fly will flip over to the water instead of blowing back at you as it would in a high-thrown delivery. You can accentuate the power of this cast by using the double haul to get extra line speed and put even a fair-sized, fluffy dry fly out thirty or forty feet into a stiff breeze.

This same driving throw is good to get a fly in under overhanging limbs or banks, or under a bridge, since the purpose is the same. In one instance you are getting out under the wind, in the other you are getting out under an obstruction.

2

Crosswind Cast

Sometimes an angler finds himself casting where the wind is blowing hard from right to left, so it carries his backcast across behind him, and when it comes forward it catches in his clothing or hat, or bangs into his arm or rod. The reason often is that in attempting to circumvent that crosswind blast he is hurrying his forward cast. The thing to do is to take it easy, slow down and allow the backcast to blow down and drop a bit, almost to the water. For the forward cast, aim slightly upstream of the spot where you want the fly to drop, continuing the slow, non-pressure throw. As in the change-of-direction cast, the line will follow the impulse of your wrist and come up

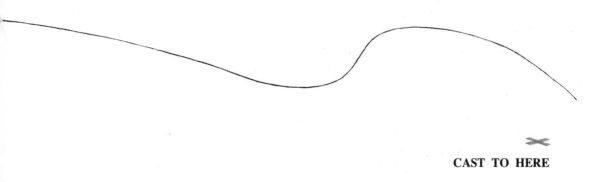

CAST TO HERE

TARGET

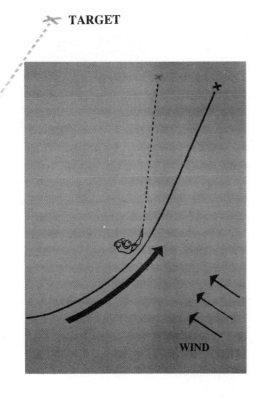

WIND

over your head and on out. For better accuracy and to get length, you can follow through after starting the forward cast and bring the rod down almost to the water. The fact that you are not pressing is what brings this cast off.

If the wind is very heavy you can also get out a crosswind cast by letting the fly drift all the way over to your left on the backcast. Then it will come through almost like a backhand cast, on your left side as you make the forward throw. A third way to beat a crosswind is to hold the rod low, almost horizontally, out to the right, and make both backcast and forward cast at that same low level.

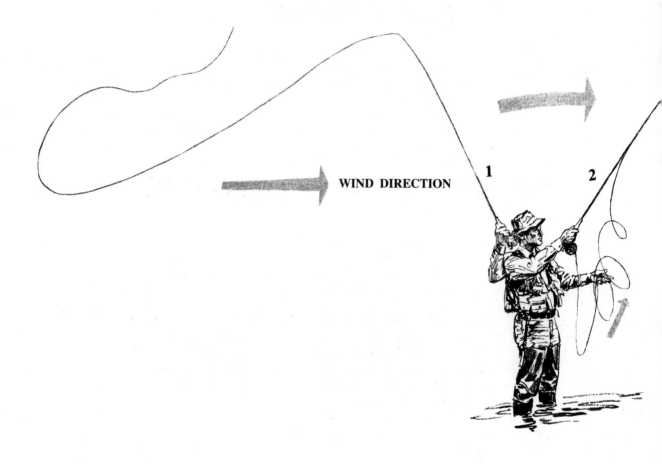

WIND DIRECTION

1

2

Downwind Cast

Many fly fishermen find more difficulty in casting with a stiff wind behind them than if it is blowing in their faces. The wind knocks the backcast down and on the forward throw it sinks into their hat or the back of their fishing vest. One way to outwit the wind is to use it. Shorten the backcast to about fifteen feet, retaining lots of line in your left hand for shooting.

When your rod has reached the eleven o'clock position in front of you, shoot the rest of the line. The wind will then take hold, and at the end of the cast the line will straighten out parallel to the water and drop down.

You can also make a horizontal cast in this situation by allowing the backcast to drift back behind you, to your left, then aiming the forward throw well out to the right. End this cast by stopping the rod high, at head height, which gives room for the line to be curved around by the wind to a point straight downwind.

Cast Across Incoming Fast Current

You often see trout rising in the slow water on the far side of a current from you. If you were to make the usual cast, letting the line fall to the fast water in front of you, it would be whisked downstream in a jiffy, dragging the fly away from any trout that might have ideas of taking. In such fast current it is almost impossible to mend the line, either, to get any more float.

The thing to do in this situation is to make an S-cast, then hold the rod as high as you can reach, trying to keep the line above that fast current so it is not touched by it until leader and fly have time to go naturally over the trout. As the fly floats down you can get still more coverage by moving the rod tip downstream.

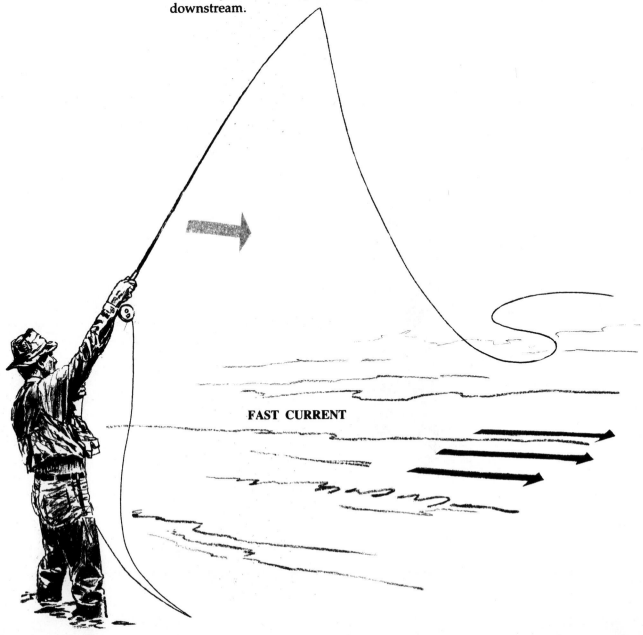

FAST CURRENT

Bow-and-Arrow Cast

Every once in a while an angler finds himself in a spot where he is completely hemmed in, can't make a backcast or a roll cast. There just seems no way to get that fly out. In such a situation, you can use the fly outfit something like a bow and arrow. Hold the fly in the left hand, by the bend of the hook, and strip several feet of line off the reel. Then push the left hand back, and at the same time bring the rod hand forward, so the line is tight between rod tip and fly. Then push the rod into a bow. Using a lot of wrist, give a hard, forward snap. The line will go forward, pulling the fly from your fingers, and shoot out for the length of line you have stripped. You can get a cast of about twenty-five feet in this way, often sufficient to take a trout from a particularly barricaded spot.

The Double Haul

The double haul is the cast to use when you need power to get your offerings out to where fish are lying.

To execute the double haul, strip off extra line from the reel and hold it in loops in your left hand or lay it in coils on the bottom of a boat or in a shooting basket if you are using one. Hold the line just below the butt guide in the left hand and with this hand pull down hard as you begin the pickup (1). The pickup itself is done with extra vigor, as is the backward and upward flip of the wrist at the end of the pickup. This hard pull, working against the downward pull of line and the bend of the rod, will give great speed to the backcast. So as not to slow this speed, allow the left hand, still keeping hold of the line, to drift to head height (2). Then at the same second that you begin the forward cast, rip the left hand down hard (3), again providing tension in the line, and when the forward impulse has been imparted to the line, release it from the left hand and all the line which has been stripped from the reel will shoot out (4).

You can practice this double haul in sections, mastering first the hard down-pull of line with the left hand, to synchronize it with the cast, then the drift up, which seems to be one of the most difficult steps for casters to master; and finally the forward throw and release of the line. The best way to practice this is to put thirty-five or forty feet of line in the air, pull down with your left hand as you send the line to the rear, pull down again as you make the forward throw, and keep it up, time and again. Suddenly you will have it, and once in the stream you will find yourself doing it automatically, without even thinking.

**RETRIEVING THE
FLY LINE**

Retrieving the fly line is one of the most important parts of fishing for trout. I remember one day when I was watching a fisherman in the next pool laying out a beautiful line. It went straight back and high up, the rod bent just right when he started the foward cast and the line shot out sixty feet and dropped quietly to the surface.

"That man's a fine fly caster," I said to my companion.

"But he never catches any fish," he replied.

I watched the caster, then, for a few minutes. I soon saw why he didn't catch fish. He was in there concentrating on the cast, all right, but once the fly and line were on the water that was the extent of the effort he put into his fishing. When the line had drifted through and was straight below him he pulled it in. This type of retrieve might bring a few fish, but not many. He didn't realize that it's what happens to the fly after it is on the water that matters to the fish. By your retrieve you make the artificial fly ape the natural food on which trout feed.

Retrieve does not always mean handling the line so as to impart motion to the fly. It can mean preventing movement—that is, unnatural movement, as with the dry fly (*see* Dry-Fly Fishing).

There are two well-known ways to retrieve the fly line. One is to bring the line back entirely with the left hand, twisting the wrist and picking up the line with the fingers and tucking it into the palm in a figure 8. But I prefer the strip method of retrieve, which enables the angler to bring in line fast or slow, and always have control. While this is often regarded as a modern innovation, I have found mention of it in fishing literature as far back as 1885, when Henry P. Welles, in his book *Fly Rod and Fly Tackle*, described the method only slightly different from the way we do it today.

To retrieve by stripping in the line, hold the rod so the thumb of casting hand comes over the top and protrudes from the grip, while the second or third finger, whichever is more comfortable, comes around under the grip and extends to meet the thumb. Grasp the line between this finger and thumb and use the left hand to grasp the line, between the right hand and the reel, and pull the line between thumb and finger, in strips of varying length. At the conclusion of each pull of the line, thumb and finger clamp down on the line and hold it taut while the left hand comes up for the next pull.

The line that is stripped in can be held in loops in the hand or allowed to drop to the surface of the water. The latter procedure is fine on still water, but in a fast-moving current the line will be whipped downstream and perhaps be dragged under so that it is impossible to shoot it on the next cast.

On the other hand, sometimes when you hold the line looped in your left hand the wind tangles those loops and again it is hard to shoot the line. The loops bunch up and form knots at the guides. This is just one of the hazards the fly caster on foot has to deal with as best

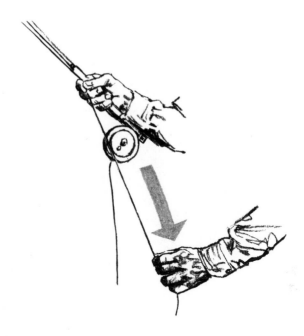

he can. But if you are fishing from a skiff, on a lake, you can coil the shooting line in the bottom of the skiff, then tuck the line nearest you, as it comes up to the reel, into your pants pocket. When you make the forward throw the impulse of the cast will pull the line out of the pocket and you can get a long cast without the line twisting.

One thing you must remember in using the strip method of retrieve is to keep the rod tip high, pointing up at a forty-five degree angle at least, to cushion a hard strike as a fish takes. I have lost a great many good fish through carelessness this way, big brown trout and steelhead that broke me on the strike. I knew exactly what was happening but I would forget or become careless and often as I retrieved, just as I made the forward pull of the fly, a big fish would hit and the combination of my pull and his hard strike would be too much. Finally I learned to do it automatically, just push the rod butt in against my stomach and keep it there, and the rod tip up, throughout the retrieve. I seldom lose a fish on a hit these days.

One sure way to be broken off when you are fishing a nymph, wet fly or streamer is to start wading downstream as you retrieve. Invariably you will drop the tip of the rod as you move, and then when you get a hit the fish has a straight pull, and tic! That's all that is needed. He breaks you off.

This is particularly important when you are using light tippets. It doesn't take much of a shock to break a 4X tippet, which is geared to only 4.3 pounds pull. With anything as light as a 6X or 7X you do not even dare to strike; simply hold the rod at the right angle and let the fish hook himself.

**MENDING
THE LINE**

In almost every form of fly fishing the angler needs to mend his line at some time or other. The purpose of the mend is to maintain a longer drag-free float, if you are using a dry fly, and a broadside float if you are using a bucktail or streamer. When you make a cast across stream, the current is constantly working to snatch the line and belly it downstream (**1**), thus pulling the fly and defeating the drag-free float you want. To prevent that line-belly and keep the dry floating without drag, or the streamer broadside in the current so it is more visible to the trout, you have to mend the line upstream. To do this, push the rod out in front, low, towards the position of the fly. Then make a slight flip and a half roll of the wrist, up and outward, very much as in the roll cast, only horizontal, close to the water (**2**). The motion imparted to the line by this thrust will pull the line off the surface and

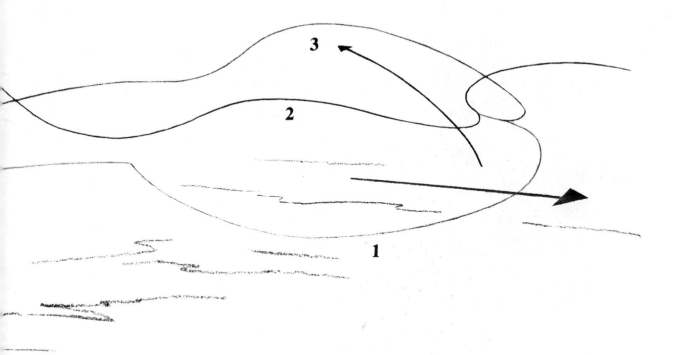

roll it over and up (**3**). When it falls to the surface it will be in an upstream bow, and until the current grabs it again you will get some more free float. It is often possible to make several mends during a single float. Considerable delicacy is required to mend the line when you are using a dry fly, to avoid moving the fly.

The comparatively new floating/sinking lines are made especially with the possibility of this mending in view. The first ten or thirty feet of the line sinks, according to your choice of line (*see* TACKLE), while the rest of the line, called running line, floats. You mend this running line in order to keep that sinking section out in the current floating your fly over the fish for a much longer distance than would be possible without mending.

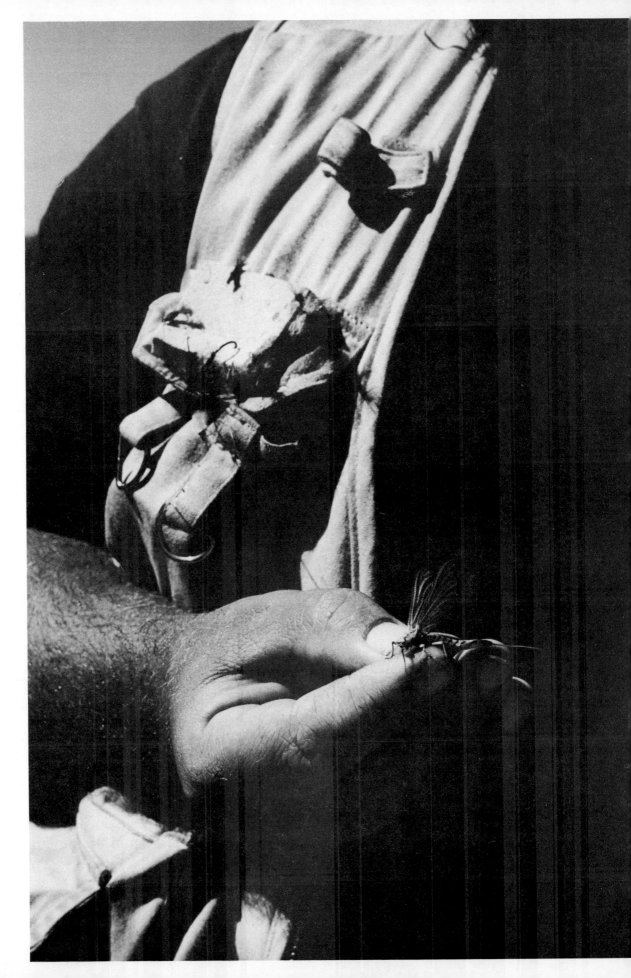

5 DRY FLY FISHING

So much has been written about the difficulties of dry-fly fishing that most beginners start out with either a wet fly or nymph or streamer, and often never overcome their initial fear of the difficulties of the dry. Actually, I believe that the place to start your trout fishing is with the dry fly. Here, everything is on the screen in front of you. You see the trout rise or you select a spot where you think he should be lying. You make your cast to put the fly over him and you see the fly land, observe its float, see the fish take, or see that he does not take. In the latter event you may often discover the reason he does not take and correct it in your next try. You also may see around you clues to the food he is likely to be feeding on—a hatch of small flies, or large, or a serving of grasshoppers being blown from the banks onto the surface of the water.

Since most dry-fly fishing is done upstream, you are coming at the trout from behind, where he is less likely to see you. A trout on a feeding station looks out at the world in a special way. His vision operates in the field of an inverted cone, the point at his eye, the form of the cone extending upward from his eye towards the surface, the base of the cone forming his circular window, small or large, depending on the depth at which the trout is holding. Outside the window, the undersurface of the water acts like a mirror, reflecting the stones and grasses on the bottom. Because of the refraction of light rays, the trout's view outside the window shows a foreshortened angler, and the trees on the bank are so foreshortened as to appear like grass growing there.

This phenomenon of the mirror is more obvious in shallower water; in deeper areas the bottom must look uneven and indistinct, and when the surface is windswept, the window, too, must be blurred. When ripples sweep the pool, the trout's window must appear as a shattered windshield glass, and the same thing must be true in fast water. In such places, fish often hold only an inch under the surface when they are feeding, the more readily to grab the fly that flashes past that broken window.

107

Most authorities are of the opinion that the trout on his station first sees the light flashes off the indentations of the feet of a natural insect as it floats down towards the window; then, as it comes nearer, he sees the wing sticking up just outside the window, and then the fly enters his window and he sees the entire insect.

All the explanations and diagrams I have seen illustrating the vision of the trout have applied to the classic position of a trout on a feeding station in a clear, slick pool. In such a position it is easy to understand the points from which you can approach a trout safely, from behind, or from the side, as long as you keep below the line that marks his eye-to-window field of vision. But it is unwise to assume that this is the only way he sees. Consider the case of a cruising trout. I have seen such a fish suddenly change his course and go straight for a downed fly seven to ten feet away, outside his supposed field of vision. He either hears the fly or line fall on the surface and moves over to investigate, or he sees the light flashes sent out by the fly.

But when the trout is feeding, maintaining a certain place in the water to take the naturals as they come over him, he is near the surface and you must come in beyond his field of vision. You can get very close to a feeder by coming in from behind, or kneeling on the bank or in shallow water.

Even though you are out of his sight, you must also make your approach quietly. If you step heavily on the bank or splash water as you wade out, the noise quickly reaches the fish. Especially in a placid pool, sound and water motion push their way upstream. As you work your way up from the tail of the pool, the nearest fish will run upstream and scare other trout up there. The alarm precedes you up the pool in chain reaction. Where a moment ago the surface was dimpled with rising trout, it will suddenly be as dead as a midwinter day.

If you do inadvertently scare fish in such a way, you can sometimes wait it out and eventually take them. Stand perfectly still for five or ten minutes, making no move, and sometimes they will forget you and begin to accept the sight of your pillar-like form standing there, and start to feed again. But the successful trout fisherman always comes in gently, quietly.

LIFE CYCLE OF A FLY

The dry-fly man's ideal pool is as slick as a skater's rink, the clear water edged by watercress. Towards one bank or the other, midway up the pool, perhaps a couple of moss boils show, the long strands that stream out from it working in the current, the ends, just under water, occasionally causing a disturbance that could be mistaken for the swirl of a trout. The shores are edged with matted grasses, too, and here and there between the shoreline foliage and those midstream growths, the current has cut gravelly channels. That's where you will often see the trout, lying there with a clear upward view of anything that comes riding down that current.

In this idyllic scene we're talking about, there is a hatch of mayflies taking place, let's say the well-known Light Cahill, a fly comparatively common on North American streams. To understand a hatch, the angler must know the life cycle of aquatic insects. The story starts when the female flies down and places her tail in the water, washing the eggs off, or she drops her eggs while flying over the river and they sink to the bottom or adhere to underwater grasses, stones or old logs. The eggs hatch after a period of time, in many cases about thirty days. Out of the eggs come small nymphs which hide in the grasses and under rocks on the bottom, feeding on microscopic matter. As time goes on they grow and break out of the first nymphal case, or shuck, and another one forms and covers them. In this manner they go through variations for one or two years. As emergence time approaches they become more active, moving around a lot, and finally they swim to the surface film and float with the current while the nymphal case splits and the insect comes out. It waves its wings to dry them and takes off. This is the dun stage, the subimago of the scientist. They are weak, slow flyers and often go only a foot or so, then drop back to the surface, float again, fluttering and drifting, and take to the air again. Finally the dun makes it to the bushes, grasses and trees along the river bank, where it lights, usually on the underside of leaves. Through a period of twenty-four hours it evolves into an insect with almost transparent wings and a gaudier overall appearance than the earlier dun. The mouth has atrophied and the breeding organs developed. The only purpose now is to breed and die, in a single day of life, hence the scientific name *ephemerid*.

When ready to mate they leave their places on the bushes and fly over the water, the males reaching there first and dancing up and down in a swarm. Then the females come out to join them. At this stage they are called spinners, and this is the imago, the perfect insect. The male attaches himself to the female from underneath and the eggs are fertilized. The male then flies aimlessly away and falls dead, usually over land but sometimes in the river. And, starting the cycle again, the female dips her tail in the water or drops the eggs while flying, then dies and falls to the surface, wings outspread, the spent spinner— hence the "spentwing" flies we use as imitations.

The intense and fascinating variety of trout fishing lies in the fact that at each stage throughout this life cycle the aquatic fly is vulnerable to feeding trout: the nymph that hatches from the eggs and lives its own varied life in the underwater world; the dun that emerges from the nymph at a preordained time; the spinner that is the breeding form, and the spentwing that has performed its part in nature and is dead or dying, wings stretched flat on the surface.

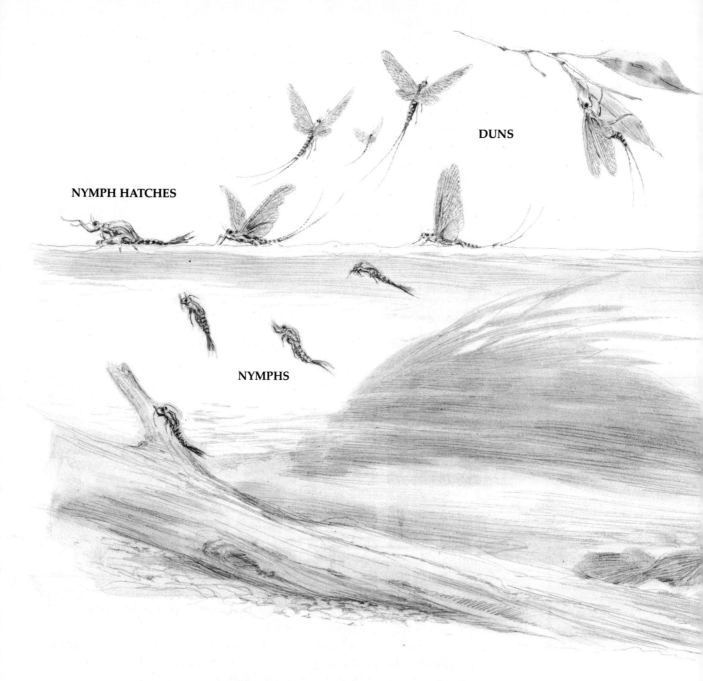

NYMPH HATCHES

DUNS

NYMPHS

The Life Cycle of Aquatic Insects
The cycle begins when the female deposits her eggs onto the water. They sink to the bottom or adhere to underwater grasses, stones or old logs. In about thirty days, the eggs hatch into nymphs which hide in the grasses or

SELECTIVE FEEDING

Such is the selectivity of the feeding trout that in most instances he will take only the imitation of the one stage of the insect upon which he is working; or something so like it that he is fooled into believing it to be the real thing. Thus if you offer a nymph, when he has his eye cast higher, for the dun, you may go hitless. But if he is feeding on nymphs and you offer the dun, you have the same result.

Of all the surface forms, the dun stage of many flies is the most

110

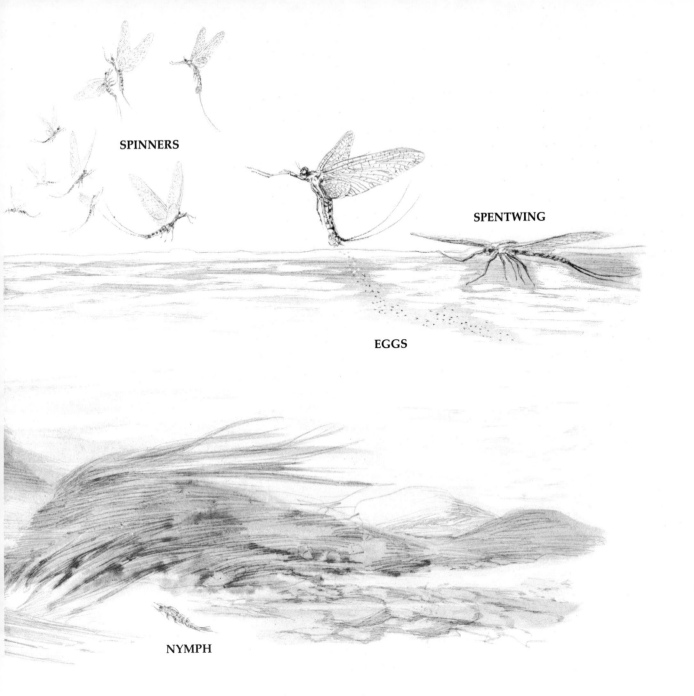

SPINNERS

SPENTWING

EGGS

NYMPH

under rocks on the bottom. Then the nymphs hatch into winged mayflies (duns) which float on the surface, take to the air, but soon return to the stream and mate, and the cycle is repeated.

important from the point of view of catching trout because this is the stage that is most seen by anglers. It usually comes off the water during the day. The spinner of some flies comes back to the river at dusk or after dark, when most anglers are no longer on the stream. The dun is commonly the most visible to the trout through the longest period, as it rides the surface in the nymphal shuck, emerges as a weak, slow flyer, often fluttering a few feet or inches, falls to the surface, floats

111

again for inches or feet, and so on until it finally becomes airborne. All this time it is moving along the thread of the current where eager trout lie watching for food.

And as if on signal, as more flies begin to hatch, trout begin to feed, a few at first, then, as the hatch forms, in greater numbers. Everywhere

PHASES IN THE LIFE CYCLE OF A MAYFLY

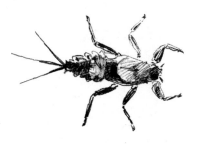

Nymphal phase of the western green drake mayfly. During this period of its life cycle, the insect lives on the river bottom.

Dun phase of the insect. The fly has just emerged from its nymphal stage; as it flutters on the surface, it is an easy prey for feeding trout.

Spinner phase: the female with its egg sac developed and ready to be fertilized over the water by the male.

Artificial Green Drake dry fly which imitates the natural insect.

A mayfly hatch on the Fall River in California. As trout begin to feed on the emerging insects, fishermen cast dry flies (*below*) that mimic the naturals.

trout rise from stations they have selected where they can face into the current. Sometimes their stations will be smack against a patch of grass or moss, where the obstruction speeds up the pace of the water and pushes it out, or again it may be against a rock that redirects the current, or over those gravel beds between two islands of weeds—all spots that are natural drifts for anything riding the surface. From those preferred locations they rise up and slurp as they snatch the floating tidbits.

CHOOSE A TARGET

Think of this natural emergence of the fly as you conduct your dry-fly fishing and you will have taken the first step towards presenting your fly properly. A trout feeding on a hatch is facing into the current, usually about three to eight inches below the surface, looking upstream for those flies to come down to him. When he sees the fly coming he moves up to take it. In a fairly slow-moving, classic limestone stream or spring creek, such as described earlier, his move will be a slow drift up and take. If you can see him, you will note that everything is moving at the same speed as he takes—the fly on the surface, the current, and the trout beneath, as he lets himself slip back with the current, decides he likes what he sees, and then gets a fin-hold, moves up, opens his mouth and inhales.

Sometimes when you step into a pool where trout are rising there are so many plops and gurgles that you hardly know where to start. In this situation the tendency is to cast fast and furiously. But if you do, you'll put the fish down, or at least alert them so they'll look over the fly more carefully and perhaps discover it's counterfeit, and refuse it. Such a rapture of feeding trout is no place for scatter shooting. A quail hunter knows that if he shoots into the middle of a rising covey he seldom touches a feather. He picks out one bird and concentrates on leading him.

So, when trout are rising freely don't cast haphazardly, hoping that your fly will go over one or another. As a trout feeds on an emerging hatch he doesn't like to move far in any direction to take a fly. He wants it right across the plate or at least clipping a corner. Choose your fish, and put your fly over him for a perfect float. The fly should light far enough upstream of his position—three or four feet—to give him time to see it and move up and take.

It is always best to start with the nearest riser. If you cast to a fish high in the pool you may be laying your line over others you have not seen, and put them down.

When you hook your chosen fish, try to keep him in close. Put the pressure on and bring him down towards you at once, so that the noise and disturbance of the strike and the subsequent fight will not disturb any fish lying higher in the pool.

Once you have chosen a certain trout as your target it pays to watch

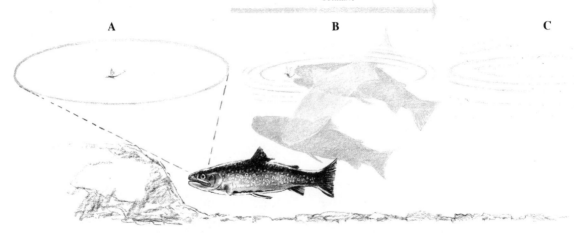

A   B   C

Circles of trout's take, drifting downstream with the current, often deceive an angler into casting below the fish's holding station. Trout sees the natural at *A*, but may wait to rise until it is at *B*. After taking natural at *B*, trout returns to holding station. Circles drift downstream quickly, and if angler casts to *C*, he'll drop fly below the trout. He should cast above the point where fish took, to *A*, or even slightly above.

him rise several times before making your throw. Try to pinpoint his position. When a trout takes a fly he leaves his feeding station. He may move up under the fly and drift back, eyeing it, perhaps eventually taking it several feet downstream from his hold. Remember, too, that after his rise the circles of his take are drifting down the current. On this account anglers sometimes think the fish is lying farther downstream than he is, and so cast below his stand, or drop the fly right on top of him.

After the trout takes a natural or refuses or misses the fly, the angler must give him time to get back to his feeding station. If you cast before he has settled down you may only succeed in scaring him, and it will be that much longer before he starts to feed again. Feeding trout, particularly in a good, steady hatch, rise with a certain regularity, a feeding rhythm. If you study his timing you can drop your fly at just about the time the fish is ready to come up for a natural, and your chances of getting a hit are that much better.

DRAG

If the fly does not come down the current in a lifelike manner, even if the pattern is right the trout will seldom take. So the angler must avoid "drag," which is what occurs when a fly travels faster or slower or in a different direction than the current, thus dragging across the flow of the stream. The S-cast (*see* CASTING TECHNIQUES) is almost always the best way to avoid drag and achieve this free-floating fly.

If you do make a mistake and the fly drags, let it float on through until it is well below the position of the trout. To lift it quickly over his head will cause water disturbance and alert him to something wrong. Let the fly float down close to you before you lift it for your next try.

In order to assure this drag-free float, before starting to cast the fly fisher should study the current and eddies, even the minor ones, near the rise, locating the thread of the main current, the lesser flows of side currents, all pushing their way at different angles downstream and ready to drag a fly out of the groove. Once the angler knows those dangers he can move into position, and drop his fly confidently so it will float free in the current that is bringing the trout his dinner.

Sometimes a change of the angler's position, even so small as a couple of feet one way or another, or up or down stream, can assure the chance of a good float.

I remember a trout I took on a Pennsylvania limestone stream. He was rising close to my bank, only an inch out, feeding hard and often. The main current came across the pool on an angle, pushing in to the bank, then skidded off and slipped on down to where I stood about thirty-five feet below. The feeder seemed to be right at the point where this fast current swept against the bank. I cast and dropped the fly

Variation in current speed produces drag, the dry-fly angler's enemy. Faster current in foreground will belly author's line when the fly drops on the slick water beyond. An S-cast will give him a longer drag-free float.

into that main current, five feet above him, and watched the fly ride the surface down to the bank. The push of the water off the bank saved it from hanging up there and it came down my way.

"A fine-looking presentation," I thought.

But after four such presentations I had not had a hit, and during that time the trout came up twice and took naturals. I decided to give this a little study. I soon saw that another current was flowing right along the bank and the fish was feeding in this one, taking his naturals an inch or two above the main current. My flies had been riding by a couple of inches behind him, and I doubt that he even saw them. There was enough food coming down that minor current close to the bank to keep his eyes zeroed in on that.

This called for a different play because if I cast from where I was in my effort to reach that second current, the main flow would seize my line and pull it and I'd immediately have drag. The fly would skid across current and the trout would know it was a phony.

I walked up the bank another ten feet and I was now only twenty-five feet below the riser. From here I could throw an S-cast to allow plenty of slack line, and hold my rod high as the fly floated down, and before the current could straighten out that slack the fly would go over the fish, drag-free. If he didn't take, I could let the fly float on through until it was opposite me, do a roll cast pickup (*see* CASTING), a false cast or two, and try again.

My first throw was too far out. The near line got into the main current and it pulled the fly downstream fast. I let it go through, and on the next cast I made it. The fly dropped an inch out from the bank, with plenty of slack line on the water, and came floating down as free as the wind. Up came the trout and took.

CRUISING TROUT

Sometimes the angler comes upon a pool where there are many risers but the rises are not consistently in the one spot. There's a pop here, then another a few feet away, then another off to the right. Or you may see the wakes made by fish as they cruise. Your problem is where to drop the fly to put it within that trout's range of vision.

A cruising trout takes his window with him. He sees those flies on the surface at the full range of the base of his cone. And you must remember that he sees you, too, if you stand out above those lines that obscure his closer view. And as he is moving all the time, at any given moment he may look straight in your direction. So care in approach and delivery of the cast is just as essential as ever. Sometimes more so, because you often find these cruisers in the slow water at the tail of a pool, or in the slick water of a shallow slough where there is little current to distort what they see. In such a situation a sidearm cast is often the only way you can get off a throw without spooking the fish.

However, when you fish to cruising trout you can sometimes attract a fish by fly movement. I recall a day when I was fishing the long, flat water in the tail of a large pool on the Big Hole River in Montana and had spotted several cruising fish. I chose my target and cast to him, matching a size 16 Light Cahill that was coming off the water. He didn't seem to see it, moved to the left away from it. I pulled back with the rod tip, bringing the fly very lightly across the surface a few inches, so it looked like an insect struggling to break away from the surface film and become airborne. That was all it took. Either the trout saw the slight movement in the edge of his window, or he heard the slight noise that even the slightest of line movement makes, and it aroused his curiosity. He changed his cruising direction, came back and grabbed that Light Cahill.

To fish such cruisers in shallow water or still water such as you find in sloughs calls for the longest, lightest leader you can manage because on the slick surface the minimum of everything is required—diameter, noise and visibility.

DRY FLY ON RIFFLED WATER

When you are fishing a dry fly on a rippled surface, be it from wind or current, and especially when you are using a very small dry fly in an effort to match a prevailing hatch on which the fish are feeding, it is often difficult and even impossible to see the fly amid the dancing waves. You miss strike after strike as those fish hit your fly and you are watching some natural that is floating three or four feet away from it. Or you strike too hard because you saw his rise too late, and the fish is there but you break him off, the final indignity in the fly man's book.

In such a situation you can get a great assist from your floating line and leader. Let your eyes follow the line out to end, then spot the leader, which makes a slight track on the water, and continue on out until you locate the fly, or at least have a good idea just about where it is. If you see a rise anywhere in that immediate area, strike. Many times you will have your fish.

It is safe to go a little heavier on your tippet on such riffled surface. True, the water commotion isn't sufficient to distort the fish's vision enough that he will mistake a totally wrong fly for the one he is feeding on, but it does seem to be enough to prevent him spotting a slight discrepancy. And the noise of the bouncing water may also prevent him from hearing the noise made by the line hitting the surface close to him, if you wish to shorten your leader a foot or so.

I had a good example of this when I was fishing the Henry's Fork of the Snake River at Last Chance, Idaho. The day had started out calm but no trout were rising. Then the wind came and really began to whistle. The surface rolled and tossed. But trout started to rise, too, wildly, splashing water that the wind blew away. The hatch on which they were feeding could be matched with a size 12 no-hackle Slate-wing Brown Dun, and knowing the independent, selective rainbows of the Snake, I was pretty sure that that was what I would have to offer them. I did so, using a seven-foot two-inch Scientific Anglers rod and matching number 4 floating line. My fourteen-foot leader was tapered to 5X.

"Too light for this wind," I thought.

I cut back the leader to nine feet, ending with a 4X tippet, still fine enough to free float that fly. The short leader was easier to throw and I could get it out into the wind by bringing the rod down hard as I finished the cast. Because of the riffle on the water, the less-than-perfect lightness of delivery wasn't quite as important as it might have been on flat water, and on my first cast I was into one of those rainbows, a sixteen-incher that ran upstream, jumped and hit with a big splash, ran some more and jumped again. A nice fish to take in any weather and doubly satisfactory in those riffles.

The same thing applies when you fish heavy water in a rapids or long, rough flow of a stream. You can afford to be a little less delicate than in the slick water—but not much. And regardless, in heavy current it is hard to achieve a drag-free float of any distance, and it is always best to fish a dry fly on a short line. Make a short cast, hold your arm high and be satisfied with a short, free drift. Use the roll cast pickup (*see* CASTING TECHNIQUES) and cast again.

THE DOWNSTREAM DRY FLY

Normally the angler fishing a dry fly wends his way upstream, casting to rising trout, confident that he is unseen from his position behind the fish as it lies on its feeding station facing upstream. He casts a serpentine line to put the fly over the fish with a drag-free float. When the trout rises and takes, the strike will pull the barb back into his mouth.

This is the classic manner of dry-fly fishing, looking always upstream, and it is the perfect way for most occasions and in the long run will bring you many more fish than any other dry-fly procedure. But you can add to your fishing rewards by looking over your shoulder every so often. Because when you wade carefully and slowly, there will always be fish that move into feeding position below you after your quiet passage from the scene. A downstream cast of a dry fly, properly executed and with proper line handling, can get you to many of these fish which would ordinarily be considered out of bounds. As they become increasingly skillful in casting, modern anglers are fishing the dry fly downcurrent more than ever before.

One day I was well out in a pool trying for a riser that kept making mighty slurps as he took naturals from the surface about thirty feet above me. I got a good float over him and he took my matching artificial. He was a fine fish, a good two-pounder. After I had landed and released him I stood there for a few minutes, resting the water. Then I heard an even mightier slurp, this time from behind me. The sound brought my head around in time to see the concentric rings spreading out from a nice rise forty feet below me. If I wanted to fish that trout in the conventional dry-fly manner, from below, I would have to wade ashore very carefully, to avoid scaring him, then go well back from the bank so I wouldn't be seen or heard, and make my way down to where I could get back into the river and wade out into position below him for the upstream throw. It meant a lot of work and I might put him down anyway, he was so close.

"I'll fish him from here," I thought.

I turned around carefully, false cast a couple of times, then dropped the fly three feet above the position of the fish, using the S-cast to avoid drag. The float was good. The fly went over him and he came up and took. I hesitated a good five or six seconds, then lifted the rod tip to strike and had him.

The reason for the S-cast is the same as in the upstream cast. The fly must light a few feet above the riser, with enough slack line to allow it to float over him naturally, free of drag, and ahead of the leader tippet. A good S-cast also keeps the line enough back from him that he does nót hear the sound of the line hitting the surface close to him, which will scare him off his hold.

Sometimes on a windy day as you throw the downstream S-cast, you may find that the wind will straighten out the curves. However, everything is not lost. Let the line, leader and fly drop to the surface in a straight line and finish with upheld rod, then drop it fast. You will get a couple of feet of drag-free float before you run out of line. The fly goes over him first, and when he takes, he should be hooked.

I once saw Hans Gebetsroither, Fishmeister on the Traun River at Gmunden, Austria, take a nice grayling on his own version of the downstream float. Hans and I were standing in hip-deep water about seventy feet from shore. We were facing upstream, seeing before us the sharp green V of the steep-sided valley through which the Traun runs down from its lake, the Traunsee. Beyond the lake a series of ridges pushed up to the Traunstein, a six-thousand-foot block of rock fifteen miles away. It was a beautiful sight. But our eyes were on the river and above us we found not a single riser.

Then we heard a plop. It came from behind us. We turned gently, so not to disturb the water, and there about thirty feet below us was a big, widening circle.

"A nice fish made that rise," said Hans.

It rose again with a satisfactory slurp.

"Downstream," I said. "Why don't you try him anyway?"

Hans got his line in the air and dropped the fly about twenty-five feet below us. Then he slowly brought the rod back to the side until it pointed almost straight upstream, pulling the line slowly along the surface.

"What are you doing?" I asked.

"Watch," he said. "Just a way of getting the fly over that fish without his seeing the leader tippet. The fly will go over him ahead of line and leader."

As fly, leader and line started drifting along in the current, he brought the rod downstream, moving it slowly along, keeping the line just tight enough to avoid drag. As he ran out of line he extended his arm to get a little more float. Altogether he got a drift of some six feet, all with the fly riding ahead of the leader. As we watched, that grayling came up and took, a nice fifteen-incher.

While the S-cast is generally the throw you will use for the downstream dry fly, there are other ways of getting the fly to a downstream fish. When you see trout rising along a bank across from you and slightly downstream, you can achieve a drag-free downstream float by using the curve casts either to the right or the left (see CASTING TECHNIQUES). But first study the flow of the current around that fish. A careful observance of the currents and counter currents, glides, riffles and eddies will tell you the most efficient cast for any particular spot.

If you make a curve cast and the fish doesn't hit, then you can carefully bring line, leader and fly back upstream and away from the trout and try another cast. Quite often that first try will give you a look at the currents and their actions and give you a hint as to what to try next—a curve to the right or left, or the serpentine.

In all downstream fishing, remember that when the fly goes over the trout he is facing you, and when he rises to take, his mouth will be wide open. You must steel yourself not to strike too quickly. It is hard to do when you see the fish take, but a quick strike will only pull the fly out of his mouth. Try to hold your strike for a few seconds. When a trout takes a fly he often sinks down with the fly held in his mouth, so you have time for this slow strike. Sometimes he will move his head from one side to the other and a strike will then set the hook.

When a fly goes over a downstream fish and he refuses, you must be extra careful with your line work on the retrieve, making as little commotion as possible as you bring line, leader and fly upstream. Strip it in slowly and quietly until the fly is ten feet from you, or closer, then lift line and leader gently from the surface by raising your casting arm. Then give an upward and backward flip of the wrist to pick the fly off the surface with no stir at all.

With the downstream dry fly, as indeed in all fishing, it is never wise to try for too long a float. There is such a thing as letting line, leader and fly float downstream and then feeding line through the guides to lengthen the float. Sometimes you can achieve a drift of as much as twenty-five or thirty feet in this way, trying to go over a fish you have seen below you. You may take a fish in this way now and again, but you seldom get a true, drag-free float. And in addition, at such a distance it is difficult to strike and set the hook. It takes too long for the impulse to pass down all that line to the fish and you fail to hook him. Better to creep quietly ashore if the fish is that far below you and then go downstream and come at him in the conventional upstream way. The only time I recommend a long downstream line-feed of this kind is when it is absolutely impossible to get at the fish in any other way. The chances are too great that you will down him, rather than hook him.

TERRESTRIALS

The dry-fly man is not limited to aquatic hatches in his fishing. There are many terrestrial insects that fall, fly or are blown into the water and present a floating temptation to trout and that, when matched by the angler's imitation, will bring many strikes. These land-born insects have long been imitated by anglers and they fill a vacuum between hatches. They include such tasty teasers as grasshoppers, ants, both crawling and flying, inch worms, jassids, daddy longlegs and other spiders, beetles and so on.

While all these elements of streamside life have been known to anglers all over the world, to a degree, it was not until about 1950 that the eyes of the dry-fly man were really focused in on them. That was the year that Vince Marinaro of Mechanicsburg, Pennsylvania, published his book *A Modern Dry Fly Code*. Helped by his friend Charles K. Fox (*Rising Trout, This Wonderful World of Trout*), over a period of twelve years he had been observing both the hatches and the terrestrials on the Letort River, one of Pennsylvania's most famous limestone streams. They had found that in midsummer, when the seasonal hatches were pretty well past, and it was almost impossible to take a fish on conventional flies and nymphs, nevertheless, every time they went astream they would see an occasional trout feeding. They soon came to identify a characteristic rise, not breaking the surface but merely bulging it, the bulge producing a V-shaped mark on the surface.

At first they thought those fish were nymphing, but one day as Vince lay by the stream studying such a fish, he noticed many small greenish and black insects riding the water. He used a fine mesh net to strain them out. In his collection he found the small duns, tiny beetles and ants he had expected, but as the trout had been steadfastly refusing his finest imitations of these, he started concentrating on the balance of the little creatures in his net, myriads of those tiny terrestrials he had seen on the surface.

Back to his prone position on the bank went Vince, and now, with his eyes clued-in to what he wanted to see, he could follow the little creatures more easily. The first thing that struck him was that they floated awash in the water, rather than on the surface. He took a small dun, size 20, clipped off all the wings and cut down the hackle so the dun floated awash. He hooked a trout on his first cast.

To convince himself that it was no accident, he took three more fish before he performed the autopsies that bore out what he had begun to suspect. Each of those three fish was crammed with the tiny terrestrials. Vince took his collection to an entomologist, who identified them as Jassidae, or Cicadellidae, as they have been termed more recently.

Vince set out to tie a fly which would represent those little insects. He named his invention the "Jassid," and as such it has taken its place in trout fishing lore as one of the greatest American contributions of all time.

The Jassidae family of leaf hoppers was so numerous and varied in color that Vince concluded that the important thing in tying his representation would be silhouette. He tied a fly without body, using a flattened junglecock wing, a "nail" as it is called by fly tyers, which made the wings opaque. Now he had the silhouette and this formless fly would float awash. And small as it was, it was readily visible to the angler because of the conspicuous junglecock eye.

With that fly Vince took trout after trout from the midsummer Letort, and since then the Jassid has continued to take fish in many streams when all other flies fail. I have used Jassids successfully in nearly every part of the United States where trout are found, and in European streams as well, always with the same success. On the Bann River in Ireland, trout that were cruising in very shallow water just below the wide apron of a dam would look at no conventional fly, but they took a Jassid. The same thing happened on the Dove. The Jassid took fish that were passing up the conventional local flies.

In 1959, while fishing in Tasmania, I showed a Jassid to David Scholes, author of *Fly Fisher in Tasmania* and *The Way of an Angler*. He looked at it, then handed me a fly from his own box.

"It is of the order Hemiptera, family Jassidae," he said. "I call it the black and red leaf hopper." He had discovered it five years earlier, a few years after Vince's similar development of the Jassid.

David's fly, which he named Guinea, is tied on a #1 down-eyed hook. It has a clipped body of scarlet chenille and wings of white-flecked guinea fowl tied as a flat-winged sedge. The hackle is black cock, sometimes tied full, on the underside.

Thousands of miles apart, these two enterprising anglers had come up with similar discoveries of a favorite side-dish of the trout, and had tied flies to imitate them and take fish.

The American Jassid is tied on #18, #20 and #22 hooks, and some tyers even go to #24. It requires a very fine tippet on the leader to float such a light fly delicately, 5X being the maximum in size and 6X even better to use with a Jassid. The light tippet calls for extreme delicacy in setting the hook, a mere lift of the rod tip rather than a strike. Trout also seem to take a longer look at a Jassid than they do an oridinary fly, and for this reason you must get a good float of at least four feet over the fish. Counting the distance you want the fly to land above the riser, this means you need plenty of slack line so your fly will float free for about eight feet altogether. You can do this by throwing the line out with more power than needed for the distance to be covered, and then stopping the line high. The line is brought up short by the reel core and falls in a series of loops or S-curves, which allows you a good float before the current straightens the line and starts to pull the fly sideways.

The Jassid may be tied in many colors, but I have found that black brings the most hits.

ANTS

The ant in its many forms is a terrestrial and has long been a great favorite with anglers. Hewitt once said, "Ants are trout's greatest love." In my own experience the Black Flying Ant has proven one of my greatest fish-takers throughout all my fishing life.

While working on the various terrestrials of the Letort, Vince Marinaro found that he had great success with a very small ant in black or cinnamon. He tied them on size 22 hooks, using the hackle to look like wings and make the tiny fly float. The tie has the body of 3X nylon dyed cinnamon, the back part of the body built up, then hackle tied in the middle of the fly, then the body built up again in front and tied off. No wings, no tail.

GRASSHOPPERS

Grasshoppers, which are also terrestrial insects, are certainly high on the list of any trout's favorite foods and you find the artificials in a myriad guises, from the renowned Joe's Hopper of Michigan to the Pontoon Hopper tied by Charlie Fox. Whatever pattern of hopper the dry-fly man chooses he is assured of some strikes, even in the midst of a hatch of aquatic flies. Even a trout that is feeding on such a hatch, and feeding heavily, seems to regard the silhouette of the hopper as an invitation to eat.

Silver Creek, Idaho, is a stream which is famous for its fantastic fly hatches, and for the difficulty of finding just the right artificial to offer at any given time. Some anglers who know the creek well claim that there are as many as twenty different mayflies that hatch in Silver Creek. Sometimes several hatches are progressing at once, and the fly man is kept busy frantically switching from one artificial to another. Many a day goes by without the frustrated angler ever really discovering which patterns the trout are really feeding on. On such occasions, my friend Don Anderson, who was Sports Director at Sun Valley Lodge, often takes fish, and big ones, with his own pattern of a hopper.

"When they're looking at 18s and 20s that they should take, and are refusing them," Don told me, "I use my Rebel Joe, my version of a modified grasshopper, in sizes 8 to 14. I've seen trout come twelve feet to a Rebel Joe."

Hoppers have always been an old standby in the streams of the

Middle West and the Rocky Mountains, and many of the top fly tyers have produced their own versions. Dan Bailey's of Livingston, Montana, sells a Bailey's Hopper that takes its full share of fish. Paul Stroud of California ties his Mountain Hopper, another good one; and Dave Whitlock of Mountain Home, Arkansas, produces his Dave's Hopper, which is a good taker of large fish. While meant to ride low in the water, it floats well, and best of all, does not twist the tippet on the cast.

A less common terrestrial is the Green Oak Worm, which has been tied variously by Bergman, who used cork, Hewitt, who used the pith of the elderberry, and three well-known Pennsylvania anglers, the late George Phillips, George Harvey and Bus Grove, the latter two formerly of Pennsylvania State College. All three Pennsylvanians used deer hair to form their versions of the green oak worm. For another distinctive tie, Charlie Fox uses tips of wing quills of ringnecks, dyed grassy green inside and out. The hook is long-shanked #16, with a little cork at the head. Specific ties for these and many other forms of land insects that end up as trout forage are found in the book *Tying and Fishing Terrestrials* by Gerald Almy, Stackpole Books, Harrisburg, Pa., 1978.

Yet another terrestrial of universal popularity is the Daddy Longlegs. It takes fish in many places, and on one occasion in my own experience this pattern outclassed any other fly. It was on the Omme River in Denmark, a small stream winding through flat farmlands. I was using a Light Cahill, size 18, and wasn't getting hits.

"Try this," said Sven Saaby, one of Denmark's greatest artists. He handed me a size 12 Daddy Longlegs.

"This water is so slick," I said. "I thought a small fly would be better."

"The Daddy Longlegs is tops here," he assured me.

And it was. I used it for the balance of the morning and landed trout from fourteen inches to three pounds, as good a few hours trout fishing as anyone could ask for.

SKATING SPIDERS

There are many spiders tied as dries and fished in the conventional manner with great success. A spider that is skated across the surface is even better. The late Edward Hewitt was one of the most inventive anglers of all time. As far as I have been able to discover, he was the first man to skate spiders for trout, and in 1935 he did a piece on skating spiders for *Spur* magazine, and called it "Butterfly Fishing." He theorized that the trout takes the spider for a butterfly and that when the fish comes out, as he occasionally does, and slaps the artificial with his tail, it is with the idea of knocking the butterfly to the surface, then turning and picking it up.

He called his big spiders "Neversink Skaters" after the trout stream where he developed the fly. His original tie called for a wide hackle,

2 to 2½ inches long, tied on a light-wire size 16 hook, sans tail or body. Today, the term skater refers to a tailless, wide-hackled fly, while spider usually means a skating type fly with tail. Hewitt's fly was big and fluffy, yet delicate, so the angler could skip it across the surface in jerks and skates, skidding it over the lie of a trout in what Hewitt described as "an attempt to jump him."

"If I needed to catch a trout to eat and the brownies were down," he once told a roomful of anglers, "I know the way to bring them up."

His way was the skating spider.

The late artist John Atherton, another student of angling, went a step further. He said that if he had to choose only one fly to fish with his choice would be a spider.

"A spider fished like any other fly will take trout," he said. "And a spider skated across a pool is deadly."

Yet with these examples before our eyes, very few trout fishermen followed the lead until the Pennsylvanians picked up the cue. Charlie Fox's book, *This Wonderful World of Trout*, contains probably the first mention of skating spiders in ten or more years.

These big spiders should be tied from special materials, and the right kind of hackle is so scarce that the late Dan Bailey, well-known fly tyer of Livingston, Montana, claimed that a commercial tyer would have to charge $10 per fly for a perfect skating spider.

"A perfect skater should be tied from the long-fibered throat hackles of game chickens, as big as you can get," Dan said. Some necks don't have even one first-grade long-hackled fiber, or they are too short in the stem. Our tyers could spend a whole day sorting feathers looking for enough hackle to make one perfect skater spider."

"Anyone who insists on a perfect skating spider," he concluded, "had better tie his own or at least find a good friend who will do it for him. But if you are willing to compromise a little and be satisfied with what is, after all, a pretty good spider, then you can use second-grade hackles. They make into flies that work very nicely and bring plenty of strikes."

The late Norm Lightner, another avid Pennsylvania fly fisherman, was a great user of skating spiders. He tied his version with saddle hackles placed in the middle of the shank of the hook and shellacked on both sides to keep the hackles fast in their moorings. This makes the fly skate well, too, and if the hackle gets out of shape you can usually pull it back into its former position.

Norm favored a hook with a straight eye for his spiders.

"If I can't get a straight eye, I'll use the down eye," he told me, once. "But never use an up-eyed hook for a skating spider because when you strip the line the fly will pull down instead of sitting up."

Although Hewitt claimed that any hook larger than a size 16 was too heavy for effective skating, many tyers now use size 14 and even size 12. There is no doubt in their minds that the 16 makes for a lighter, better-skating fly, but the small hook is apt to lose the angler a big trout, either through straightening out on the strike, or when the fish makes for cover and the angler must hold him out from a sure breakoff under a brush pile. On big western rivers the 12 and 14 are much safer and while not as light on their feet as the 16 they will skip along the surface smartly enough to bring many a rousing strike.

Since Hewitt tied his first Neversink Skaters there have been many variations in color. Atherton used a badger hackle spider, and another of his favorites was a mixture of badger and furnace. Norm Lightner favored the Adams hackle, all black, black and brown, two black and one brown hackle tied together, all dark ginger hackle, all honey, and all badger. Charlie Fox likes the all black, all slate and the Adams hackle combination. And Vince Marinaro adds a bronze, blue and black hackle faced with green.

Vince figured this tie out on his own, and years later when he showed it to Hewitt's son, he found that it was exactly the same as Hewitt's own. Vince ties his skaters with slick nylon instead of silk and wax. He ties the hackle, advances the tying thread, wraps the hackle, then jams everything down towards the bend. He keeps this up until the two hackles are on, shiny sides out. He likes to use more turns on the back hackle because that's the one that takes the beating as the angler strips line and makes the skater dance.

If you are going to skate a spider, special care must be given to line and leader. Both should be well greased so they are light and easy to handle and will impart real zip and buoyancy to the skater. The rod may be anywhere from 8 to 9½ feet. Whichever rod you use, the double haul is almost essential in casting these big fluffy flies. It takes all the line speed you can get to put such wind-resistant flies out where you want them (*see* CASTING TECHNIQUES).

This is one of the exceptions to the rule of a long, light leader. The leader should be from nine to twelve feet and tapered to a 2X tippet. Because of the size of the spiders a very light tippet will twist so badly that it is almost impossible to fish the fly. The twist will often go all the way up the leader and cause the first foot or so of the fly line itself to twist. The lighter terminal tippet is not so important as in floating a dry because the trout is not as cautious when he spots a big fly speeding across the surface as he is when he looks carefully over a fly that floats serenely into his window.

I like to throw the spider slightly up and across stream as a rule, and as Hewitt recommended, start it back at once. Sometimes the spider lights on its side but a pull of the line or rod tip will bring it to its feet and then a longer pull makes it dart swiftly forward. The upstream cast will occasionally take a fish but nowhere near as often as up and across, straight across, or across and slightly downstream. If I see a fish straight down from me, I throw off to one side or the other and try to skate the spider across in front of him. A curve to the left, with the retrieve started at once, will usually bring the fly across his nose and get a hit. But a straight downstream throw makes the fly heavy-footed and leaves a deep trail on the surface.

The best place in a pool to start to skate a spider is just at the end of the riffles made by the incoming current. Then you can work down through the slick part of the tail. The shallow water at the tail is an almost sure payoff spot.

Once a spider has become waterlogged it will not skate with the lightness required to bring hits. When a fly becomes soggy I continue to work it in, however. Often it will come to the top again and you can skate it the rest of the way back. But regardless, the bringback should be fished out in order to avoid scaring nearby trout. The quick yank back and pickup of a drowned fly would cause so much noise and water commotion that nearby trout would head for the deepest cover.

When you have retrieved the fly, all wet and sodden, take it off and replace it with a new, dry spider that has been sprayed with silicone. There are many fly dressings on the market and those that can be sprayed on are best for spiders, to be sure that very little filament is covered. However, never respray a wet spider. Even if it has dried somewhat a new spraying will not give back its original lightness. Have half a dozen dressed ones ready in your fly box. Put the used one away in a special compartment where it will not dampen the others, and you can dry it out overnight, then respray it in the morning, ready for the next fishing trip.

It is possible to take fish sometimes by skating smaller dry flies of standard patterns, too, even as small as size 18. Occasionally you see trout taking duns that are coming up and fluttering across the current as they try to take off. A fish will not usually leave his feeding station to follow such a fly but if you drop your fly a couple of inches or even a foot from the line of drift that would take it over the plate, then pull back with the rod tip and skate the fly into that drift line, the trout will sometimes take. I don't recommend this moving of a dry fly in most circumstances, but if you have tried all else and are getting no response, it is worth a try. And as mentioned earlier, you can sometimes attract a cruising trout by skipping a dry across the surface.

MATCHING THE HATCH

Sometimes a hatch can be very confusing. You see several phases of a fly on the water at once, and it seems natural that the fish will be feeding on all of them. But many times it takes the imitation of a single phase of the hatch. The fish will not touch any other. One morning I fished a small stream in Pennsylvania with a delegation of dry-fly specialists including Vince Marinaro, fine fly tyers and anglers Wayne Leonard of Harrisburg, John Snider of Chambersburg and Sid Neff of Pittsburgh. We were all equipped with short fly rods from eight feet down to six feet in length. My own was a seven-foot two-inch stick with matching DT-4-F line. With these we were using fourteen- or fifteen-foot leaders tapered to 6X or 7X tippet, a breaking point of 2.1 and 1.2 pounds, respectively. Plenty light, but invisible to the trout and that's what was needed in this clear, slick water. The flies used on most of these Pennsylvania limestone streams are usually small, sizes 18 to 28, to match the aquatic hatches and also to ape the many terrestrials such as the jassids, mentioned earlier. I always allow myself twenty minutes to tie one of these small flies to a 7X tippet. It takes steady fingers, tremendous patience and a great will to get the job done.

I needed it all that morning because Vince handed me a couple of size 24 Caenis Spinners. Though we originally called them this because the flies were of the family Caenidae, they are more properly *Tricorythodes* (Tricos for short), one of three genera in the family.

"This fly matches the naturals the trout are feeding on," he said. "And they won't touch anything else. See those flies out there?"

I looked where he indicated and saw a loose ball of flies in a cloud above the water, a couple hundred of them, or maybe a thousand, they were so small, rising up and down a few inches, moving forward, then back, up and down, very busy indeed.

Fly fisherman selects a tiny midge from his collection to match the aquatic insects rising on the stream.

Most spinners hit the water at night, usually out of bounds for the angler. But *Trycorythodes* cooperates and you see them as we did that day, in great clouds rolling up and down above the stream. They change form and mate in midair and the female starts dropping her eggs and falls spent, and the male flies off into oblivion.

"Soon they will be on the water and you'll see the fish take them," Vince said. "And listen, too! They make a smack as they inhale the fly. When you hear that smack you know they are feeding on Tricos. They don't take any other fly that way."

I crawled in to the edge of the river, keeping low to hide from the trout, and finally wound up on one knee amid the watercress about thirty-five feet below where I had seen a trout rise. I saw his nose come out, his shoulders, and heard a loud smack, and knew what Vince was talking about.

My first cast landed the fly three feet above that riser. But it was about five inches too far to the right and the trout was too intent on naturals traveling the thread of the current to move over to take. I tried again, but this time my fly dragged a bit. The third float was right, drag-free, over the inside of the plate, as natural-looking as a natural. It fooled the trout. He came up and took with an extra loud smack, and I gently pulled the rod back and felt him. He dashed down past me and thirty feet away came out in an arching leap, a nice fourteen-inch brownie that landed with a thud. I held the rod tip high to keep him from diving into the grasses and breaking off. Then he switched ends and ran upstream, broached up there and got on top and started thrashing around. When he was tired of that I pulled back on the rod and finally got him in. I took the hook out and put him back in his wonderful home, a stream any trout would be proud of, with a nicely gravelled bottom, weed patches packed with nymphs, watercress-lined shores, plenty of oxygen, and best of all, unpolluted water. Through his window a trout on his feeding station could easily spot those Tricos drifting down the slick current to him.

I looked around. A hundred feet upstream I saw Vince creeping silently into the river, and above him the concentric rings spreading from a rise told me he had his eye on a trout. I eased ashore, went well back from the stream and then walked up to watch Vince. I was in time to see him make his first throw, a fine, accurate cast that resulted in a beautiful, drag-free float. The trout liked the looks of the offering, rose, and took, and Vince lifted the rod tip and was into him. He tore upstream and came clear out, just as mine had. But this brownie of Vince's was a good four pounds, one of those really hefty trout that live in these limestone streams. Vince took one look and lowered his rod tip and pointed it right at the fish because this makes for less drag than when the line goes over the tip of the rod. Vince knew that the slightest resistance when a four-pounder goes into action can snap a delicate 7X tippet such as he was using.

That trout had plenty of action planned, too. He raced upstream, he turned and ran down, with Vince after him, trying to keep him from getting out too much line and running around weeds or watercress. It was nip and tuck, a hard-fought battle on both sides, back and forth, in and out, for twenty minutes. Then Vince began to win. Wayne Leonard, who was standing by with a landing net, moved down to the edge of the water. Vince backed up, to pull the fish in. And then the hook came out.

I breathed a great sigh. I heard a moan from Wayne.

"Tally ho and goodbye!" said Vince.

A lost fish is a lost fish, but you don't mind so much when you have fooled a suspicious old brownie into taking and he has waged such a grand fight. And as Vince was going to release him anyway, he didn't feel badly at all. Getting him to take that perfect match of the tiny *Tricorythodes* was the thing.

Seconds later a shout from further downstream told us that John Snider was into one. It turned out to be a 2½-pound rainbow, which knew a good Trico when he saw one. John released that one, too, and before the sun was too high overhead we had all hooked, landed or lost fish. Then there were no more flies on the water. The fish, well fed on that hatch, went down and that was that for the day.

GENERAL REPRESENTATION

To carry the perfect match, in form, color and size, for every hatch he may encounter, a fly fisher would have to carry hundreds of patterns in dozens of sizes. In his fine book *The Fisherman's Handbook of Trout Flies*, Don Dubois lists some fifty-four hundred ties. Although it is great to have the exact match for the hatch, it isn't always possible, and there is considerable evidence that it is not always necessary. Every dry-fly fisherman has had the experience of taking fish on a fly that does not correspond to anything hatching or otherwise occurring in the river.

I recall a day in May 1968, when I fished the South Island of New Zealand. With my guide, Ted Tapper of Invercargill, I stood well back from the bank of the Clutha River, looking things over.

"There's a rise," I said, "and another."

"They're coming up good, now," said Ted. "The hatch is on. Go get them."

I waded into position, leaned over and looked at one of the natural flies as it came floating past. This was a new one to me. A mayfly, I was sure, but I knew that nothing in my box would match it. Then I remembered something Dan Bailey of Livingston, Montana, a great fly tyer, had said to me many years earlier.

"It's always good to use the imitation of the prevailing fly on the water when you are fishing," he had said. "But if you are caught without the exact imitation there are three standard flies that will give you an approximation of almost any of the mayflies. Those three patterns are the Light Cahill, the Quill Gordon and the Adams.

"I believe that color and size are the two most important points in a fly," he said. "If you match those, you don't always have to have an exact imitation of the fly which is hatching."

Now, ten thousand miles away from the man who told me that, I nudged gently through my fly box with my forefinger. I was looking for an Adams, because one of my own long-time sayings has been, "When in doubt, use an Adams." I found a size 16 and it looked right in size for those natural insects that were coming down the Clutha, and the color was close. I tied it on the 5X tippet at the end of my fourteen foot leader, got line in the air and shot it out, trying to hit the surface three feet above the concentric circles spreading out from where a trout had risen.

The fly dropped lightly, came jauntily down the current without drag and over the place where the trout had shown. He was there and he inhaled that American tie, one he surely had never seen before, but whose size and color must have made it look like a familiar South Island mayfly. I raised the rod tip and felt him and he splashed on top, lunged upstream and cut through the surface water, whizzing along on a seventy-foot run that made the click on the reel clatter as loud as a kingfisher's call. I landed that three-pounder and eight more that apparently didn't see anything foreign about a size 16 Adams.

Many patterns that have been tied for the fast rivers of the Rocky Mountains, and particularly for use at the top of a pool, where the water comes pouring in with a vengeance, are more or less flash flies. They are conspicuous enough for the angler to see in the heavy water, so he is ready to strike. And they are close enough to some real insect to fool the fish that are lying up there drinking in the extra oxygen of the turbulent water. The Sofa Pillow, the big Wulff hairwing flies, the bucktail Caddis flies, the large Trudes and Stone Flies, the Joe's Hopper, the black and the brown Norwegian sea-trout flies, the size 6 Gray and the same size Brown Hackle, the bigger spiders and variants, are all good takers in fast water, even when there is a hatch of some other natural going on.

The hatch of big flies variously called stone flies, salmon flies or willow flies can be followed for as long as five or six weeks from Colorado to Montana. On any given river it starts in the lower altitudes and moves upstream as the water reaches temperatures suitable for the hatching of the flies. If the weather becomes really warm the hatch progresses rapidly and can be over in a short time, but if there is a cold spell it will be delayed.

During this hatch, on whatever river, the trout are very unselective. Anything that floats and bears a faint resemblance to the natural will do. The most used fly is probably the Sofa Pillow, which doesn't look much like any natural I can name. The Bird's Stone Fly is another popular tie. The Muddler, floated dry, is good. But almost any large fly, no matter how crudely tied, will get hits as the fish smash into the rafts of stone flies that are drifting on the surface of the river.

WHEN TROUT ARE NOT RISING

When trout are not rising you can still coax many a fish to your dry if you think of all the likely lies they could take, and put your fly over them. On hot, bright days trout seek the shade. They hide beneath grasses in the stream and those that hang over the banks. They shelter behind rocks and under them. Every shadow should be explored with your fly.

George LaBranche popularized the method of "Manufacturing a hatch" to bring a deep-lying and non-feeding trout to the surface to take a fly. This system consists of dropping the fly again and again on a spot where you know from previous experience there should be a fish. Perhaps after six or seven casts you see him move, deep down, then repeated casts cause him to come higher, and finally after more floats he takes. Most of us do not have the patience to do this very often, but it will get a fish every so often, and is certainly good practice.

As you wade, too, you learn the geography of the bottom of a stream or lake, and this can tell you where fish may be even though they are not showing. One day on the Beaverhead River in Montana, I was casting from the shallow shore towards the deeper, far bank—a likely-looking spot for trout—but I was not getting any hits. Then I made a poor cast and my fly fell about two yards out from the shore. It floated about three feet and a fish took and I fought him in, a nice two-pound brownie. I made my next cast purposely to that same area where he had hit and had another fish. I took three browns all from that same drift, rather than in along the bank where I had figured they would be.

When I reached the top of the pool and looked downstream I saw why. In this light I could spot a long ledge running down the middle of the river, a couple of yards out from the far bank, and there, in the deeper water, in the shadow of that ledge, the fish were lying. Now when I go back there I know exactly where to drop my flies, and those trout always seem ready to take.

A dry fly must really be dry to perform to its best ability. It usually starts out that way, but as soon as you have made a few casts, or caught a fish, the fly needs to be dried and treated again with a commercial spray. I use amadu to dry the fly, amadu being a fungus from the English beech tree. You can squeeze the most fragile fly between folds of amadu without hurting it and it will come out dry enough to treat it with dry-fly solution. A more practical alternative to the hard-to-get fungus is dry-fly powder or borax. A little is held in the palm of your hand while you dredge the soggy fly through it. The powder quickly absorbs wetness, rendering the fly fishable in a few moments.

6

WET FLY FISHING

The forty-foot-wide stream was in spring flood. Runoff from a heavy rain of the previous night had swelled its waters and it came plummeting down the mountains, banging into upjutting rocks, splitting against them and fuming by on either side of the obstruction, leaving an eddy in back. It swept the shore grasses into a downstream curve, washed the feet of the alders and reached for the roots of a stand of bull laurel farther back. The water was colored with dirt and mud washed in from open fields above.

But now, six hours after the rain, the stream, although still discolored, was beginning to drop and this was the time to start to catch trout. Along the banks were more peaceful pockets where the water slowed and swirled, and where fish might be lying, pushed in by the current. And they would be finding resting places in eddies like the one behind those rocks and under logs and in back of ridges and earth clumps.

I opened my fly box and looked for something I thought those fish could see. Dry flies were out for this spring scene. I chose a size 12 Black Gnat wet fly, tied it on, lowered it into the water at my feet, and let it sink. I could see it there, fifteen inches down. A trout should be able to spot it even in this discolored water.

I made a cast and dropped the fly forty-feet downstream and a foot from a point of the bank. I let it drift into the slower water below, then after three feet of float I started it back in short pulls, very slow, to give the trout, if he was there, time to see it. He did. The rod tip dipped and the trout darted out towards the middle to take advantage of the heavy water. I pushed the rod in towards my bank and pulled him in there, then slowly worked him up and in. He was a twelve-inch brownie, who had had no trouble spotting a wet fly in that turgid spring water.

FATHER OF FLIES   The dry fly and the nymph have taken such prominent places in American fly fishing that many anglers nowadays completely overlook the use of the wet fly, and that there are many times when it is their best choice. As a matter of history, the wet fly is the father of flies. The first fish recorded as having been taken on a fly hit a wet. Writing in the third century A.D., Aelian tells of an angler who fastened red wool around a hook and added feathers, to imitate a natural fly on which fish were feeding, but which natural fly was too delicate to fasten on a hook. With this innovation the angler caught a fish with "spotted skin," in the Astracus River in Macedonia.

Later fly fishermen produced many such tries at copying insects on which they saw trout feed. When Dame Juliana Berners published her *Treatise of Fishing with an Angle* in 1450 (*see* HISTORY) she gave the dressings of twelve wet flies which were in common use. And Charles Cotton, writing in 1676, in the second part of Walton's *Compleat Angler*, describes sixty-five wet flies and gives the best month for each fly. The Black Gnat, which I used on the day just described, and the Cowdung, were two of Cotton's listing. In 1681 Chetham mentions the March Brown and in the 1830s Tom Bosworth, coachman to the royal family of England, originated the Coachman fly. These are still popular patterns wherever trout are fished. They were among the wet flies brought to North America by early settlers.

The immigrant anglers added patterns tied to meet special conditions of local waters, notable among them the "Canadian flies" for brook trout. They were big and gaudy, a flashy come-on of vivid reds and showy whites, and they wore such euphonious names as the Scarlet

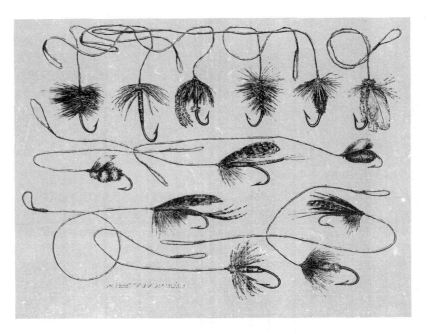

Wet flies were tied by Americans in the 1850s to meet the special conditions of local waters where brook trout were abundant. The flies were big and gaudy, with colorful dressings. This plate is from a fishing book of the period.

Ibis, Parmachene Belle, and Dark Montreal. To the fish they may look like a bit of meat or the fin of a brook trout or a very small brook trout. At any rate, wherever eastern brook trout were found, from 1850 on, these flies have filled creels. (The same patterns were tied later on much larger hooks and proved very successful for bass.)

To fish the tumultuous mountain rivers of the new continent the early North American anglers tied their flies on fairly large hooks with heavy dressings; and added others among more classic lines to match the naturals they saw on more placid waters. The Western Bee, Royal Coachman, Rio Grande King, Light Cahill, Quill Gordon, Adams and many others put an American stamp on the fishing scene.

NATURE OF WET FLY	

NATURE OF WET FLY

Wet flies are tied in two ways, either with wings and hackle, or all hackle. Either way, the fly is designed to be fished beneath the surface, to imitate a drowned aquatic fly that had inadvertently got into the water, has been caught in the surface film and finally pushed under by waves or dragged under by an eddy. Trout hit such a fly because they take it for a downed natural, or sometimes they may think it is a nymph that has been battered about by the current. This is the theory of it. But I believe that they also hit wet flies because they look like small minnows. The Coachman is a prime example. When you give it action with short jerks, the white wing makes it look very much like a small, silvery minnow darting along.

While feathers are the basis of many of the old favorite wet flies, many other materials are used, including wool, fur, and synthetics. Hair wet flies were originally popular in the West, but are now used across the U.S.

To help get a wet fly down without commotion, and to ensure it good action once under the water, tyers slant the wings back and up a bit along the shank of the hook, towards, but not reaching, the bend. Soft hackles are used to further resist buoyancy, and for action. All this, together with the weight of the hook, is usually sufficient to get a wet fly down, but to help it to sink, especially in slow water, I often hold the fly by the bend of the hook and place the head and dressing in my mouth and soak it with saliva. "Spit on the hook for good luck" has real meaning. It helps to get the fly down. (I am speaking here of using wet flies on a floating line. For use of the sinking line, *see* TACKLE.)

Some wet flies are not meant to look like food but rather to attract by color. They are called "attractor," "flash" or "fancy" flies. The trout, seeing them moving or floating through the water, gets mad and hits them because he wants them out of the pool or simply wants to mouth this strange-looking object and find out what it is. Even though the flash fly is not tied to look like a natural, there is enough of the color, shape and size to cause the trout to take it for one or another phase of a natural or a terrestrial fly. Such bright flies often pay off in the heavy runoff of spring, when the waters are clear, although high.

However, color, like beauty, may all be in the eye of the beholder because in my experience, particularly in eastern waters, I have found that black, brown and yellow flies produce far better in early water conditions. I generally use a Black Gnat, Leadwing Coachman, Brown Hackle/yellow body, Cowdung, March Brown or Black Ant. To give these flies plenty of exposure, so the trout will have time to spot and take them, I slow the retrieve, sometimes stopping it altogether, especially in eddies and back of rocks, where the swirling and jiggling water can make a fly look very alive.

HOW TO PLAY THE WET FLY

When working a wet fly to look like a darting minnow, I like to cast across stream and bring the fly back in short jerks, breaking up the retrieve with longer, slower pulls interspersed. Again, if I want it to look like a downed fly, I let it drift and float free in the current for several feet, then give it a couple of eye-catching jerks, then let it float free again. When the fly finally swings in below me, I bring it back for several feet, again in jerks, before lifting it for the next cast.

Some wet-fly fishermen like to let the fly float right on through without any action, until it swings across the pool and winds up straight below. Then they bring it back in short jerks, until it is near enough to pick up. But I am inclined to think that over a day's fishing, the more active use of the fly will get more hits. Mix it up, pull it, let it float free in the current. Above all, whatever wet fly I am using, I try to keep constantly in mind exactly what this fly is supposed to represent, and I play it accordingly. As an example, I have watched many a trout take a Coachman wet fly, one of my favorites. When the fly is retrieved in short jerks, its white wings make it look like a very tiny minnow darting along. The trout nearly always take it broadside in their mouths, evidently crushing down to stun or kill it, then turn it and swallow it headfirst. The Alexandra also looks like a minnow and is one of the all-time greats in producing strikes. Gray Hackle/yellow seems to me to be a small moth or spider that has fallen into the stream and drowned or has very little life left in it. I like to fish this fly in a dead float, letting it go down current several feet, then giving it a short jerk, then another, and when it swings through across current down the pool, I impart short jerks to make a trout think the insect is making a last desperate effort to escape.

Other flies, especially those that have been used for some time and have lost part of their hackles or feathers, so they really look beaten up, must appear to the trout to be nymphs, and I handle them accordingly. Sometimes you see trout bulging, taking their food within a few inches of the surface, causing a slight upwelling of the water as they turn their bodies to take. Strictly speaking, this is a situation that

Easiest way to fish a wet fly is to cast down and across stream, let the current sweep the fly downstream, then retrieve it in short jerks. Giving the fly action as it floats freely in the current will produce more strikes.

CURRENT

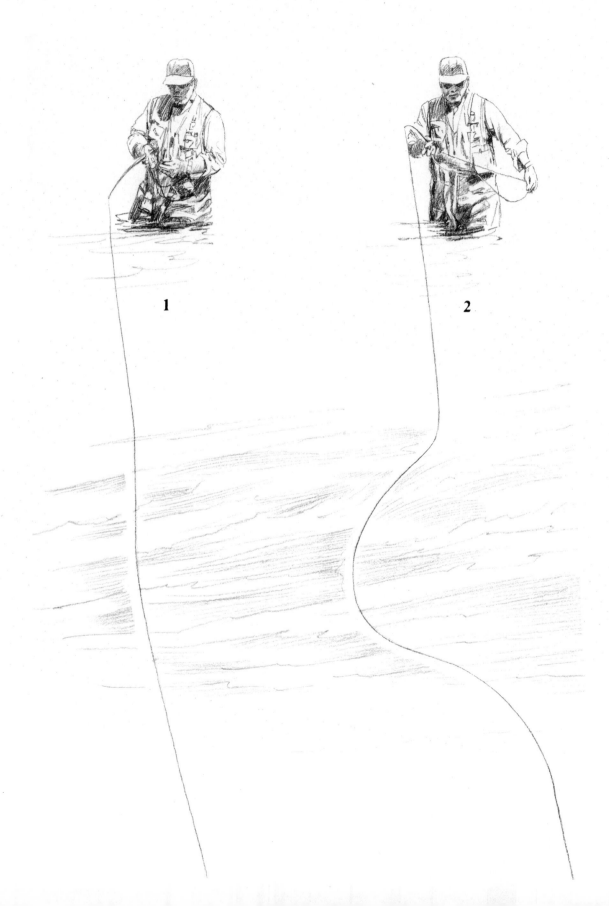

1

2

When a wet fly is cast directly across stream (**1**), the current often bellies the line (**2**), causing the fly to float unnaturally, or "drag." By mending the line (**3**), that is, flipping the belly upstream, you can give the fly a longer, drag-free float. At completion of the float, fly is stripped in short jerks.

calls for a nymph (*see* NYMPH FISHING FOR TROUT), to match the food on which the trout are feeding, a nymph coming up to change to a dun. But you can adapt your wet fly to such a situation by greasing the line and leader down to within three or four inches of the fly. This will let line and leader float on the surface, so you can mend it lightly and easily; all the while the fly drifts high in the water, only a couple of inches under the surface. While it is not the exact imitation of the food, it will be within the view of the fish as he watches for the real thing, and since he is definitely on the feed, it will look good enough to bring hits.

Whenever you fish a wet fly it is just as important to approach a pool carefully and read the water thoroughly as it is with a dry fly. Haphazard casts and floats will take some fish, but for a consistent catch you must make a noiseless entry on the scene, cast accurately to the right spots, where fish should be lying, make a minimum of motion with your arm as you cast, and retrieve the fly properly. This is especially true when you fish a wet fly downstream or across and down, as most fishermen do, and it is doubly important on a small stream that calls for real stealth, very light presentation and a more gentle retrieve than you might use on bigger rivers. Too much action imparted to the fly in small streams or shallow water will often flush the trout. The same goes for too-quick motions on the part of the angler. Make your moves slowly and carefully and take up a casting position against a high bank or a clump of trees with the idea of blending into the background, to be as inconspicuous as possible.

Before you make your first cast, take time to locate the separate runs of current which are found in every pool and riffle. In most cases the main current comes into the pool with a heavy rush that's obvious, and is a natural spot for fish to lie. But there are usually small currents on both sides, with some amount of riffle or waves, and trout like to nose into these minor currents where life is a little easier than out in the mainstream, looking for food and savoring the extra oxygen. If you have your eye only on the main current you may wade right over many a trout lying in that small inshore current. So start your fishing before you even put foot in water.

FISHING DOWN A POOL	To fish the average pool it is best to start your series of casts well up in the incoming water because many a fine trout lies high in the rough and tumble of the rapids at the head of a pool. Make your initial cast to the water close-in, then extend the throws a couple of feet each time, until you are covering all the possible holding water. Depending on the width of the pool you are working, this may be thirty feet, or in some of the big rivers, seventy feet or more. Once you have covered the water from your first stand in the pool,

move down ten or fifteen feet and start over, the first short throws, then the series, extended a bit at a time.

The middle of the pool is the least likely spot to take a trout because usually that is the deepest part and the water is moving slowly and there is not as much oxygen as at the top or tail. But fish do lie there, just resting, and if you put a fly in front of them you often get a hit. And these are frequently extra-big fish. Sometimes they will rise to your wet fly drifting over them; and occasionally you can stir one to zoom up by moving the fly fast, erratically, almost the same way you would make a skating spider dance. But in most cases, to reach a trout lying in the depths of the deepest part of the pool calls for a weighted fly or sinking line.

As the wet-fly fisherman works down past this deeper part of the pool he usually finds that the river narrows, and often down towards the tail there are rocks studded across, some of them head-size, others only the size of a clenched fist. Trout will often hold in front of and in back of these rocks, watching for food to drift past. Out in the open, too, over a gravelly bottom, they will lie facing into the current, letting the water wash past their heads and shoulders and press in around their bodies so as to hold them there with seemingly no effort.

All this is usually in fairly shallow water, and you have to be extremely careful to present a fly from your upstream position without being seen. And if the fish does not take, the fly must be retrieved very carefully and quietly back upstream, and then lifted equally carefully and quietly, to avoid disturbing the water.

| WET FLY UPSTREAM | On any river, the faster riffles between pools may hold many trout, but because of the speed and overall rush of water it is difficult to pinpoint the likely lies and be sure of getting your wet fly to them with a downstream throw. |

On any river, the faster riffles between pools may hold many trout, but because of the speed and overall rush of water it is difficult to pinpoint the likely lies and be sure of getting your wet fly to them with a downstream throw. In such cases it is possible to fish the wet fly upstream, just as you would a dry fly, seeking out the best spots and dropping the fly there for a short float over that likely holding place. This is a situation that calls for a short cast and quick retrieve. Drop the fly on that chosen spot, then retrieve as fast as necessary to try to meet the speed of the current, so your line does not get pulled in against you and jerk the fly out of there before a trout could see it. It is like fishing a dry fly in fast water—the short cast for control of line and fly, a float of twenty or twenty-five feet, the rod held high to keep the fast current from sweeping line and fly downstream and to keep your line tight so you can strike. Or so, as it comes in near you, you can make a roll cast pickup for the next throw.

When you fish a wet fly downstream, the strike is usually hard enough for you to feel it at once. But when you cast your wet fly up into this fast water it is difficult to see the strike, and you do not get that hard pull because the line is coming towards you. You want a short line so that when you do feel the fish your strike will get to him in a hurry and sink the barb.

There are times, too, when the wet-fly angler wants to cast his fly up and across, mend the line and let the fly float down the current for several feet, then bring it across current in short jerks, either all or part of the way in, with more pauses interspersed. This is a very good way to fish a wet fly in a big pool where there is an undercut bank across from you. It will often pull a big fish out of there to follow your fly and eventually hit it. As in fast water, you have no chance of observing the strike, so you must watch the end of the fly line, or the leader, and if you see it hesitate or stop, or move forward, strike hard.

While I like to fish a single fly, many wet-fly fishermen use a dropper, or even several flies. My first experience with this was at Loch Leven in Scotland, where four wet flies are fished at once, a tail fly and three droppers.

"Size 22, with double hooks," the gillie told me. "Cast them out, keep the rod high, and when they drop to the surface bring the rod back slowly, keeping the first two flies skipping across the surface, the next one just under the surface, and the tail fly a bit deeper. Retrieve them about ten feet. If you don't get a hit, make your backcast and try again."

My first cast with those multiple flies resulted in such a tangle as I hope never to see again, but the next try was a slight improvement and eventually I got the swing of it. I caught seven trout in the next three quarters of an hour, nice brownies averaging a bit over a pound, the largest a pound and a half.

I was itching to try a single fly, so finally I took off the Loch Leven's fearsome foursome and for half an hour I fished a single fly, first a Black Gnat, size 12, then a size 12 Royal Coachman, and finally a size 4 Muddler. I had one half-hearted strike, saw a couple of fish come up and look and fade away again. I put the multiple flies back on and caught fish at once. Whether it was the combination of the extra flies, the dancing of the bobbers over the surface, the sight of several rather than one fly, that excited the trout, I don't know. But there, as in many other European lakes and rivers, I found that multiple wet flies often produce more than a single fly.

Nevertheless, I usually fish only one fly, because I like the art and pleasure of casting so much, and the finesse of real casting technique is not possible with multiple flies, which all too easily become snarled in each other. I also like the challenge of trying to present and then play my artificial as nearly as possible like the natural coming down the stream.

Most North American anglers who use multiple flies only go to two, a tail fly and a somewhat larger dropper. The leader on which they use these flies is usually about seven feet long with eighteen inches between the dropper and tail fly, the better to avoid tangles in casting.

The dropper itself is eight or ten inches long, tied into the leader with a blood knot. The end of the tie is left about ten inches long to act as the fly leader, the other clipped off tight to the knot.

One summer day I was wandering up the Yellowstone River in Montana when I met Homer Langley, then county assessor at Livingston. He was just moving out into a big pool, and I stopped to watch him. He was using two flies, a size 12 Black Gnat for a tail fly, and a size 12 Cowdung as a dropper. He made his cast, let the flies settle and drift downstream. Then as they began to move across the current down there, he used his rod tip to impart short pulls to the flies. Suddenly he gave a shout.

"A big one!" he yelled.

The fish had taken off downstream the second it hit. It was well into his backing before he could stop it. Then, out in the middle of the pool, a big broad tail came into view, disappeared again and the reel sang. On went that fish and Homer had to follow him. It finally stopped and headed upstream and now Homer had to reel fast to keep tight to him. Gradually he beat that fish and reeled him in close, all the time working his way slowly to shore. The beach was low and gravelly, and he eased the trout in as far as he could against the small rocks along the shore, then scooped him out, well back from the water.

He straightened up, smiling broadly.

"That's the biggest trout I've ever caught," he said.

It was a 7-pound 3-ounce brownie, a fish that was 27½ inches long, and had a girth of 13 inches, a real Yellowstone many-spotted brown trout. Like his forebears on the Dove, away back in the 1860s when Charles Cotton wrote of fly patterns and used them so effectively, that big Montana brownie had liked the looks of a Cowdung wet fly.

Homer Langley, of Livingston, Montana, with 7-pound 3-ounce brown trout taken on a brace of wet flies in the Yellowstone River.

7 NYMPH FISHING

To fish a nymph well and successfully is certainly more difficult than to fish a wet fly or a dry, but it generally pays off in bigger trout. And it often produces trout when nothing else will. This was the theory of G.E.M. Skues, the English barrister who pioneered fishing for trout with artificial nymphs (*see* History). Skues lived and fished and wrote in the same period as Halford, who had so thoroughly touted the art of dry-fly fishing as the "only" way to fish for trout in a chalk stream. But Skues was equally vehement in his exposition of the nymph. He spent many years studying the subject, and experimenting. He used to open the stomachs of the fish he caught, place the contents in a shallow white bowl filled with water, gently stir the tightly packed mass until the particles separated and the insects assumed more or less their natural shape. Then he tied artificials to match, fished them, and wrote about how he fished them and how successful they were. He soon had a following as vociferous as Halford's, and became known as the father of nymph fishing.

Many experts have stated that eighty-five percent of the diet of a trout consists of nymphs. It is certainly true that the nymphal forms of the aquatic flies are available to the trout in more phases and for longer periods of time than the other forms. And since there are so many aquatic hatches and each has a larval stage of some kind, the number and variety of nymphs that could be copied by the nymph fisherman could well be described as infinite.

BASIC NYMPHS

Every trouter cannot become an entomologist, and it is not necessary to be one, to fish a nymph. For practical purposes it is possible to fill your nymph fly book with the right patterns for almost any occasion, if you are familiar with certain basic nymphs found commonly in trout waters.

The mayflies, Ephemeridae, are found in most streams that are capable of holding trout and where pollution has not destroyed both the hatches and the fish. The evolution of the mayfly (*see* Dry Fly) is typical of many aquatic hatches, and in spite of its name it occurs throughout most of the warm months of the year. Nearly every trout angler at some time meets a situation that calls for a mayfly nymph.

147

The stone flies, Plecoptera, are found mostly in fast rivers, where there is plenty of oxygen. In early summer they furnish some fast and furious fishing. They are big insects and bring up big trout. When they are on the water trout smash into them fearlessly. This is the time when the fly fisherman on the big rivers of the Rocky Mountains can take big fish.

The female of the stone fly drops her eggs into the water individually, not as a cluster, and they then sink to the bottom. After they emerge from the egg, the nymphs stay on the bottom for about a year, during which time they grow legs and wings, in fact everything that will be needed when they enter the world of air rather than water. When they are ready to emerge they crawl out and attach themselves to rocks on shore, and the imago, the perfect insect (stone flies have only two stages, the nymphal and the imago), breaks out of the nymphal case, crawls under a rock or log, and after about two hours its wings are dry. The male finds the female in this situation, they mate, and then the female flies off and drops her eggs on the water, to start the cycle again.

At any time the nymphal form is in the water, Plecoptera is prey to the trout; in fact, an artificial Stone Fly nymph will take fish at any time of year, not just during a hatch. On a trip to the Williamson River in Oregon, in early July, when no big flies were hatching, the biggest fish I got, a five-pounder, fell to a big nymph tied by Klamath Falls fly tyer Granny Granstrom. Called the Granny's Creeper, it produces at any time of year.

The caddis flies, Trichoptera, have still a different cycle. The eggs are laid by the female dipping into the surface or dropping them while flying over the water, or by crawling down a reed or branch of some kind and fastening the eggs to a rock, log, or base of a reed. The small larva comes out of the egg and, in many species, constructs a case around its body for protection, using tiny bits of bark, leaves, small pebbles, sand and slivers of twigs. It sticks its head and shoulders out of the forward open end of the case and crawls along dragging its house behind it.

As it grows it enlarges the case. And then after a year the larva goes into the pupa stage and encases itself in a cocoon of silk and seals it up. Deep in its nest it forms legs and wings, and when it is ready to emerge it bites out the end of the cocoon and goes to the surface and emerges as the imago, the perfect fly, and flies away, to mate. Thus, in this fly, we have the larva and the pupa, or still stage, both nymphal forms that are available at one time or another to a feeding trout, and all suitable to be matched with your artificials.

In my opinion nymphs are usually tied too big, probably because fishermen shy off from the very small sizes, which do indeed some-times look infinitesimal. It's one thing to fish a small dry fly that is matching something equally small that you see on the surface. It's quite another to be able to picture a correspondingly small nymph

Stone flies are found in fast rivers where there is plenty of oxygen. Drawing at right shows three stages of the stone fly: (from left) nymph, partly emerged adult, and the adult insect.

A caddis hatch on Idaho's Silver Creek. At right, caddis larvae in their cases on an underwater rock. The larvae construct these protective cases of bark, leaves, small pebbles and sand. Eventually, they will pass into the pupa stage, and then emerge as winged insects.

drifting along under the surface and to believe that a fish will see it and take it. So we are inclined to go to the larger sizes. But I firmly believe that if more nymphs were used in sizes 16, 18 and 20, more trout would be caught. After all, the small mayflies we match with a size 24 dry fly came out of an equally small nymph—so why back off?

The midge nymph is probably the least used of any of the commercially tied patterns, but this nymph has been taking trout for a long time, tiny flies tied on size 18, 20, 22, and smaller hooks. When you find a swarm of midges, smuts or other small natural flies working above the surface of the water, hovering and falling and rising, you can often use those midge nymphs with telling effect.

One time I was fishing a mountain lake in Wyoming, close to an outlet where a small stream ran out, an ideal place for nymphs to hatch. There were so many midges working about a foot above the surface that it looked like a small black cloud. I had a size 20 Black Hackle dry fly on and I dropped it four times in among those flies, let it sit still on the surface, then gave it short jerks as I retrieved it. Not the first hit. They didn't want a dry. I changed to a size 12 Olive nymph. Still no hits. Then I recalled that in my fly box I had a couple of black midge nymphs. I put one on, a size 20, threw it out there through the ranks of the swarming midges. When it dropped to the surface I let it sink for an inch, then started it back, drawing it slowly along. A fish had it. With that same nymph I took four more trout from beneath those swarming midges. That was a day that was won by having the right nymph with me—a small one.

It is often difficult to find the very small nymphs in tackle stores. You frequently must order them from a commercial tyer, direct, or tie them yourself. On the other hand, there are plenty of large nymphs available, and plenty of these are good fish takers regardless of what is going on in the way of true nymphal activity at the time you are fishing.

One of the great favorites on Rocky Mountain streams is the Gray nymph, weighted. It is made with a heavy, fuzzy muskrat fur body, gray hackle and badger hair tail, in sizes from 6 to 12. Cast and allowed to sink, then retrieved slowly, in pulls and pauses, it produces well in all types of water.

The big Stone Fly nymphs are great producers in the fast water at the head of a pool, and again, they are good regardless of season. I have had great fishing throughout the trout season with various stone fly patterns that Dan Bailey ties, under the name Nature Nymphs.

TIME FOR THE NYMPH

Often you see trout "bulging," taking the nymphs just before they reach the surface, and turning their bodies as they do so, thus causing the water to bulge a bit. Novices may mistake this for a rise to a dry fly and wonder why they don't get a hit to a dry that matches the flies coming off the river. But when the trout are working on nymphs they usually ignore the fully hatched fly. So look carefully, and if they are bulging, without breaking the surface, go to a nymph, particularly one tied as an emerger.

When trout are bulging, taking nymphs right at the surface like that, almost at the point of emergence of the dry fly, I like to fish the artificial nymph very much like a dry fly—upstream on a floating line and with a long leader, tapered to a very fine tippet. I like to grease the floating line to make it even more buoyant, and also grease the leader down to within three or four inches of the end of the tippet. The line and leader then float nicely, but that few inches of ungreased leader tippet allows the nymph to sink an inch or two beneath the surface and go over the fish at that depth, right where he has his eyes fixed.

The cast should be made well above the bulging fish and the S-cast is the one to deliver it free of drag, just as you like a dry fly to float.

Many times you will be able to spot that telltale bulge as the trout takes your nymph, but as in dry-fly fishing that rise can fool you. The disturbance of the trout bulging will rock the water and fade out well below the spot where he actually took the nymph. Be sure to take time enough to fish that spot of the first bulge of water in your mind, or you may be casting below his station. If you make several casts to the fish and do not get a strike, try extending your throw to drop the nymph from eight to ten feet above where you have been casting.

At all times, keep your eyes on the end of your line as it floats downstream, and when you see that line move forward, or stop, then strike, whether you have seen the fish or not.

Again, as you stand at streamside you may see the flash of a trout's sides, and at such a time you can be sure that the fish is feeding on nymphs that he is digging out of the gravel or snatching as they scurry across it. As the trout noses down and takes, he turns his body and the light glints off his sides, an underwater heliograph that gives him away.

When trout are intent on those nymphs down in the gravel, in shallow water, say 2½ to 3 feet deep, you can take them with a floating line. Cast upstream, then pay out plenty of line so the nymph will float deep and into the range of the trout. Or you can increase the chance of getting down there by using a weighted nymph cast upstream and allowed to sink and come bumping across the gravel. Some nymph fishermen pinch a bit of split shot onto the leader about a foot above the fly, and it is effective, as the split shot bounces down the stream bed and the nymph jerks erratically along in back of it with a lifelike action. But if I am going to use weight, I prefer to go to a weighted nymph.

Any time you are fishing a nymph deep in this way, you must watch the line carefully because there is no way to see the trout take your offering. When a trout takes, the line will stop moving or it will jerk forward. Every time you get such a line reaction, that's your cue to

Angler studies contents of trout's stomach, to determine what fish are feeding on, and tries to match it with an artificial. G.E.M. Skues, a British angler, used this method to devise the first artificial nymphs in the early 1900s.

strike. Your nymph may only be caught on a rock or bit of grass down there, but on the other hand you may have a fish.

If there is no strike throughout the float, start the fly back in short jerks, keeping this up for several feet, then stop it all together, then start the short jerks, and so on until the nymph reaches the surface. A trout may hit at any stage of this retrieve.

If I am not getting the hits I think I should to an upstream nymph, I often cast up and across and bring the nymph back immediately, in short uplifts of the rod tip, to make it jerk and dart as I bring it along. It should move not too fast, but briskly, so the trout will have to chase it; and the rod must be kept at a fairly high angle so the bend of the rod can absorb the force of a hit.

To fish a nymph deep upstream, strip line as current brings the fly toward you and to the surface; watch carefully for the slightest hesitation or forward motion of the line.

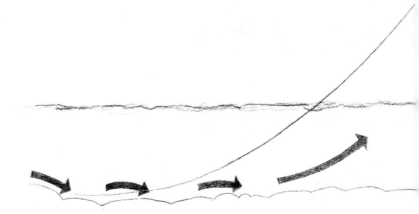

On the whole, however, I think that when you make a cross-stream throw, the dead float pays off best; and that when you are fishing a nymph in dead water, a fast retrieve is best. In the still water of a slough, for instance, a cruising fish might never even see a nymph that is dropped and allowed to float dead. But pull it across in front of him a foot or so, and he spots that movement, and if it looks right, he comes for it. This is the time, however, when you must use a very long, very light leader because in such still, clear water it is easy to line the fish and spook them.

In general, such shallow-water fishing always calls for a light outfit. I remember once when I fished the Little Pine Lagoon in Tasmania, Australia, with Jim Wilson of Lake St. Clair. We found the trout tailing

amid stumps and grasses in water only two feet deep. I got out my 7½-foot rod, matching double-tapered #5 floating line, and used a 14-foot leader tapered down to a 4X tippet. Then I greased the line and the leader down to six inches from the fly, and was ready for business. I dropped a brown and black nymph a foot away and slightly beyond the nearest tailing trout and retrieved it slowly past him, hoping he would think it was a nymph he had scared out of the grasses. It worked, and he chased after it, took with a swirl and a splash, and the fight was on.

For most nymph fishing the leader should be long and light. The trout has a close-up look at a nymph that rides along right in front of him, and he will shy away from a heavy tippet. I like to use a leader not less than ten feet long, to assure that the line will fall far enough away from the fish not to scare him. And for most nymphs I like to go down to a 5X, or at the heaviest, a 4X tippet. The light tippet allows the nymph to swim freely, with a much more lifelike action than if it were riding into the trout's vision on the end of a stiff, straight stick of nylon.

When nymphing fish are lying very deep, on the other hand, and it takes a sinking line to get to them, the leader must be shortened considerably, to six feet only, so the current will not wash the leader high, and drag the nymph up out of the fish's area of interest. The weight of the line should also be adjusted to the river or lake you are fishing, according to depth. The floating/sinking line, of which the first thirty feet sinks while the balance floats, is good for deeper streams and lakes; while the shorter sinking line, of which only ten feet sinks, serves better in shallower water (see LINES).

Usually as you walk along the river bank you can find some evidence of a nymph that might have value in that time and place. One day a few years ago I was wandering up the Big Hole River in Montana, having great fishing with a dry fly. Several times during the day I noticed a big, dark nymph floating down the current, and I saw the shucks along the rocks onshore, too. But I was doing so well with a dry fly that I didn't change. Then just before sunset the situation altered. The fish stopped rising to dries. I was at the head of a run where the white water rushed madly into the pool, then subsided gradually and rolled out into a smooth surface further down.

"There must be some trout holding somewhere along this heavy current," I thought.

I opened my nymph book and looked. There were a couple of large nymphs tied by Dave Whitlock, the Whit Bronze nymph and the Whit Black Stone nymph. Dave had told me that the latter was good towards evening and at dark, so I chose that in size 8.

But the current up where I thought the fish would be was very heavy. My floating line was not going to get that nymph down to them. I reached into my vest pocket and pulled out the extra spool I usually carry, loaded with a #6 wet-head sinking line, and complete with the necessary short six-foot leader. I threaded the new line through the guides, tied on Dave's nymph and was ready.

I moved down a bit, to just where the fast incoming water smoothed off. I made my throw upstream for forty-five feet and held the rod high to keep the current from snatching the near line and pulling it in to me, which, of course, would bring the fly nearer to the surface. I stripped off several more feet of line from the reel and wiggled the rod tip from side to side to get it out, then aided it a bit by roll casting to put the line farther out.

Now I knew that the nymph would ride close to the bottom and I turned the rod downstream, following the track of the line. Almost immediately I saw the line shoot forward, and I pulled back with the rod and was tight to a fish. Tight to a rollicking projectile that tore downstream like a bolt from the blue, racing, making the spray leap up from the line as it sizzled through the water. On he went for fifty feet, seventy-five, a hundred, and then he was into my backing. Just about then I saw the line coming up towards the surface and the water flew apart and I saw the deep body of the fish, his long length and sides afire with crimson. That beautiful, wonderful and wild rainbow went two feet into the air and I guessed him at five pounds.

But this was no time for guessing games. I was too busy. He turned the smooth part of the pool into a shambles, in and out, up and down, and I held the rod high and each time he jumped I dropped the rod tip like it was a live coal. That gives slack line, and it is a good move that keeps a wild fish from falling on the leader and breaking it, or from getting a hard, straightaway yank at it, which might snap the flimsy tippet.

I hung on and met all his tactics and gradually he tired and I got him in close. Then he saw me and off he went again, and wound up that flurry with a halfway-out jump. But he was cooling off, and now I slowly pulled back on the rod, and finding him receptive I gave him the butt and pulled him my way along the top, nose out. I unlatched my landing net, held it in the water and pulled that beautifully colored trout into it. He was long and deep, with a small head on his powerfully built body. He was silvery, too, almost like a steelhead fresh from the salt, but liberally sprinkled with black dots, the crimson streak along his side seemed to glow, and the red splash on his gill covers completed a masterpiece that only nature can produce. I gently unhooked him and slid him back into the river where he belonged.

8 STREAMERS AND BUCKTAILS

Basically, a streamer is a fly tied with feathery wings and tail. A bucktail is a fly tied with bucktail or other animal hair, ranging from bear, goat or wolf to a few strands clipped from your favorite dog or cat. Some flies, such as the renowned Muddler (*see* FLIES) combine several materials. The Muddler is tied with a clipped deer-hair head, a bucktail throat and wings and tail of turkey feather. I nevertheless class it as a bucktail because in its conformation and in the way it works—practically without any action from the feather wings—it is more like a bucktail than a streamer.

The majority of streamers and bucktails are tied to represent minnows, but they may also ape a drowned grasshopper, a crawfish, a large nymph, and sometimes I suspect that to the fish they may look like a mouse, a prime attraction for large trout. Other bucktails and streamers may be flash flies, not necessarily copying any particular form of underwater life or trout food, but merely by color and flash attracting the fish and making him mad, so he will strike at this foreign thing that he sees swimming through his pool.

BREATHERS

Many of the larger streamers and bucktails are tied to do a little "breathing." This means that the feathers of the wings are placed high on the shank of the hook, two or three on each side, and flared outwards so that when you strip in line, pulling the fly forward, the feathers close in on the hook shank, and when you stop the pull they flare outwards. When you pull, stop, pull and stop again, the fly is really breathing in and out with a great come-on action.

There are times when a dead-floating bucktail will take fish. I have caught big brown trout many times by letting a big bucktail drift still with the current. I feel that the browns take it for a mouse, which they particularly like, and plow into it with vigor. But although you can often take fish by allowing a bucktail to drift like this, if a feather streamer is treated the same way its wings will droop so the offering loses its shape and looks dead, unattractive to the trout.

Marabou streamers are possible exceptions in that they are great breathers intrinsically. The wings of the fly are made of marabou stork from the East Indies or Africa, each delicate fiber alive and pulsating in the water. When you strip, the wings press in on the hook, so the streamer assumes the shape of a minnow. Stop, and each of those fibers moves and twitches and breathes, to attract the attention of the trout and make his gastric juices flow like Niagara. Even in a dead drift the marabou seems to live. One of the best fish taken from the Letort River in Pennsylvania in recent years fell to such an offering. Ed Shenk, fine angler and fly tyer of Carlisle, figures that he had spent 150 hours trying for a large brown he had seen feeding. He hooked and lost it five times on five different flies, and between those times he tried almost every other fly in his book. He finally caught it on a white marabou streamer dead-drifted, on a 2X tippet. That fish weighed 8½ pounds.

Bucktails that try to incorporate the breathing principle are usually tied with the wings fore and aft on the top of the hook, so they breathe up and down, rather than in and out. That they can be just as effective is clearly proven by the tremendous success of the blonde patterns in bucktails (see FLIES).

To produce the action these flies are capable of, so the wings will work, flatten as you pull, then open up as you stop. The strip retrieve is all-important (see CASTING TECHNIQUES). Remember that a trout (the prospective predator) and a minnow (the prospective victim) often live side by side in apparent peace. But let something happen to cripple the minnow, to make him limp along, or suddenly dart, as in fright, and watch that trout grab him. So everything you do with your retrieve to make the fly look alive, like the real thing, will add to its attraction for the trout.

BROADSIDE FLOAT One day many years ago I was working slowly upstream on Yellow Breeches Creek in Pennsylvania. It was a beautiful spring day, the water was low and clear, and there was practically no wind. As usual, I was wearing Polaroid glasses for better vision through the water. As I stood at the tail of a small pool I saw a fourteen-inch trout suddenly shoot into view. There was a flash of silver in front of him and he opened his mouth and I saw him grab that shiner. He took it crosswise, held it that way a moment, then turned and swallowed it head first.

I've seen saltwater fish hit baitfish the same way. Few fish of any kind take their prey head-on or from behind. They chase it down and grab it in the middle, then turn it. It is probably a protective maneuver. If the baitfish were taken tail first the upright spines of the dorsal fin might lodge in the predator's throat. When he takes it headfirst, the sharp spine folds down to make for easier swallowing.

It was that particular moment on the Yellow Breeches, in my early fishing, that got me seriously started thinking about the most advantageous way to present my streamers and bucktails to trout. The answer came out "broadside." I needed to use the greased-line technique

Streamer should pass over trout so he sees it broadside and can hit it the way he would hit a baitfish. Diagrams below show how current will belly line and spoil a broadside float unless line is mended by flipping the belly upstream or down.

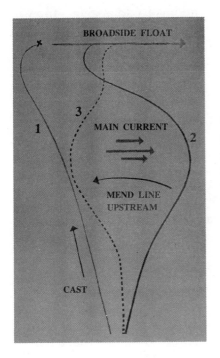

Up-and-across cast (**1**) swings through stronger current in midstream, which bellies the line during the float (**2**), pulling the fly headfirst toward any fish in its path. Angler must mend line upstream (**3**) to bring the fly broadside for a better presentation.

In this instance, the strong current grabs the *fly* and sweeps it downstream ahead of the line, also defeating the broadside float. Angler must mend the line downstream to bring the fly broadside to the fish.

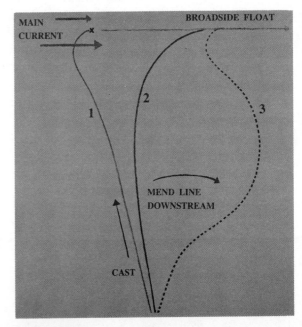

of fishing for Atlantic salmon, a method designed to show the fly broadside to the fish. The method was invented by a famous Scottish angler, A.H.E. Wood, and described by Jock Scott in *Greased Line Fishing for Atlantic Salmon* published in London by Seeley, Service and Company.

In order to achieve the broadside presentation and to cover the entire water, I like to start my series of casts at the top of the pool. I make a short throw first, in the fast water up there, because good fish often lie in that turbulence. Then I extend each cast until I have reached as far across as I can and still control the line, or until I have covered all the water. Then I move down about fifteen to twenty feet and start the series over again. This way I can be sure of putting my fly past the mouth of almost every trout in the pool.

I make the casts across and slightly upstream, and lead the line slightly with the rod tip. If the line begins to belly, I mend the line upstream with a sort of backward and outward flip (*see* CASTING TECHNIQUES). This means that instead of the fly being dragged headlong down the current, far too fast, by that bellying line, it floats freely, broadside to the current and the fish. All he has to do is give a flip of his fins, rise up and grab it in the middle, the way he likes to grab a minnow. A mere lift of the rod tip sets the hook. After a long cast you can sometimes mend the line three or four times and keep the fly floating broadside that much longer.

To handle the retrieve of such a cast, the strip method (*see* CASTING TECHNIQUES) is by far the best. It allows you to make a short, slow pull or give a long yank, or a series of jerks, so a bucktail comes to life, darts and swerves, or a streamer flirts its tail at the fish.

As mentioned earlier, this is the same broadside float often used by anglers using the greased-line technique for Atlantic salmon, as they work over a fish on a known lie. I fish the streamer or bucktail for trout the same way, treating the pool as if I knew that a trout was lying at each suitable spot. I make my cast so the fly will swim through the water broadside to that trout as he faces upstream. Time and again when I have neglected to stick to that broadside float, I have missed a good fish and then, suddenly recalling my good sense, have taken him by that method.

I recall one time when I was fishing the Rio Grande River on Tierra del Fuego with Bebe Anchorena of Buenos Aires. We knew that a fresh run of sea trout had come into the river, some of them twenty-pounders. That's a lot of trout. I was using a red and yellow streamer on a six-pound-test leader tippet, hoping to connect with one of those silver-clad sea-going brownies. On my first cast I had a nice rise but the fish missed. I tried again but this time the fast current bellied the line and pulled the fly under the surface immediately. There was a mighty explosion right in back of the fly, but again the fish didn't touch it. I stopped and waited for him to get back to where he had been lying.

"I saw him," Bebe shouted from the bank. "A big one."

I realized that in my excitement I had been simply heaving the fly out and retrieving it too fast. That fish was willing, as he had plainly shown, but I wasn't presenting the fly so he could really see it and get a hold on it. It called for a broadside presentation.

On the next throw I put the fly out the necessary distance, let it float a couple of feet, then mended the line, and I knew that fly was going along out there, broadside, right over the place where that trout had been. He was still there, and that was what he wanted. The fly was over him the right way for the first time, and he took. There was a toss of water, a heavy pull that made my rod tip bounce down. He took off so fast I couldn't get the tip up, so I pointed the rod right at him and let him go. He ran 150 feet and stopped and then I pulled, but I couldn't move him. I walked his way, and when I got down opposite him I finally could pull him off his perch. He went the other way this time, sixty feet upstream, and jumped. He tore that pool apart, smashed the water into splinters. He was a long slab of beautiful silver, a fifteen-pound sea-run brown.

Occasionally as you fish the broadside float, you find that you need to mend your line downstream rather than up. For instance, you are standing in still water and casting your fly out into a fast current. Then the force of the current sends the fly barrelling down while the shooting line, which has dropped to the surface on your side of the current, in the still water, lies motionless, thus putting a pull on the rest of the line and on the fly. A mend downstream will allow you at least to straighten that line so it's even with the part in the current.

In a similar situation, if all your line is floating high in the water, you can raise the rod high and make a regular roll cast and send part of the shooting line out in the current, and again you will have a free fly, floating broadside for a good number of feet. This is not a mend, but it does give you more free float.

RETRIEVE

When stripping in a streamer or bucktail, always keep the rod pointed above the parallel to the water, to absorb a sudden strike. The bend of the rod will cushion the shock. If the rod is pointed at an angle of about forty-five degrees above the parallel to the water it will bow down with the force of the strike and prevent the fish from breaking the tippet. Fish hit a bucktail or streamer in different ways under varying conditions. Sometimes a trout, especially a smaller one, will charge and sock a fly hard. A bigger trout will often be more deliberate, take more slowly, with majestic aplomb. Again he may simply rise up under the streamer you are retrieving across the pool and suck it in, then sink back to his holding position, and then, when he feels the pressure of the line, give a couple of hard lunges of his body, from side to side, hard enough to disjoint the rod tip—usually a signal that you have a good fish. But whatever way he hits, unless you have that rod tip up to absorb the sharp strike, you are going to have a long list of lost fish.

If a big fish—three, four or five pounds—hits when your rod is pointed at him and you are retrieving, the chances are that any tippet up to 2X (breaking point of 6.3 pounds) will lose him, as the combined strike and the quick lift of your rod to set the hook come at the same time. Pop goes the leader. But if your rod is held at the proper angle, it will absorb some of the shock and will aid you in hooking the fish. All you need to do is lift the rod tip gently. In fact, in such a case the trout will usually hook himself.

The bucktail or streamer fisherman should never move downstream as he is retrieving. Almost invariably you will unconsciously let the rod angle drop, and every time a whale of a trout will hit and snap the leader. I have learned to jam the rod butt into my stomach and keep it there as I retrieve a streamer or bucktail, an automatic position, with the rod up at the forty-five degree angle. And I stay pegged in that one spot until I have completely finished the retrieve, then move down as much as I want to make the next cast.

Sometimes you find yourself fishing across a fast current to the position of a trout you have seen, or where you know from previous experience he will be. Despite your mend, the line gets ahead of the fly, which, because of water resistance, rides along more slowly. The speed of the line pulls the fly downstream headfirst and there it is, ten feet or so behind the end of the line. If you jerk back hard with your rod, it will hasten the swim of the fly and bring it level with the end of the line, and then you can mend that line again and show the fly to the fish in the proper manner. This yank should be done with the rod held low to keep the fly from coming to the surface and making any noise that might scare the fish. If it is done well above the position of the trout he will not be disturbed.

TACKLE

When you are casting the larger streamers and bucktails in large rivers you need a good, powerful rod and matching line to throw them. An 8½-foot rod with a WF-7-F and a 9-footer with a WF-8-F will handle the 1/0 blondes, just about as heavy a fly as you will use for trout. This outfit provides enough power to reach the holding water in most rivers without having to press too hard. In all streamer and bucktail fishing, when you are using a floating line it should be well greased so it will float high. You can mend such a light-floating line without too much water commotion, it retrieves better and allows for more vigorous action of the fly, and picks up better for the next cast.

In a big river with four- or five-pound trout, the leader should be from twelve to fourteen feet in length and tapered down to a 3X or 4X tippet, depending on how big you think the fish may be. The 4X is heavy enough if the pool is free from sunken logs or trees, and provided you do not strike too hard or hold the rod pointed directly at the fish, or even slightly above the parallel to the water. He'll break you off in that case. In many instances you can even use a 5X tippet, but you must watch the rod position on the strike.

In really big water, where the fish are extra large, you can up the tippet to 3X or even 2X. Towards dusk it is often wise to go to 1X. In early morning and late evening trout seem to lose some of their gimlet-eyed vision so it is safe to use a little heavier tippet. And when you fish water that you know holds seven- and eight-pound fish and even heavier, especially towards dark, the veteran angler will even raise the tippet strength to eight- or ten-pound test. After you have been broken off by a couple of these hefty babies you begin to see the point.

CHECK THE FLY

When using these large flies the angler should check the hook frequently, to be sure it has not been blunted or broken as it hit something behind him, especially when he is in waist-deep water. The heavier flies are inclined to drop down behind as you cast, and if you are close to shore even a reasonably high backcast will often allow the hook to touch a rock. A broken hook has resulted in the loss of a lot of good fish.

It is also necessary to check the wings of streamers and bucktails frequently, as the wings often get twisted round the hook. You could fish such a fly all day without getting a hit. It has lost the look of being alive. When you discover that the fly you are using does this, you can often correct the fault by taking hold of the long wing, where it is tied to the shank of the hook, just in back of the eye, and pulling on it, upward, hard.

FISH ALL THE WATER

When fishing streamers or bucktails, it is important to start your casts close in to the point where you are standing. Make the first throw only twenty or thirty feet, across and up, then let it drift downstream a foot or so, then begin to impart short pulls to it. Keep the rod tip up, to absorb a sudden strike. When the fly is within ten or twelve feet of you, pick it up, and make the next cast, again across and slightly up, and about two to three feet farther than the first try. Keep doing this until you are throwing the fly out there for sixty to sixty-five feet. Then move down about ten feet and repeat the process.

Always fish carefully, moving as quietly as you can, so as not to knock rocks or grind gravel. Even if the water is only a couple of feet deep at the top of a pool there are often some good-sized fish up there and careless wading will scare them away. If you walk out, say, thirty-five to forty feet in water from ankle to knee depth, you can bet that you are stepping on trout and scaring them off.

When you have fished out a chosen area, look around you for possible fish lies. Check the currents and upjutting rocks. Fish the fast water. Don't waste time casting into slow water on either side of the current. Trout are in that fast water and will follow your fly into slower water on your side to take. That is another good reason for the across-stream cast. The fly covers more holding water. A fly cast straight downstream or only a bit to either side is not going to be seen by many trout.

While the fly is in fast water it is often a good idea to allow it a little free float. In the first place, the current itself is moving the fly along fast enough that the fish does not have time to spot any phoniness. And the eddies and swirls will keep the wings of either a bucktail or streamer moving so it looks like a minnow in trouble. To let a fly float thus for a few feet, then give a couple of quick jerks, will add to the appearance of a hurt minnow, struggling; and a nearby trout will come for it, his dorsal fin quivering and his mouth watering.

Most big-river fishermen who use streamers and bucktails limit themselves to the big pools. They make a great mistake in not trying the runs, bankside glides and pocket water, often only two or three feet deep. Especially towards dark, trout move into the shallows, sometimes stay there through the night, and only move out in morning when the sun warms the water or when fishermen start walking the banks and disturbing them. If they are not disturbed they will often stay in the shallow water throughout the daylight hours, particularly if the sky is overcast. In such water the smaller streamers will be better because you can present them more gently. And with these smaller flies, the leader should be correspondingly lighter.

While the streamer and the bucktail is essentially a fly to be fished at least a few inches under the water, there are times when you can use them to take fish that are lying very close to the surface yet not taking top-water flies. That's the time I like to grease the underside of a muddler, cast it out, and with rod held high, strip fast. This brings the fly zipping across the surface and often gets a thudding hit.

SMALL STREAMS

In streamer and bucktail fishing, size can be just as important as it is in dry-fly fishing, not so much because you are trying to match a natural hatch as because of the size of the water you are fishing. A big fly in small water where there are only small trout is more likely to scare the fish than is a smaller one. Remember that the trout has very keen eyesight, sharp enough to readily spot a natural that can be matched with a tiny #28 hook. So in small water a fly as large as a #2 or #4 streamer might well scare him enough to pop a few scales. Even a small streamer should be dropped quietly and retrieved with a minimum of fuss. It often pays to drop the small fly up into the fast incoming water of the pool, and let it float down into the deeper part

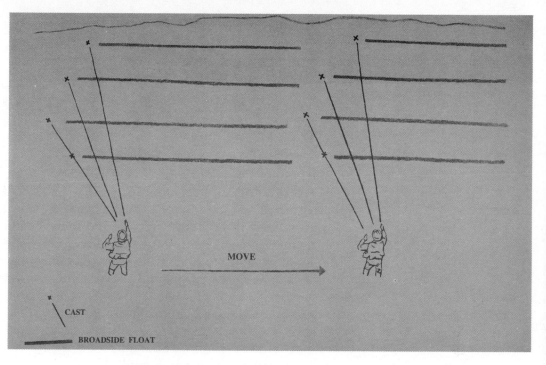

MOVE

CAST

BROADSIDE FLOAT

Proper way to fish all the water is shown in this diagram. Starting at the head of a run, angler makes his first casts to the near water so as not to spook fish farther out, gradually extends casts until he has covered all the water between himself and the opposite bank. He moves downstream about ten feet, continues the series of casts, and so forth down the stream.

without any motion whatever, looking like a drowned natural or an injured minnow moving in the eddies.

Once I watched Red Monical of Livingston, Montana, work such a stream. He tied on a #10 Muddler, crept and catfooted into position near the tail of a fifty-foot-long pool. He made his throw well up to the top, let the fly float motionless for about two feet, just under the surface, then used his rod tip to impart a twitch to it. It looked like a drowning grasshopper struggling for the surface. Just then a brownie came from nowhere and took the fly on the run, a nice fourteen incher that shattered the surface.

The thing that put the catch over was Red's handling of his equipment. He used a short line and kept most of it off the surface to avoid a line track which could be seen by the trout, and he avoided the noise of the line being stripped near the fly and the fish. With his high-held rod he was ready to pick up the line gently for the next cast. All the while he had good control over line, leader and fly, and when the fish came to the fly all he had to do was pull back gently with the rod and set the hook.

In small mountain streams and clearstone streams everywhere, trout have a tough time getting enough food. There is an occasional flurry of aquatic flies, never heavy, plus the nymphs of these flies, and some terrestrials that arrive on the water by mischance. But at best these are lean pickings. A minnow looks like a whole meal to the trout, and he will go for a streamer or bucktail good and hard.

AUTUMN WINDFALL

Come autumn, most sportsmen's thoughts just naturally turn to hunting, and many of them put up their rods for the season. The fly hatches have come and gone and they let a few cold days convince them that winter has arrived. They miss some of the greatest streamer and bucktail fishing of the entire year. I nearly did that myself the first time I went to the Rocky Mountains to fish for trout. When a snowstorm roared in around the first of October I made ready to head east. But the storm blew through in two days and then, in a bright blue sky the warm sun melted the snow from the low foothills, like rolling back a rug, all the way up to timberline and above, leaving a white coat only on the peaks. And as if to enjoy a last splurge of feeding, trout were on the move everywhere. I had the greatest fishing of the entire season. Since that time I have been a confirmed autumn fisherman.

This is the time when the country is at its most spectacular, the wonderful Indian summer season. In the mountains, above six thousand feet, aspen leaves shine gold. Along the rivers the cottonwoods and willows are a medley of yellow and brown and green. Sparked by the fall air, wildlife moves, too. You come upon deer that stand and stare at you with wide eyes, ears pitched forward and legs set for a fast start. They cross the river, stepping high, and bound into the bush on the far side. A mink flows sinuously along the bank, and slips into the water and reappears fifty feet downstream. Muskrats swim the river, dragging bunches of watercress to store for their winter diet. And overhead the ducks stream southward in wavering lines. You hear the whistle of wings as a single shoots low over you and you see him turn his head as if to discover if you are into a fish.

On the rocks alongshore a water ouzel, or dipper, walks to the brink of the stream, and straight into it, goes under the water to pick a nymph from the gravel, and casually emerges on a rock. He stands there blinking his white eyelids at you, all the time bending at the knees, dipping and dipping, then takes off upstream on wings set like a duck's, well back on his body, a honey of a bird that makes you stop fishing just to look.

Many western streams only reach their prime in autumn. They are still high and sometimes murky with snow runoff as late as mid-August in places. But by early September the bigger rivers have started to drop and by the middle of the month they are low and clear. You can wade in spots that have been out of bounds all summer, and reach pools and runs you couldn't touch in high water. And because of the lower water the trout are packed into well-defined pools. There is a definite migration of the fall-spawning brownies at this time, to favored pools or towards smaller streams which, in a month or two, they will ascend to carry out their reproductive activities. But meantime, they are crowded together in the pools, restless, cruising, feeding, ready for your offerings.

One such fall day when the river was low and clear, I was fishing the Yellowstone, and the fishing was so good you could hardly stand it. This particular day I walked towards the pool, stepping carefully over the head-sized rocks along the water's edge, rocks that earlier in the season had been under water. While I was still twenty feet back from the river I stoppped and made a forty-five-foot cast so that the #4 Muddler fell lightly some twenty feet out in the water, in two-foot depth. I made a couple of strips of line and there was a flurry of spray and a hard yank as a trout took, turned and headed at astounding speed down the two-hundred-foot-long pool. Halfway down he jumped and tumbled back in. Then he stopped and bucked and thrashed and had the rod tip bowing in all directions at once. He was some fish! Then I got him in close and saw he wasn't the four-pounder he acted like. But he was two pounds, a good brownie, fat, firm and as brilliantly colored as the leaves along the banks, his fins sparked with the extra vigor of the cooler water of autumn.

After I had released him I moved carefully out into the head of the pool where the water tumbled in fast, making four-inch waves. This time I cast the Muddler across current and up a couple of feet and watched it hit, ride one wave and disappear into another one. I held the rod tip at about a forty-five-degree angle to absorb a strike to my 4X tippet. Then everything stopped. It felt as if a giant hand grabbed the line, held it for a second, then gave a couple of hard yanks. I struck, then dropped the rod tip fast as that fish pulled line from the reel spool and headed downstream. Dropping the tip like that lessens the strain so the line pays out more easily than it would if it went out over the tip of an upthrust rod.

Halfway down the pool he jumped, a big block of a fish. He jumped going away and just kept on running and went well into the backing. He jumped again and again, fourteen times in all. Each time he came out I dropped the rod tip so he wouldn't fall on a tight leader and snap it. He slowed at last and I stopped him and started him back. In close, I saw the bright crimson of his gill covers, then the wide streak of red down his sides. He was as big a rainbow as I had taken in some time and right then and there I decided to keep him for a mount. When I beached him, he checked out at five pounds five ounces, and he hangs above my desk today to remind me of that fine day that was just the right time for streamers and bucktails.

If the weather becomes very cold and the water correspondingly so, it will sometimes send the fish down to lie close to the bottom, and then you may have to go to a sinking line to get hits. There are several different types of sinking lines and the choice has to be made according to where you are fishing. For big, deep pools, the best line to use is one of which the first thirty feet sink while the balance floats. You can mend this floating part easily and thus keep the sinking part and the fly out in the current where you want it. I never recommend a line that sinks in its entirety of river use because all too often this line is pushed sideways by the current and driven into the slower water at the angler's feet. The fly is snatched away from the lie of the trout, out there in the current, and he has no chance to see it.

My friend Jack Bannon, of Stuart, Florida, used a sinking line and streamer fly in the fall of 1970 to take a seldom-equaled string of big trout, four, five and six pounds. And on October 12 he topped them all. He was casting the weight-forward sinking wet head, already mentioned, of which the first thirty feet sinks, while the rest floats. His fly was a #4 Spruce Fly, a streamer, on an eight-foot leader with a 1X tippet. As he worked down the pool he had a hit that shocked him, so hard that he automatically struck and was fast to a fish that went into a steaming run, busting through the water like a ten-second man returning a punt. He went sixty feet up the pool and jumped clear. He was a long, deep rainbow—so big he scared Jack.

That ball of lightning turned and rushed back to where he had started. Jack couldn't begin to keep a tight line, but he reeled as fast as he could. Then the fish stopped and Jack got line back. Immediately the fish headed out again, jumped again, and this time continued up the 150-foot pool right to the top and Jack's reel spool was showing. But luckily the fish stopped before those last few winds of line had gone, and Jack began to get the fish back. It took thirty minutes to finally beach him. Jack picked him up and staggered back from the water. That big, beautiful rainbow weighed eight pounds fifteen ounces, and gave Jack a place on the Wall of Fame in Dan Bailey's Fly Shop at Livingston, where fly-taken fish caught in Montana waters and weighing better than four pounds are recorded.

For smaller streams, say only five feet in depth, the ideal sinking line is that of which only the first eleven feet sinks and the balance, or shooting line, floats. A longer length of heavy line in such water would go down too fast and become caught around rocks. With the shorter sinking section, as the heavy head works down the pool you can mend the floating section and keep the fly out where you want it, where the fish are. If you want to fish a spot where the current is running fast over a shallow stretch, send the cast across and slightly downstream, then hold the rod high and the speed of the current plus the upheld rod will usually be sufficient to keep the eleven feet of sinking line from being caught and will allow you to swim your fly enticingly over these shallow holding places.

One of my favorite ways to work a river with bucktails and streamers on these fall days when there are few other anglers on the river, so that moving along is no problem, is to choose a pal and select a stretch of river we would like to fish. We drive one car to the spot where we plan to end the day and leave it there, then in the other car go upstream as far as we want, and fish our way down, alternating pools or fishing the larger ones together. It's the same procedure as used in floating a river, only you do it on foot. If you carry a lunch in the back of your fishing vest, you are all set for the day and can cover a lot of river without having to look ahead to a long walk back to your car at the end of the day when you are tired. We often cover three to four miles in a day's jaunt, with plenty of time to fish each pool. At the end, we both hop into the car that awaits us there, and drive back and pick up the other car. For 10 years this was an annual event for Dan Bailey, his partner, Red Monical, and myself, on the Yellowstone River. We had many wonderful days, taking trout over five and even six pounds, and lots of others not so big. We always used streamers and bucktails as we were after those extra-big ones, and we all agreed that a big streamer or bucktail was what the doctor ordered for those trout.

Regardless of how you are fishing, there's no need to start early on these autumn days. You can sleep as late as you want because at this time of year the night-time temperature often drops low enough to chill both air and water and it takes a few hours for the sun to warm things up and get the trout stirring so they will hit. From October 1 on, the good fishing will usually start about 11 A.M. and continue until almost dark.

9 HOW TO PLAY AND LAND A TROUT

The fisherman in the pool was into a trout that was shaking his head back and forth, thrashing with his body, throwing surface water all around. It was a good-sized trout, maybe sixteen inches, and the angler was holding his rod up and there was a big bend in it. As I watched, the rod snapped back and the line flew high in the air.

The luckless angler retrieved his fly and turned to me.

"Look," he said, "he straightened the hook out."

Naturally. That fisherman was using a fly tied on a #16 light wire hook. His leader, on the other hand, was a 2X, big enough to haul in a ten-pound trout. Something had to give and the tippet, usually the weakest link in the fly-fishing outfit, was stronger in this case than the light wire of the hook. It had to straighten out.

"Your tippet is too heavy for the hook," I said.

"But on a lighter tippet I might lose him," he protested.

"You've lost him now," I pointed out. "You are always going to lose some fish, but it shouldn't be because of mismatched tackle. There are tricks that will help you land a good fish even on the lightest of gear."

LET HIM RUN

When you hook a fish and he starts to swim away, let him go, working only against the slight drag of your reel. Too much pressure may straighten out a light hook, as happened in this case, or break the tippet, if you are using a delicate strand. Let the trout take line, and when he tires he will slow and stop and then you can get into the picture. But at first, raise your rod high and let him go. Trout do tire quickly and all the while the bow in the rod is working against him, wearing him down, without any further effort on your part, giving him no quarter. When he stops you can start to reel and get him coming your way.

When a fish runs, and takes line from the reel, it is better to play him from the reel. If he runs again, let him go, and when he slows and stops, start to reel again. At all times, be ready to let go of that reel handle in a flash, when he makes a sudden pull or starts to run again. If it happens to be a small trout, you can often strip him in fast,

173

of course. He doesn't have the weight or strength to move out. But if he has any size, you are always safer to play him from the reel.

If a fish dives under a brush pile or takes the leader around a rock or cuts it on some underwater snag, you may lose him on this run. But otherwise you will probably be able to land him, even on a 5X tippet. And the chances are that if you don't use the light tippet, you will not get the strikes. So what have you got to lose?

GO BELOW HIM When you hook a big trout that sulks and hangs in the current, walk along the shore until you are below him, always keeping a tight line, then pull back with the rod. This will usually unseat him, and then you can go ahead and fight him.

Any time a fish is out in the current and you are having trouble moving him, bring your rod in towards your bank, holding it parallel to the water, and pull backwards with it, towards the bank. This will pull him out of the current and your way, and you can fight it out with him from there.

FOLLOW THE FISH If the fish runs downstream into the pool below, keep a tight line and follow him down, reeling as you go. If he keeps ahead of you, keep following, and fight to get line on your reel. When a trout gets a lot of your line out he can get freeway enough to run in back of a rock, a fallen tree, a small point or under grasses. And with the fly line and a hundred or more feet of backing out, the drag is increased so much that it is all the easier to break him off. It is much more difficult to play and land a big trout or a steelhead that has gotten into the backing, than it is to play him off the fly line on the reel. The backing is smaller in diameter and harder to control with your fingers than is the fly line so a sudden jerk of the fish may yank it from your fingers. And at that distance you must play a trout lighter. You can't put the butt of the rod to him, or you stand the chance of the tippet breaking or the fly pulling from the fish's mouth.

So in all cases, your first effort should be towards getting the fly line back on the reel. After the fish has made his first run and stopped, pull back with the fly rod, then drop the tip and reel fast, and continue doing this as long as he will come along towards you. This is called "pumping" a fish. If he does not stop, of course, you must go after him, following him down the shore and reeling as you go, eventually getting close enough so when he finally does stop you can play him.

It is important to wind your line evenly onto the reel while fighting a fish. To begin with, the spool should not be overloaded to the point that the line and leader scrape on the crossbars of the reel case as you bring in line. But even with properly loaded reel, the line will hump up and finally stick tight against the crossbar, unless you use care. And when such a hump appears, the line tends to fall off on either side. A fast run by the trout, plus a bit of drag on the reel, will cause the loose line to dig in and stick. With a reel that has a wide face, you can guide the line back and forth across the spool as you wind, using the little finger of the rod hand, as you reel. Even on a narrow spool you can control the line between your thumb and first finger, and steer it back and forth to place it evenly on reel.

At all times, in fact, it is important to be sure that the line has been reeled in evenly. If you put a reel away one evening with the line carelessly reeled, so the leader is under two or three loops of line, it may cost you a fish the next day.

LEAD THE TROUT

You can also lead a trout away from danger, pull him upstream for a couple of hundred feet in a big river, or fifty feet in a small one, to get him away from some obstacle that threatens. Leading a trout is a great maneuver and has saved me many a fish, including the biggest brown I have ever taken.

It was in Argentina, on the Chimehuin River in the pool just above the Gargantua del Diablo, a mad rush of rapids where the roaring river shot out of the tail of the pool, a rush of racing white water and upjutting rocks where it would be impossible to hold or land a fish of any size, let alone this $18\frac{1}{2}$-pounder with fire in his eye. I had to keep him out of there. He had raced upstream after being hooked, and then up-pool about two hundred feet he turned and busted down my way and I thought he was going over the rocks into the rapids. But he stopped, perhaps as reluctant to go into that maelstrom as I was to have him do so.

I was tight to him now, so I started walking slowly up the pool, rod out over the water, and he came along quietly, no head shaking, no protest at all, just swam slowly along at the pull of the line. I walked him for 250 feet, until I could go no farther. A bush stopped my progress on land and the dropoff at the bush was too steep to allow me to wade around. It was from there that I had to wage my fight. I immediately pulled harder on the fish, pulling the rod in towards the bank, and he came to life and ran across stream for a hundred feet, then back again to the rim of the rapids. He stopped there again and once more I went after him reeling all the while for a tight line. I went down as far as I could, to the very spot where I had started that first upstream walk of the fish and again I led him up. I had to do it the third time but then he was weakening, and standing some 150 feet above the tail of the pool I gave him the works and pulled him in, on the top, his head halfway out, from which position he just couldn't get his head down to swim off again.

There was no place to slide him up on the beach so I pulled his snout against a protruding rock in six inches of water and he lay still. I reached down and got my four fingers under his gill cover and lifted him up and out.

I had to use the same maneuver once on a big rainbow in Wyoming, and later in British Columbia with a steelhead that kept running downstream and stopping right in front of a tree that had fallen into the river. I led him upstream for 150 feet, and by that time he was tired and I got him in.

GIVE SLACK

When a trout runs around a tree limb or protruding log or rock, you can often wade into position to free him. But if you cannot wade close enough, try giving a little slack, take the pressure off and wait for a couple of minutes. If the leader is not snagged tight around anything the fish will think that he is free and start to swim away, which often lifts the line or leader clear of that snag. Then you can tighten up and fight it out.

TO GET A TROUT OUT OF WEEDS

Heavy stands of grass and weeds are the main obstacles in many trout streams, and when your fish gets himself entangled in such growth, it is very difficult to get him out. I always try to note where he goes in, and wade in as close as possible, then pull back and try to bring him out from the same direction he went in, to avoid the line catching across any growth. If he is so far into the grass that this is impossible, I sometimes wade right into the grass and take hold of the leader and gently try to lift him, straight up. Sometimes you can pick handfuls of the grasses from above him and clear the leader this way, all the time keeping a very slight pressure on the line. Then, if you see him, you can pick him up, or sometimes you can pick him out of the water in the midst of a handful of that grass.

When a fish is so deeply imbedded in the underwater growth that you cannot reach him in any other way, you can sometimes use your foot to move the fish. While fishing Silver Creek in Idaho, with Bill Rae, then Editor of *Outdoor Life*, I saw him save the day this way. He had hooked a good fish, but it dove and went into a big patch of the aquatic grasses with which the stream abounds. No matter what Bill did, he couldn't budge that fish.

"I'll have to use my foot to get him out of that grass," said Bill. "But gently," he added, remembering his 5X tippet.

He moved out towards the patch of grass, and when he reached it he held the leader lightly in his left hand and shoved one foot along the bottom, slowly, poking and probing, so as not to come up against the leader hard. It took a bit of doing, but finally his foot found the fish, and a gentle push got him moving. He dashed out of there into clear water and Bill landed him.

Any time your fish gets into such a situation you stand a chance of losing him when he makes a sudden lunge and the line is tight around something; but better to lose him trying than just to lean back and break him off for sure.

| KEEP HIS HEAD UP | Some limestone streams and spring creeks are crammed with floating weeds and grasses and you have to cast over them in order to reach a riser. |

KEEP HIS HEAD UP

Some limestone streams and spring creeks are crammed with floating weeds and grasses and you have to cast over them in order to reach a riser. The best approach in this situation is to wade as close as you can without disturbing the fish. You want to be near enough to use a short line.

For instance, picture yourself in a stream where the matted grass lying on the surface extends out for twenty feet in front of you. In the clear water beyond that, fifteen feet from the edge of the grasses, you have spotted a rising trout. Drop the fly four feet above him and let it float through. When he takes, his pull on the line will cause the line on the grass to jump up and come tight from rod tip to trout. When he takes, immediately raise the rod high, your arms straight up, and strip line fast. This way you get to him while he is still on the surface and you can keep his head up. Often you can just keep on stripping and bring him to the edge of the grass, then strip a bit faster; because he has already been started in your direction, and is on top, he slips onto the grass. You can keep him skidding across the top of it, and bring him to you and pick him up.

Sometimes the top of the grasses will be so matted that when you pull fish over on it he will lie there, almost as if on land. All you have to do is reach down and pick him up.

When landing a fish, then, the main thing to remember is to keep his head up so he cannot dive. When you have him in close, head up, pull gently, bringing his head above water to start him your way. But be sure to let out more leader before you are ready to land him. Pull back with the rod tip, still keeping the fish's head up, until you have a length of line and leader about equal to the length of the rod, or a little more. Then extend your arm back, rod high, and this will pull the fish in to you, to net or to pick up. If you have a greater length of line out, you can't reach the fish. But if you pull back with the rod when you have less line out, you won't be able to reach him and will swing the trout into the air and probably break the tippet. Always try to have the length of leader and tippet, from rod tip to fish, as long as, or a foot or so longer than, your fly rod, then the push back brings the trout in to you.

LOWER ROD TIP

When a trout jumps, the angler should drop the rod tip, and when the fish is back in the water, lift the tip gently to come tight to him again. Dropping the rod tip helps keep the trout from falling on a tight leader. If you hold tight, and he is jumping away from you and comes up against the non-giving line, he will pop your tippet. Or if he falls on a tight leader that has perhaps a small nick in it, he will break it.

Too much drag can give you the same result. If a trout makes a sudden dash away, lower the rod tip fast. Point it right at the fish. There is much more drag pressure on the line over the tip of an unheld rod, than when it comes off the reel through the guides and goes straight out.

NETTING A TROUT

The choice of how you are going to land your fish has to be made according to how and where you are fishing. If you are fishing from a boat, in a fairly large river or a lake, it is often best to use a net. It is difficult to reach over the side of a boat, while keeping the line tight, and lift a fish from the water. The net should be placed in the water so the frame is under the water before you attempt to bring the fish over it. Hold him out, say ten or twelve feet, lower the net beneath the surface and then lead him over it. If you wait until the fish is right there beside you, then thrust down with the net, he will make an extra effort to get away. When you pull him over the net, he will lie still and you just lift up and there he is.

Sometimes as you fish shallow water from a boat, the guide will go overboard and hold the craft while you cast the near water. When you start to bring a fish in close, you have the problem of being sure to keep your line and leader away from his legs, as well as from the prop of the outboard motor. You must be ready for all his sudden darts and surges. If you are in deeper water and the line threatens to go across the motor or around the guide's shoulders, shove your rod arm high, raise as much line as you can, so it goes down into the water at an angle sufficient to clear these danger points. If the fish is too close for this, and is under the motor or the boat, do the opposite. Thrust your rod down into the water and try to guide the line so the fish cannot pull it around these obstacles.

If you are wading, and someone else is going to net your fish, you still may have problems. You can be fairly sure that a guide will handle things right, but I long ago learned never to trust a friend. I've seen willing helpers wield the net like a club and bring it down on the fish itself, or on the leader, usually managing to break him off with that wild swing.

If you are in a river, never allow the helper to wade downstream from you and then out and try to net your fish while you have a lot of line out. The netter should stay with the angler, and when the latter

Proper way to land a trout is to lead him over the net, nipping line against rod handle with the fingers. Frame should be thrust into the water before bringing the fish over the netting.

has brought the fish in close enough to reach without wild lunges, slip the net under the water and scoop him up. The fish should be netted headfirst. If you try to net a good-sized fish tail first, he often gets leverage on the edge of the net with his tail, gives an extra flip, and takes off, perhaps snapping the light tippet if you are not quick enough to give free line.

Just at the moment of netting, the angler should give slack, a mere drop of the rod tip, perhaps six inches, to avoid the rim of the net hitting a taut leader tippet.

If the fish is not successfully netted on the first effort, don't make another try for him right then with a sudden stab. Let him go a little, and work him back into position again. If you go at it frantically, the fish will start lunging around and before you know it he may have the leader around your legs or that of your netter—and snap, he's gone.

While nets are fine in boats, they are something else again when you are fishing on foot in wooded country. I still have bumps on the back of my head from earlier days when I used to wear a net slung on an elastic on my back. As I made my way through bushes, moving from pool to pool, the net would hang upon something, then suddenly let go and come forward like an arrow, hitting the target area of my neck, ear or skull with a thud and a whop that I felt for the next hour. A net tangles in every fence you try to cross, it swings down in front of you as you lean over. If you are wading in deep water it gets caught in the current behind you, and even sometimes in your line. You don't need a net for the average river trout, anyway.

There are several ways of landing a trout. You can pick him from the water, if he is not too large, beach him by skidding him up on a gravel bar, or with his head against a rock, as I did with that big trout in Argentina.

TO BEACH A FISH

It is always easier for me to beach a fish, either on a sloping shoreline or atop grasses, or even on a shallow gravel bar in the middle of a stream. In such situations a trout seldom struggles hard, and it is fairly easy to manage him. You can then pick him up by sliding your fingers under his gill covers, being careful not to touch the gills, and lift; or, if the fish is not too large, you can simply slide your hand under him, palm up, then close the fingers gently around him. A fish lifted in this manner will seldom struggle unless you clamp your fingers tightly. If you clamp down on him, grab him hard and squeeze, he will spurt out of your fingers and swim away. Sometimes you have to bring a fish in a couple of times, if he is still fresh. But keep working at him until he is a little tired, then lift him up, gently, and he will lie still in your half-closed fingers.

To land a trout without a net, simply slide your hand under him, palm up, and close the fingers gently.

Many streams today have catch-and-release regulations. Even on those that don't more and more anglers are releasing their trout in order to ensure good fishing for the future.

10 HOW TO WADE A TROUT STREAM

I was about thirty feet from the bank, in knee-deep water, when my right foot slipped on a round rock and I started to fall to my right. I was holding my fly rod out in front of me, and automatically I pushed the rod through the air, hard, to my left, then immediately snapped it back to my right. The spring of the rod broke the impetus of my fall and kept me erect. I finished the trip ashore in safety.

Later that same day I was wading in water that was waist deep. I was going altogether too fast. My toe bumped a rock with such force that I began to pitch forward. This time I swung the rod hard into the water in front of me and pushed down for three feet. The strong, continued drive of the long fly rod against the density of the water stopped my fall and gave me enough leverage to regain my balance and straighten up.

THE FLY ROD IN WADING

These are only two of the many ways you can use your fly rod as a safety device in wading. The average fisherman who finds himself about to tumble into the water instinctively thinks of saving his rod. He is afraid he will break it in the fall. This might very well happen if you fall on land but not so in the water. Certainly waving it in the air or thrusting it down into the water, however hard, is not going to do it any harm. Its use as a balancing agent can save you tumbles that range from the merely laughable to disastrous. For a good many years I have used my rod boldly as an aid to wading and have never yet damaged one in this way. In an emergency you can even use your rod as a wading staff, butt down in the river, without hurting it. Your fly rod is tough, your life is short, so don't worry about the rod.

Balance is the most important part of wading. The rod can be used to help achieve balance. If you are in fairly shallow water you can wade with both arms outstretched, parallel to the surface, and wield the rod as a balancing agent in the air. When you get into a heavy stretch of current you can lower the rod on your downstream side, slanting it into the water, so it is a foot under the surface, right up to the butt. You'll be surprised at the sudden ease of wading, at how it takes the pressure off. If you should slip you can immediately push

183

down with the rod, or backward or forward as the occasion demands, and save the day. Time and again I have done this and marveled at the extra balance I can achieve through the use of the rod.

You don't have to be falling in before you discover what the rod can do for you. Most falls happen so quickly as to call for instant reaction, so you should practice using the rod in this way. Next time you are in a stream hold the rod in the water and swing it from side to side and up and down. Try the same thing with the rod held in the air to see how its flex works as a balancing agent. You will soon get the feel of it as you realize that both water and air have a certain amount of resistance you can take advantage of. When you are wading and slip even slightly, work your rod, and soon you will bring it into play automatically whenever necessary.

Few anglers realize how easy it is to fall when wading and how dangerous a tumble can be. Wet rocks along shore are almost always slippery and a fall there can be rough because there is no water to cushion your fall. You can break an arm, a leg, even your head. In the river you may merely down the trout around you as you splash in, but on the other hand you may find yourself in a serious situation and have a bad time getting out. There are a few each year who don't make it back to shore. Yet most falls could be prevented by careful and intelligent wading.

FAST WATER

It is nearly always easier to wade in waist-deep water than in rapids where the fast-flowing current hits you any place between the ankle and the knee. In shallow water the force of the river tends to push your feet downstream and on occasion can take them right out from under you. If you have a chance, therefore, it is always better to wade where it is a little deeper and the current is slower. If you do have to cross a heavy, shallow rapids, plant each foot firmly, squirm it around until it is settled securely on good footing, then move the other foot up to it, probing for obstacles. When you find a good spot, squirm that foot around, just as you did the other, and get it set.

When you are fishing with friends, and it becomes necessary to cross a heavy flow of water, it is a good idea to line up, holding hands with the biggest man at the upstream end of the line. He should use a staff in his upstream hand. As you wade across in this way, the big man breaks the current to some extent, so that those below him are walking in a sort of eddy. The clasped hands provide additional balance, and if one person does slip the others can help him.

It is basically the same principle you use when crossing a clear-water river where you can see the bottom. You can pick your way across by using advantageous spots where the footing is extra good, patches of gravel that have formed where the force of the current is broken by a

When wading in fairly shallow water, you can extend both arms and use the rod as a balancing agent (*above*). If you get into heavy current, you can lower the rod into the water and prevent yourself from falling (*below*).

rock that splits the current. In the eddy back of such rocks you often find a smooth gravel patch. Stepping from gravel patch to gravel patch is like walking down Fifth Avenue.

LOOSE ROCKS

A wading hazard that is all too often forgotten is the rock that is not solidly imbedded in the bottom. Each year a river in flood washes down new rocks and changes the position of old ones. Often they are left lying loosely when the river drops, not anchored to the bottom. Or they are so rounded by centuries of washing by the river and gravel that they roll easily underfoot. You should always test a rock before stepping on it. Use your forward foot to shuffle around a bit, making sure that stone is firmly set. One of my own most dangerous falls occurred when I stepped carelessly on such a round rock as I was wading the Yellowstone River. The rock rolled, spinning me so that I lit facing upstream. I was only in knee-deep water but the current was so heavy that it kept pushing me downstream towards the deeper part of the pool. I couldn't get to my feet in that current. I finally crawled and scrambled back to safety on hands and knees, emerging from the water only a yard above the big, deep pool below, where I would really have been in trouble.

The top of a pool and the tail of a pool can be treacherous spots to cross. The water here is sometimes very swift, more so than it looks, and could wash your legs out from under you. Where rocks cushion the flow, watch carefully those little runs between the rocks, where the entire force of the flow is narrowed and plunges down with extra force. Sometimes it is sufficient to take the angler's feet out from under him.

ANGLING ACROSS CURRENT

A wader should never move straight upstream or straight downstream. You are almost bound to stub a toe and fall flat. You are presenting the full width of your body to the current, too, when you face directly up or downstream, so you must work that much harder. If you are facing downstream the water has that much more area to push against and throw you off balance. Get sideways to the flow and angle across the river, preferably moving slightly downstream. It is much easier to move with the water, and you do not become tired as you do when wading against it. Push one foot along, bring the other one to it, and so on, across and down. At all times in wading, you should use this method, pushing one foot forward, getting it settled, bringing the other one to it, and so on. This probing type of wading will save you from coming abruptly against many an obstacle, or from suddenly stepping over the edge of an unsuspected drop-off in the pool.

However, in wading downstream, it must always be kept in mind that you may have to come back, unless you know the stream and have already plotted a way ashore down below. And when you start back you are going to have to buck the current.

TO TURN IN A CURRENT

One of the most dangerous moments in wading comes when you must turn into a heavy current, with the water almost to the top of your waders. You may have waded out there to fish to a riser and find yourself in heavier water than you realized. Or you may have been trying to cross and then, finding the current too heavy, decide to go back. When you turn it will mean that you must momentarily present the wide trunk of your body to the current, and this is the treacherous moment. Always turn into the current, with knees slightly bent, so that you are leaning a little upstream. To make the turn, start with the feet in a fairly close stance, so you are facing across current. Gradually turn the upstream foot into the current, as far around as you can with comfort. Get it well set, then bring the other one up and around. Repeat this, continually leaning into the current, until you have made the 180-degree turn and are facing toward shore, with your narrow side to the current. Keep your feet only fifteen or sixteen inches apart during the turn. And remember, always move the upstream foot first and bring the other one to it. You can use the rod on the downstream side after you have turned, for further steadiness, but never use it as you turn, because the slightest push of the current against it might throw you off balance.

Never turn your back to the current to make a turn. The push of the water will start you moving downstream, and it is like running before the wind. It is tough to stop, and even though you dig your heels in you will have trouble getting around. If by chance you find yourself in a heavy current and in such deep water that you cannot make the upstream turn and therefore must let your back take the current, then the only thing to do is to go with it, downstream, trying to angle towards shore. Try to bounce your way to the shallows. Get up on tiptoe, leaning forward a little. Give a hard upward push with one foot, and with the force of the current to help you, you will bounce forward three or four feet. Then push down with the other foot to get a toe-hold on the bottom and again shove. It is possible to reach shallow water in this way, even in big waters.

In places where you have to resort to this procedure, the force of the water is often so great that if you do fall in it is very difficult to regain your feet when you reach the shallows, and in such case you just have to swim or crawl ashore. If in spite of your efforts the current takes you away from the shallows, you should try to let yourself float with the current and, above all, keep cool. Get yourself turned so you are going downcurrent feet first. Sooner or later you will be pushed against a bank where you can grab an overhanging bush or some roots, or you will be drifted into shallow water again. Do not let yourself be swept into the upcurrent side of long tree branches or logs sticking out into the river. You could be forced under them in heavy current, and become snagged and held there. An angler who fishes very large rivers should wear a life vest of some kind. There are now several on the market which are comfortable and not cumbersome. Also, new neoprene foam waders greatly aid in staying afloat.

WATCH FOR DROP-OFFS

Even where the bottom of a stream is gravel and apparently trouble-free, the angler who wades must move cautiously, reading the water, which changes color from light brown in the shallows to the bluish shades that indicate deeper areas. Waders should always wear polarized glasses to give better vision into the water, so they can spot hazards. There is always danger of finding yourself on the edge of a gravel bar where the bottom drops off suddenly to considerable depth. The gravel on such an edge is often loosely packed and will give beneath your weight and may deposit you feet first in the depths of the pool. If you are wading carefully, probing ahead before stepping down with your full weight, you will feel the loose gravel and will be able to back up and get out of there. If you do feel the gravel beginning to give way, turn towards the shore and dig hard and fast with your feet, in short, hard pushes, and unless you are in really deep, you will be able to climb out.

WADING IN MUCK

A further hazard on the bottom of a stream is muck. If you must wade in muck, you should test your feet often, to make sure you can move them. Sometimes you sink so far in that to try to take a sudden step would throw you and you would go down, unable to pull your feet out. If you fall in the water with your feet anchored it is very difficult to get up again. This is another spot where you can use your rod to advantage. Plunge the entire rod down hard underwater and push against it, against the direction in which you are falling, and it will give you a little leverage to regain your balance.

If you must wade in such soft stuff—and you often do to reach a vantage point from which to cast to a riser—slide one foot forward about two feet, put it down slowly and press gently to see how deep it is going to go. If you can find a firm footing, then bring the other foot up. Sometimes gravel lies only a few inches under such mud. If there is a good current, you often find that gravel swept clear of mud further out.

Occasionally every angler gets into a spot where the muck is so deep it seems there is no bottom. Your boots sink in until you are up to the crotch. That's a good spot to leave at once—but slowly. Pull one foot out first, holding your balance with the other until you are clear. Sometimes you have to pull so hard that your foot will come right out of the boot and up the leg of the wader. It is hard to get it back in again. The only way is to grasp the waders above the knee and pull up at the same time as you try to shove the foot back where it belongs. Start on your way again, freeing first one foot, then the other, never hurrying. A fast step when you are mired may only result in a face-down fall; and besides that, this is hard, wearying work, and you want to conserve your strength.

WADING STAFF

Any time you have to cross difficult water you should use a wading staff. Some fishermen carry one at all times, and there are good ones available in tackle stores. But if you are on the stream without one, you can make do with a stout stick picked up on the side of the stream. Test the improvised wading staff. Sometimes such an old stick will have a rotten spot, and you don't want it to give away in midstream.

As you wade across, use the staff on the *upstream* side, so you are leaning into the flow of the water and onto the firmly planted staff, always using the heaviest end down—the strongest end, as the lighter end might wobble or snap under pressure. Move the staff forward a couple of feet, plant it firmly, then bring the upstream foot up beside it, then the downstream. Move the staff again and repeat, and so on. When you get to the far side carry the improvised staff back from the river and put it where you can find it if you return this way, or where someone else can find it if he needs to cross.

If you use a staff on the downstream side, the current pushes hard against you and may push you into the staff and throw you off balance, or even trip you.

Always use a wading staff when crossing difficult water. Collapsible staffs are available at tackle stores; otherwise, use a stout stick found at streamside. Staff should be carried on your *upstream* side so you lean into the current.

IMPORTANCE OF STEALTH

Aside from the matter of safety, good wading means more and better fishing. It enables you to cross rivers to reach better fish in a run or pool, and enables you to move in any direction to reach more advantageous spots from which to cast to difficult lies. While the safety factor is one reason you should never stride along freely in the water as you would in walking on dry land, quietness is another reason. The quieter you are, the less you will scare the fish and the more fish you will catch. Push one foot forward, gently, get it well settled, then ease the other one up to it, all as quietly as possible. The sound of gravel grinding underfoot is sure to spook nearby trout. Similarly, when you push your legs hard against the current you send out waves that warn the fish of an intruder. In slick water where there is not much current, such rough tactics can even send waves rolling upstream for fifty feet or more. To overcome the waves and the noise made by the push of your legs against the water, you should ease your way along, swinging your legs slowly against the current.

When you are in very shallow water, only a foot and a half deep, pick each foot up carefully from the water and slide it back in on a slant, so the toe goes in first. You may look like a clumsy ballet dancer but you will get that foot in there with little disturbance and no noise, and that's what you want when you are trout fishing.

WADERS

Garments for wading come in three basic styles: hip boots, chest-high boot-foot waders and stocking-foot waders that are used with a wading shoe, made especially for the purpose. Hip boots of course will suffice on a small stream, but when you get to the larger rivers this type of boot confines you to shallow water and often you cannot reach a rising fish or maneuver to a proper spot for the presentation needed to get a strike. If you plan to fish water of any size you should have chest-high waders. The chest-high waders permit you to roam the good fishing water, to cross from side to side easily, to move into good casting position, and to get out far enough to properly fish a heavy current or make a long throw to a distant bank. I always wear a belt cinched around the waist of mine, so that if I am unlucky enough to take a tumble, the belt will prevent water from pouring in. You can be submerged for quite some time before much moisture will seep past the belt. Some waders are now being made with belt loops for this purpose.

Rubber soles are satisfactory on sandy-bottomed or clay-bottomed rivers, but for trout streams where there are rocks, felt soles, combined with aluminum cleats for the most difficult conditions, are the only choice. Wet felt will cling, as will the carpeting now being applied to some waders.

If you do only have rubber-soled waders, either hip boot or chest high, you can obtain felt soles to glue to them. Felt-soled sandals are also available; these are a little clumsy for walking but are certainly better than trying to make your way over wet rocks with rubber soles. The combination of wet rubber and wet rock is just about as bad as you can get. You can fall down without even moving. If you plan to do much bank walking between pools, the sandals can be carried in the back of your vest and put on again when you go back to the river.

During summer months many anglers wade wet, wearing shorts or long trousers and wading shoes. Here again, felt soles will provide better footing and more safety, although obviously this type of angler isn't going to mind a dunking. There are good felt-soled wading shoes on the market which may be used for wet wading or may be worn over stocking-foot waders.

Personally, I prefer the boot-foot wader at almost all times, because they are easier to get in and out of, and are better for walking in the brush as they do not tear so easily.

When you purchase waders try them on and, standing beside a chair, raise one foot and place it on the chair seat. If you can't do so, the waders are too short for you. During a day astream you will continually be stepping up banks, over rocks, and so on. Waders that do not give you enough room for this will pull you up short and cause you to fall. On the other hand, if the legs are too long, they will rub on the inside, and eventually the abrasions will wear through.

I also like to use a lamb's-wool insole in my waders as the wool cushions the bottom of the foot against stone bruises and makes for more comfortable wading.

Waders should be turned after each day in the stream, to dry the moisture that had condensed inside.

11

FLY FISHING FOR TROUT IN LAKE OR POND

The fly fisherman's approach to trout that live in lake or pond is considerably different from his approach to those that live in moving water. In a lake the trout cannot depend on the current to bring food to him and therefore he is less likely to be found on a feeding station. He has to work harder for his meals, cruising for his food, to pick a fly off the surface, or a terrestrial that has blown into the water or crawled there. He has to chase after minnows flashing past, or nymphs that are rising from the bottom of the lake to hatch into flies. The angler's problem, therefore, is to locate the spots where he is most likely to find such food in a lake. And if you learn to read the signs you can increase the probabilities of putting your fly over fish even though you see no sign of them on the surface.

LOOK FOR MOVING WATER

Since aquatic fly species in general prefer moving water for their hatching, there are not as many fly hatches on lakes as there are on rivers. But many of those that do occur will be located wherever there is some slight movement in the water, even though it is not true "current"— places like inlets and outlets of the lake, where a slight current builds up as the water piles into the lake or flows out. Here the insects seek out the shallows because they need the gravel often found in such spots, to cover up their eggs so the larvae and nymphs can develop.

In such places there is often a hatch just at dusk, particularly of small flies, midges or smuts. They are often so small that it takes a size 24 or even 28 hackle fly to match them and bring hits. Frequently, on lakes six or seven thousand feet high in the mountains, I have seen swarms of aquatic insects, dipping and dodging, falling to the surface and then rising as if in formation, like black skimmers along a salty sandbar. Trout would be sticking their noses out and taking or inhaling them, or yet again jumping clear of the water as they fed on the minute flies. Now and again a larger fly may bring a hit, but usually you have to use a size 18 or 20 black hackle. And as this situation is usually encountered close to dark, it is often impossible to see to tie on such a small fly, or to change flies once you start fishing, so it is best to have that small number already tied on. If you do attempt to change the fly, and use a flashlight to do so, don't let the light shine out on the water. It will put the fish down. Turn away from the water and shield the light all you can with your body. I carry a small pocket flashlight that I can hold in my mouth, pointed down at the fly as I hold it in front of me, close to my chest. Or you can tuck a flashlight under your arm and shield it to a degree.

GRAVEL BEDS

Even if the lake does not have an inlet or outlet creek, it pays to look for the shallow, gravelly spots, in hopes of finding a hatch; and if none is in progress, it doesn't hurt to offer a nymph in such a spot, just on the chance that there are fish around and that they will recognize your offering as something they had fed on in the past. Such shallow gravel beds sometime occur well out in the lake, as do rocky reefs, and trout like to hang around these as more likely food sources than deeper water.

SHORELINES

The entire shoreline of a lake is usually worth fishing. Some lakes have large stands of reeds and aquatic grasses that harbor nymphs and freshwater shrimp, both favorite foods for trout. Often you will spot the fish rising along the outer edge of such grasses, and can make your cast accordingly; or if they are not rising, it is always a good idea to work the edges blind, on the chance the fish are just lying there, resting, and will spot and respond to your offering. The same is true when you fish a shore where there is a brushy overhang. The trout may be lying in there in the shade.

In many lakes there is a more or less shallow area for a few feet out from shore, then the water drops off abruptly. I like to treat that drop-off as if it were the bank of a stream. I cast the fly to the edge of the drop-off, let it sink if it is a wet fly, streamer or nymph, or rest there a bit if it is a dry, then make my retrieve. Fish often cruise those edges in their search for food. Many trout are taken this way in large lakes where it is difficult to pinpoint other good spots because of the very size of the water.

MOVING THE FLY

When you fish moving water, the current imparts a certain amount of action to the fly. It takes a dry fly over a rising trout, sweeps a wet fly or streamer down to him, keeps a nymph wiggling and shivering in the current. On the still surface of pond or lake, however, the angler must supply all the activity of the fly. He must use the rod tip to impact the kind of action which will make the fly look real and alive and get hits from the trout. To cast a fly and allow it to sit motionless on the surface might attract a fish which is close by and sees it as it lights. But to leave it there a long time, hopefully; or to cast a wet fly or streamer and let it drift limply to the depths, is not going to produce many strikes. It's up to the angler to provide the action that will tempt the trout, and this action must be varied according to where he finds the fish and how they are feeding.

There are times when trout are cruising, moving along just under the surface, coming to the top every now and again to take a natural fly that has fallen to the surface or is just emerging from its nymphal case. Such feeding trout often travel swiftly. The angler must intercept them, drop the fly in front of the swimmer, leading him by four or five feet, not close enough to flush him, yet close enough that he will see it as he pursues his course. If he veers away, or doesn't see it, then the angler should give the fly action to attract the attention of that swimmer. Make the fly flutter if it is a dry fly. Pull back with the rod tip if it is a wet fly or streamer, so the fly jumps forward in the water. Let it stay still again, then move it again. Many times the trout will spot such lifelike action and turn and rush the fly.

SKATING SPIDERS

Often when you cannot see any signs of fish feeding in a lake, the skating spider can save the day. The skater, a fly with two-inch-long hackles, stands up so delicately on those hackles that you can dance it across the surface so it looks for all the world like a tarantula . It will attract nearby fish, often bringing them up from considerable depth, and it seems to drive them wild. I have seen trout act almost as if they were playing with it, jumping out and falling on the fly, hitting it with their tails.

To fish a spider on lakes you need an 8½- or 9-foot rod and by all means a floating line because lightness and quickness is all important in the presentation and working of the fly. Grease the line and the leader and be sure that the spider has been well treated with fly buoy and then dried completely. The leader tippet should not be lighter than 2X because the spider will cause anything lighter to twist, this twisting sometimes moving right up into the end of the fly line, and it is impossible to work the fly lightly because of this twist. This also weakens the tippet, and eventually it will break, probably on the hit of a nice trout.

It's great fun to use a skating spider on the still waters of a lake. Once, just at dusk, I was fishing Dailey's Lake near Livingston, Montana, and there were a few rainbows showing, taking stuff from the surface. I was casting from the shore and couldn't reach most of them. I had taken two fish, one and two pounds, using a size 12 Black Gnat, usually a good fly in this situation.

"Those fish I can't reach are much bigger," I said to Len Kinkie, of

Pray, who was with me. "And they don't seem to come any closer. I'll have to try something that will attract their attention, and maybe bring them closer. I'll try a skater," I said. "I'll skate a spider across the surface and maybe they'll see it and come in."

A big, two-inch-hackled fly is harder to throw than a small Black Gnat, especially when there's a little breeze to buffet it, but I managed to get my presentation out there about sixty feet.

"Still short of where they are," I said. "But here goes."

I thrust my fly rod up and pulled back with the tip. The spider came to life, quivered a bit, like a natural, then darted toward us, like a big spider all right, and then I stopped it and let it sit there. I didn't move it for a whole minute. Again I started it back and suddenly the surface water was shattered and out come the head of a big trout. He had it and I struck. He jumped, ran and tugged. He tried to get into the grass on the bottom. He pulled many rainbow tricks, but luck was with me and I finally got him in.

"You were right," Len said. "He's bigger. A good 3½ pounds. Give me one of those skating spiders."

During the next hour, until dark, Len and I each landed two more rainbows that weighed about 2½ pounds apiece. Those big cruisers had heard the swish of the fly along the surface, investigated, and when they saw the big juicy spider darting along, then had moved in fast for the kill.

We used Adams hackle skaters that day, tied on #14 hooks, but lots of times I use the 10 or 12, with two-inch-long hackles. They stand up on those hackles like Pavlova and some of the antics you can put them through with your rod and line work make the dying swan look like the ugly duckling.

The all-black skaters are also good producers on lakes and so is the tan. Those three have stood me in good stead over a number of years. The one thing to remember, no matter which you use, is to dress the fly well, and once you have caught a fish on it, change to a new fly. A spider that has had a good soaking is not going to sit up high again, even if you douse it with spray. Take that one off and put on a new one. You need to keep those spiders up on their toes, for the quick action needed to bring hits from trout.

The 8½- or 9-foot rod suggested for spiders is my choice for most lake fishing. With this length of rod you can give better action to the fly than would be possible with a shorter stick, and it also makes for better and easier casting. On large bodies of water you usually encounter some wind and this adds to the importance of using a slightly larger outfit than you might use on a stream. You not only may have to cast into the wind, but you may also have to make longer casts than are called for on a river. It is more difficult to approach a trout in a lake without scaring him than it is on a stream. Especially if the fish are cruising, you want to stay far enough away, whether wading or in a boat, so as not to scare the trout. Cruising fish are usually looking upward; if you move in close they will spot you, and although they may continue to cruise, hits will be few and far between.

For these reasons, when I fish a lake with surface flies, I like to use a Scientific Anglers WF-7-F line with an 8½-foot stick; or the WF-8-F line with the 9-footer. The leader should be 10 or 12 feet long, tapered from a heavy butt section to the desired tippet. The heavy butt section allows the entire leader to turn over nicely and drop the fly lightly and quietly. For spiders, as mentioned, and for large dry flies, I use a 2X tippet, to absorb some of the force of the hit, which often comes when the fly is moving, and to avoid the twist already described. For smaller flies, a 3X or 4X tippet will usually suffice, but in very clear water, and when using very small flies, you often have to go to 5X to get hits. The thing to watch when you use the very light tippet is the force of your strike. If you come back too hard you are going to leave the fly in the trout's mouth. Merely lift the rod tip a bit and that small, sharp hook point will sink in well above the barb.

HIGH-ALTITUDE LAKES

One of the great events in any trout fisherman's life is a trip to some of the high-altitude lakes of the Rockies—lakes from five thousand to as high as eleven thousand feet. Some of these lakes did not originally hold native populations of trout but they have been stocked—nowadays by airplane, in earlier days by pack horse—with rainbows, cutthroat, eastern brook trout, and occasionally with golden trout. Wherever these stocked fish find a good supply of food they thrive up to a point. Many of the stocked lakes seem to end up with a population of like-sized trout, usually not more than two pounds in weight, apparently the limit that the food supply will sustain. Occasionally the fish population may end up with only a few really big trout. Such lakes give rise to fabulous stories of some lucky angler who has hooked into one of these big fellows, or has seen one as he stood on a rocky shore and peered down into the clear alpine depths.

On a trip to Aero Lake, high in the Beartooth Mountains of Montana, many years ago, we saw such a large fish, which we believe may have been the last survivor of an earlier stocking of golden trout. He patrolled the shore in front of us for half an hour, plainly a ten-pound fish, but never once did he look at anything we offered, from dry to wet to streamer, and even ignored the flashing glint of a small gold spoon across his nose. Whether he was old and blind, or just too smart, we never did find out. However, the lake held a good population of fat and healthy and willing cutthroat trout and we soon discovered the probable source of their good health.

Walter Weber, artist and naturalist for the *National Geographic* magazine, was with me, and when he caught his first fish, on a size 20 black-and-red ant, he opened the fish to see what it had been eating.

"Daphnia," he said, pointing with the tip of his knife blade. "Water fleas."

I looked where he was indicating. The inside of the mouth of the fish was sprinkled with small black and red dots, clinging to the membranes.

Later that day we spent some time just looking down into the water, and we soon spotted those water fleas. There were hundreds of them, a cloud ten feet square and ten feet deep, looking as if someone had sprayed red and black pepper into the water. That trout must have been swimming through the swarm of water fleas with his mouth open, the way a whale absorbs plankton, just swallowing big gulps of the tiny daphnia.

That is the only lake where I have seen this particular phenomenon, but in almost every high-altitude lake I have ever fished I have found that the small ant we used at Aero Lake usually takes fish. I always have on hand a supply of black, red, and red-and-black ants, in sizes from 22 to 28.

High-altitude lakes are inclined to be somewhat individualistic, and those who fish them regularly often go to all kinds of trouble to develop fly patterns suited to just their own particular lakes. In Centennial Valley, high on the border between Idaho and Montana, there are a number of pools that have been famous for the brook trout and rainbows they produce: the Widow's Pool, with its deep, red-fleshed brook trout; Widgon and McDonald's pools, with high-jumping rainbows. They are small pools, necessarily limited to a few fishermen at a time, and although known to a few hard-bitten old-timers for many years, have only recently become known to casual anglers. They do not produce big fish, nor barrels of fish, but they do offer the kind of highly specialized fishing that is a challenge and a great satisfaction to the fly man.

Centennial Valley is about eighty miles wide, rimmed with hills, and lies at an altitude of seven thousand feet in the Montana Centennial Mountains—so be sure you have a Montana license, even though you may approach it from the Idaho side without being aware that you have crossed a border. It is a National Wildlife Refuge and was the scene of a great effort to save the trumpeter swan. When the refuge was first formed, the flock was down to 37 birds. Now it is at over two hundred. There are also sandhill cranes, Canada geese, many kinds of ducks, grebes, and you may see antelope, deer, moose, and much small game. There are several large cattle ranches in the valley and one small fishing camp, but the scene is as wild, rugged and wonderful as when the early settlers came.

In the summer of 1970 I went up there one afternoon with Will Godfrey, who runs a guiding service at Last Chance, Idaho, near the Idaho entrance to the valley, and his business partner, George Wright, a cattleman from El Cajon, California.

"We'll try McDonald's Pool first," Will said. "It holds some big rainbows. But they're finicky. Even some of us who have fished the pool again and again have never quite found the answer to what those fish want. We're always tying and trying something new."

"That's what makes fishing," I said. "The fact that we never quite get the answer."

That afternoon those McDonald's Pool rainbows wanted a small dark nymph, size 16, that Will had tied—at least, they wanted it for an hour. Then hits fell off, so we started trying other offerings. The eventual producer was a small yellow nymph, and it worked for another hour.

"We'll have to leave now, if we're going to hit the Widow's Pool this afternoon, too," Will said, as he slid a nice two-pounder back into the water.

"Let's go, then," George and I agreed, and we headed back to the jeep.

We reached the famous Widow's Pool just before dusk. Brook trout were rising everywhere, cruising in the still water that was beginning to reflect the pink sky of the near-sunset.

"The average brookie here will only go a pound," Will said. "But that's a nice brook trout. And there are plenty of two-pounders, and some have been taken up to eight pounds. They are extra bright and fat, in this pool, for some reason."

George and I rigged up with small dry flies, size 16 Black Gnats, later tried the Adams, and the Blue Wing Olives, and all those small, dark teasers took fish. Down the shore from us Will was hooking his share on a small green nymph he had tied just especially for the fishing here in the Widow's Pool.

It was rapidly growing dark but somehow those gimlet-eyed trout could see our tiny offerings and take them for what they are meant to be, the kind of small, titillating delicacies trout are used to finding in high-altitude lakes. Then only ten feet above the water, and thirty feet out in front of us, three big trumpeter swans swept past and splashed down a hundred feet beyond us.

"Let's not disturb them," said Will. "It's time to head for home, anyway."

We quietly reeled in and headed back through the tall grass to the jeep. Behind us, Centennial Valley settled down to the mysterious, eerie silence of night among the peaks.

Many high-altitude lakes are only fishable for a brief time each summer, because of the cold or snow, or both. But in those that can be reached, cold does not always put the fish down. Years ago, when Georgetown Lake, near Anaconda, Montana, was crammed with big, healthy rainbows, I used to go there in the autumn with Lee Elliott of Rock Creek Lodge, near Clinton, and sometimes we went out in the skiffs when it was so cold you almost expected to see ice in the guides.

Georgetown has fine stands of grass and reeds in the shallower parts of the lake, and the big rainbows liked to hang around them. The first time I fished at Georgetown, Lee and I ran down to a bay in the southwest end of the lake, turned the motor off and drifted, watching the edges of the reeds. We soon spotted fish feeding, making big, healthy circles as they took on the surface. I tied on a size 12 Gray Wulff and had immediate action. I had started off with a 5X tippet, and the first rainbow that hit turned so swiftly that he broke me off. The next one did the same thing, because I was too slow in getting the shooting line out of my fingers. But then I changed to a 4X tippet, calmed myself down a bit, and began to land those wonderful rainbows, fish that went from three to seven pounds, and all on dries. It's one of the great tragedies of fishing that for some unknown reason Georgetown Lake was later cleared of rainbows and stocked with cutthroat trout, all right in their way, but which provide only a small degree of the fantastic excitement the mighty rainbows used to give.

12 TROUT FLIES

Since artificial flies were first used to catch a trout, man's ingenuity has produced a geat variety of offerings to tempt the quarry. Although some are not meant to resemble a real-life insect, we nevertheless class them as artificial "flies" because the system of fly fishing is based on the original intent to match a hatching fly in one phase or another of its life cycle. Thus, in addition to dry flies, wet flies and nymphs, which are imitations of a form of true insect life, we have bucktail and streamer flies, which may imitate a minnow, crab, small snake, beetle, or even a small mouse—any denizen of the waters where trout live and on which they might feed.

And while the mention of the true representation of an insect is the first description of fly fishing we have found in literature (*see* HISTORY), primitive races used offerings similar to those we now class as flies, but which they may not have intended as such, in their efforts to take fish. In 1953, when I visited his Estancia Maria-Behety on remote Tierra del Fuego, in Argentina, Carlos Menendez-Behety gave me a "fly" that he said had been used by the Ona Indians, now almost extinct, which he estimated to be some hundred-odd years old. It was a piece of skin and fur from the *juanaco*, impaled on a hook, and tied in behind the eye. The fur of this beautiful, romantic and most graceful runner of all the deer species in the world looks alive in the water and makes a truly effective bucktail fly.

Not long after that, farther north in Argentina, on the Chimehuin River on the eastern slope of the Andes, I came upon an Auracano Indian using a sixteen-foot homemade rod, a pole cut from the stands of coligne cane on a nearby mountainside. He had tied fifteen feet of heavy line to the end of the pole, and as I watched he cast the line out, then lowered the pole so the tip was in the water and began to move it slowly back and forth. In a few minutes I saw him jerk up with the tip of the pole and out came a two-pound trout.

I moved in closer to ask what bait he was using.

"Not bait," he said. "Mosca"—a fly.

His fly was a single eagle feather, barred black and white, tied on a big hook. It was a streamer fly as surely as any ever invented by a more sophisticated angler. I traded him a Platinum Blonde bucktail for it and we both went our ways happy. I used his fly that day and took a pound-and-a-half brownie with it, then put it away in my collection of unique flies. Since he had been exposed to modern fly fishing, he may have been deliberately copying a fly he had seen—or perhaps he was only applying the modern name to a feathery copy of some minnow, just as his antecedents may have done.

Fly patterns have been designed for reasons other than a strict resemblance to a real-life form of trout food. Edward Hewitt, as inventive an angler as any that ever lived, first tied the bivisible fly to meet a need that is at some time felt by every fly man.

"So I can see it," he said.

The tie calls for white hackle at the head of the fly, in contrast to a different color for the balance of the hackle, so that the all-white fronting of the bivisible floater is readily spotted by the angler.

George Griffith, of Grayling, Michigan, one of the founders of Trout Unlimited, is responsible for another pattern of this kind. George lost the sight of one eye in 1953 in an accident while fly fishing. To help him see a fly better, with his limited vision, his friend Clarence Roberts, Conservation Officer at Grayling, originated the Roberts Parachute Drake. The pattern proved so successful that it is now popular with anglers throughout the Midwest. I give the pattern for those who would like to tie it.

Tail	Two strands of pheasant tail.
Body	Deer hair from a deer killed near October 1, to assure correct length and color. Roberts prefers to tie with hair from the forehead of the deer. The tail of the body is extended beyond the bend of the hook.
Wings	Upright, made of white belly deer hair.
Hackle	One or more hackles, tied parachute.
	Use golden yellow thread.

Those upright wings of white deer hair can be spotted for quite a distance.

Al Troth, a great fly tyer and angler, from Dillon, Montana, came up with a similar eye-catcher. He used a bit of orange fluorescent yarn on top of some of his flies.

"I tie the fly, then add the yarn," he told me. "The trout can't see it because it is on top, but I can see it plainly. It comes in handy on dull days and at dusk, and we call it the 'little red ball.' We kid and say, 'Let's follow the little red ball.' "

There are also many "flash flies" that do not claim to be true representations of either an aquatic fly or a terrestrial but simply seek to attract the trout by their shape and bright colors. In wet flies and streamers these garish concoctions may just make the trout mad enough to want to hit it defensively or offensively and get it out of his pool.

It is when the fly fisherman enters the field of exact imitation of a hatch of flies that he needs a fairly comprehensive knowledge of fly forms. This field is so great and so varied according to locale that it takes a student indeed, and would require a lifetime of study, to become thoroughly familiar with the many patterns that could be tied. The thoroughgoing expert collects his sample from the stream, has on hand his stock of supplies and fly-tying vise, and produces a match right there on the stream. Or he carries his specimens home, studies and then reproduces them in artificial form, or ties something that he thinks will look like the real thing to the fish. Typical of his approach is the work of Vince Marinaro and Charlie Fox with Jassids and other terrestrials; and of Douglas Swisher and Carl Richards with their no-hackle flies, which will be discussed later in this chapter.

But not all of us are going to do this, partly because of inability, partly because we don't have time, and partly because we are not sufficiently knowledgeable entomologists. For those of us in this group, and I am one, there are shortcuts to being prepared for almost any eventuality you may meet on a trout stream.

Certain well-known patterns have proven successful almost everywhere that trout are known. A fine example of this is the Adams. This most famous of all Michigan ties was designed by Len Holliday of Mayfield, Michigan. He fished it with great success himself, the first day he tried it, and that same day he gave a couple of his creations to his friend Lon Adams of Lorain, Ohio. When they came off the river that evening, Adams told him how well the pattern had produced for him, too.

"It has to have a name," he said. "What are you going to call the fly?"

"Since you were the first to see it, I guess it will be the Adams," said Holliday.

It proved a great pattern not only on the Michigan streams for which it was designed, but almost everywhere else it has been used. And as mentioned earlier (*see* DRY FLIES), my favorite admonition to a dry-fly man who has come up against a blank wall in working a succession of patterns is: "When in doubt, try an Adams."

The mayfly family is the most numerous and widespread of all North American aquatic insects. To match each particular one would be a hopeless job for the average trout fisherman. But it is easy enough to stock your fly box with a few basics. For instance, the size 24 Blue-Wing Olive will be taken by the trout for some twenty-four members of the mayfly family, so close is it in shape and color to the various hatches.

Based on this general resemblance theory, a fly fisherman starting out in the world, could have a fair degree of safety by including in his initial collection of flies certain specific patterns given below.

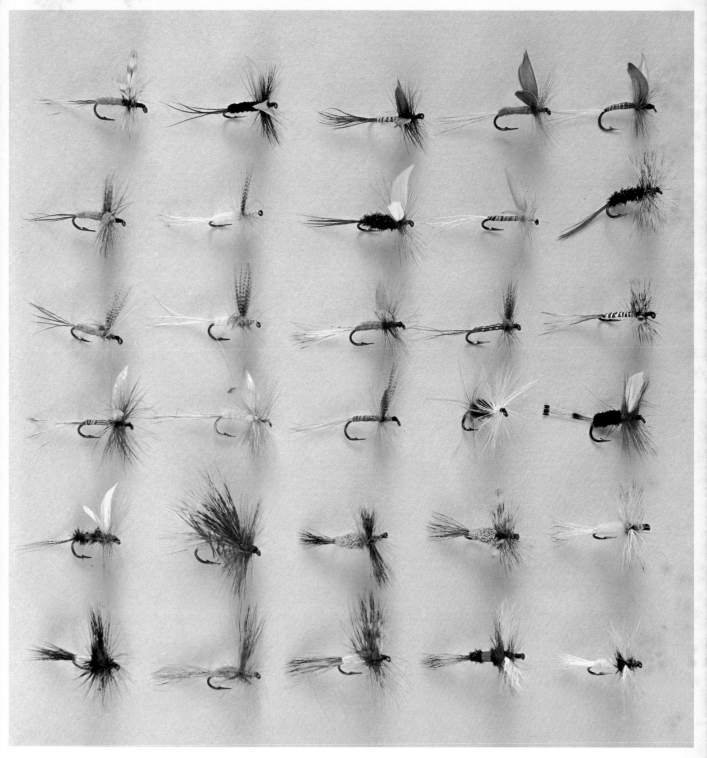

DRY FLIES

(Dressed by Dan Bailey, Livingston, Montana)

ADAMS	BLACK GNAT	BLACK QUILL	BLUE DUN	BLUE QUILL
DARK CAHILL	LIGHT CAHILL	COACHMAN	GINGER QUILL	GRAY HACKLE PEACOCK
DARK HENDRICKSON	LIGHT HENDRICKSON	IRON BLUE DUN	MARCH BROWN	MOSQUITO
DARK OLIVE QUILL	LIGHT OLIVE DUN	QUILL GORDON	RENEGADE	RIO GRANDE KING
ROYAL COACHMAN	BUCKTAIL CADDIS	IRRESISTIBLE	RAT FACED McDOUGALL	BLONDE WULFF
BLACK WULFF	GRAY WULFF	GRIZZLY WULFF	ROYAL WULFF	WHITE WULFF

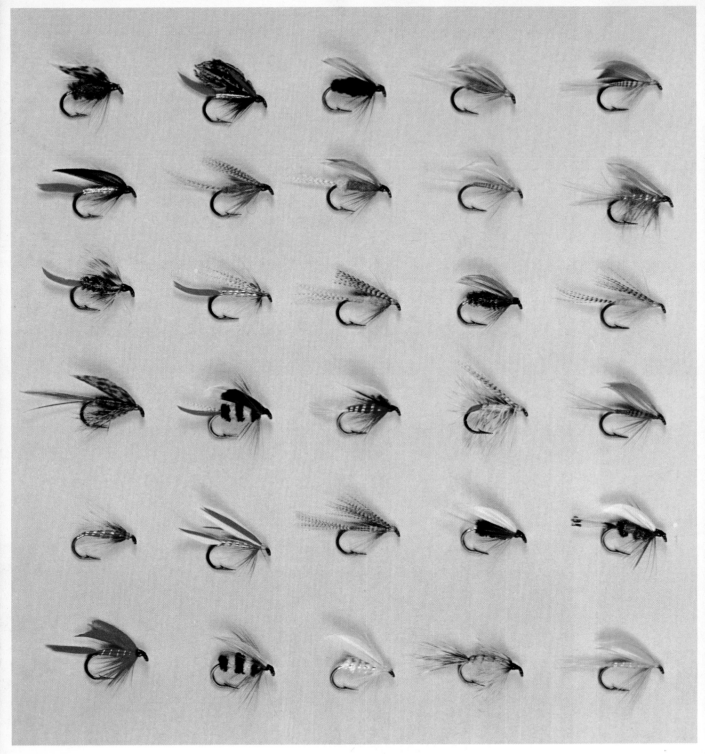

WET FLIES

(Dressed by Robert V. Jacklin, Jr., Roselle, New Jersey)

ALDER	ALEXANDRA	BLACK GNAT	BLUE DUN	BLUE QUILL
BUTCHER	DARK CAHILL	FEMALE BEAVERKILL	GINGER QUILL	GOLD RIBBED HARE'S EAR
GRAY HACKLE PEACOCK	GRIZZLY KING	HENDRICKSON	LEADWING COACHMAN	LIGHT CAHILL
MARCH BROWN	McGINTY	MONTREAL	MORMON GIRL	OLIVE QUILL
ORANGE FISH HAWK	PARMACHEENE BELLE	QUILL GORDON	RIO GRAND KING	ROYAL COACHMAN
SCARLET IBIS	WESTERN BEE	WHITE MILLER	YELLOW BODIED GRAYBACK	YELLOW SALLY

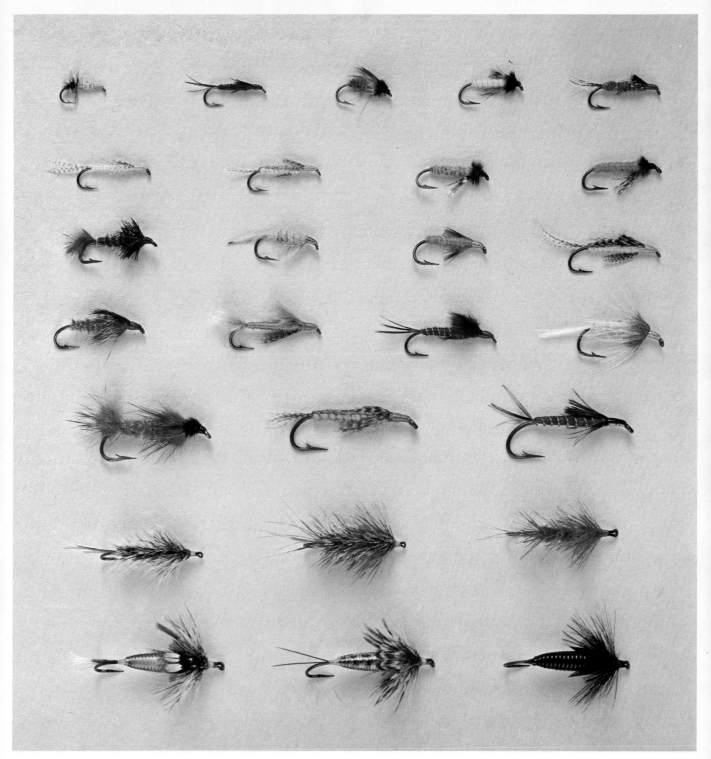

TYPICAL NYMPHS

(Top 5 Rows by E. H. Rosborough, Chiloquin, Oregon)

(Bottom 2 Rows by George F. Grant, Butte, Montana)

BLACK MIDGE PUPA (12*)	LITTLE BROWN STONE (12)	HARE'S EAR (10)	LIGHT CADDIS PUPA (10)	BLACK DRAKE (10)
YELLOW DRAKE (10)	LITTLE YELLOW STONE (10)		MUSKRAT (10)	GREEN ROCK WORM (10)
NONDESCRIPT (10)	SHRIMP (8)		DARK CADDIS PUPA (8)	YELLOW MAY (8)
FLEDERMAUSE (8)	GREEN DAMSEL (8)		BICOLOR WALKER (8)	BLONDE BURLAP (6)
CASUAL DRESS (6)	GOLDEN STONE (4)			DARK STONE (4)
BLACK CREEPER	ROUGH BADGER STONE			BRASS BUG
LIGHT HELLGRAMMITE	MOTTLED HELLGRAMMITE			BLACK HELLGRAMMITE

(* = Best Hook Size)

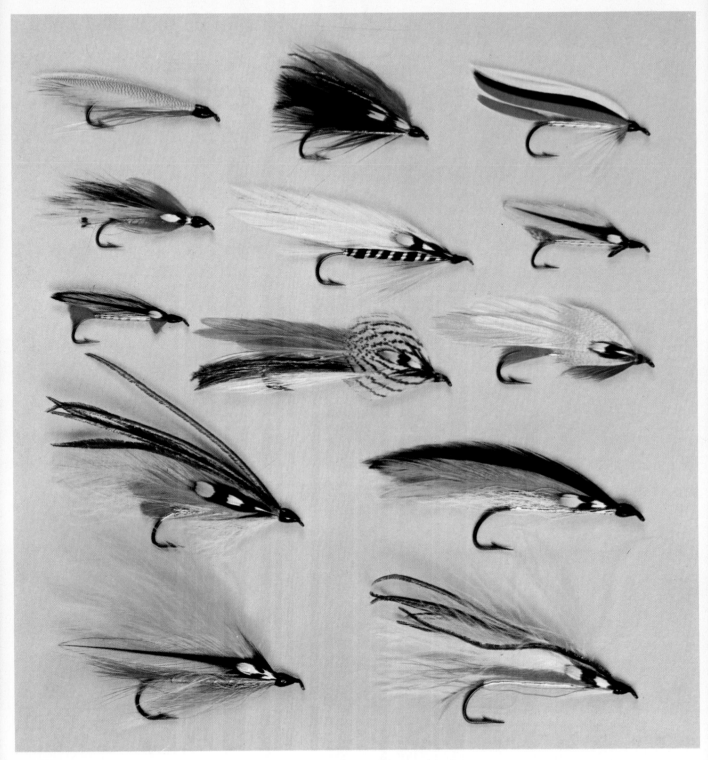

FRESH WATER STREAMERS

(Dressed by Originators, or Exact Copies)

COWEE SPECIAL	BLACK MARABOU	TROUT FIN
MILLER'S RIVER SPECIAL	BLACK GHOST	GOLDEN DARTER
RED FIN	GRAY GHOST	COLONEL BATES
SUPERVISOR		NINE-THREE
BLUE MARABOU		BALLOU SPECIAL

FRESH WATER BUCKTAILS

(Dressed by Originators, or Exact Copies)

SHUSHAN POSTMASTER EDSON DARK TIGER GHOST SHINER
MUDDLER MINNOW HERB JOHNSON SPECIAL FULSHER'S SILVER MINNOW
MICKEY FINN POLAR CHUB ROYAL COACHMAN
LITTLE BROWN TROUT LITTLE RAINBOW TROUT LITTLE BROOK TROUT
GOVERNOR AIKEN BLACK NOSED DACE TRI-COLOR

UNUSUAL DRY FLIES AND TERRESTRIALS

GOOFUS BUG   PLASTIC-WINGED MAYFLY   FLYING BLACK ANT   "WONDER-WING" MAYFLY

PLASTIC-WINGED BEE   CATERPILLAR   DEER-HAIR BEE   GRUB   BLOW-FLY

LETORT HOPPER   GREEN LEAFHOPPER   JASSID   PLASTIC-WING DRAGON FLY   ROCKWORM   COOPER BUG

GRASSHOPPER   PARACHUTE MAYFLY   BLACK ANT   PARACHUTE SPIDER

KING'S RIVER CADDIS   RUBBER LEGS

DEER-HAIR BOMBER   BLACK AND ORANGE WOOLY WORM   JACKLIN'S BIG BLACK WOOLY

STREAMERS AND BUCKTAILS FOR FRESH WATER TROLLING

STREAMER WITH UPTURNED SINGLE TRAIL HOOK

STREAMER WITH UPTURNED DOUBLE TRAIL HOOK

STREAMER WITH DOWNTURNED SINGLE TRAIL HOOK

TANDEM HOOK MYLAR BODY MARABOU STREAMER

TANDEM STREAMER WITH MYLAR STRIPS

LONG SHANK SINGLE HOOK STREAMER

MYLAR BODY STREAMER WITH MYLAR STRIP THROAT

BEADED BODY BUCKTAIL WITH DOWNTURNED SINGLE TRAIL HOOK

BUCKTAIL WITH UPTURNED SINGLE TRAIL HOOK

PACIFIC STEELHEAD FLIES

(Dressed by Irwin Thompson, Sebastopol, California)

BLACK ANGUS	BLUE SHRIMP	BOSS	BRINDLE BUG
BUSTLE BACK	BROWN SHRIMP		THE CANADIAN
FALL FAVORITE	FLUORESCENT COMET	GOLDEN ANGUS	GOLDEN COMET
GOLDEN WOOLY WORM	KLAMATH RIVER SPECIAL	LITTLE JAK	THE OAKIE FLY
RED BARRON	SADDLE BACK		SILVER BOSS
SILVER HILTON	SYLVIOUS DEMON	THOMPSON'S RED COAT	WINGED BOSS

Dry Flies, *hook sizes from 20 to 10*

Adams

Black Flying Ant

Black Gnat

Black Quill

Black Hackle

Blue Dun

Blue Quill

Dark Cahill

Light Cahill

Royal Coachman

Ginger Quill

Hendrickson

Light Hendrickson

Iron Blue Dun

Red Fox

Tups

Quill Gordon

Blue wing Olive

Red Variant

Gray Midge

Jassid

Gray Wulff

Royal Wulff

Grasshopper

Wet Flies

Adams

Alexandra

Black Gnat

Brown Hackle, Yellow

Black Ant

Light Cahill

Blue Dun

Coachman

Leadwing Coachman

Royal Coachman

Cowdung

Gray Hackle, Yellow

Gray Hackle, Peacock

Hare's Ear

King of the Water

Mosquito

March Brown

Olive Quill

Mormon Girl

Professor

Queen of the Water

Red Ant

Rio Grande King

Western Bee

Quill Gordon

These should be on hook sizes 10 and 12 for bigger rivers and lakes. For smaller streams, and for most eastern rivers, regardless of size, many anglers use very sparsely-tied wet flies on smaller hooks—12, 14 and sometimes even 16.

Nymphs

Gray nymph, sizes 12, 16

Montana nymph, sizes 6, 8, 10

Yellow May nymph, sizes 12, 14

Dark Olive nymph, size 12, 2X long

Olive May, sizes 12, 16

Zug Bug, size 12

Hendrickson nymph, sizes 12, 14, 3X

Blue-wing Olive nymph, sizes 18, 20

Light Cahill nymph, size 16

Dark Mossback nymph, sizes 8, 10, 12 long-shank

March Brown nymph, size 12, 2X long-shank

Brown Drake nymph, size 12

Narrowing the scene to those areas in the United States where most of our trout fishing is found, there are certain flies that are basic for each area. I give my own selections for each area.

Basic Eastern Dry Flies

Adams, sizes 12, 16
Black Gnat, sizes 14, 16
Blue Dun, sizes 16, 18
Royal Coachman, size 12
Jassid, sizes 18, 20
Flying Black Ant, sizes 18, 20

Red Variant, size 16
Tups Indispensable, sizes 12, 14
Tiny Blue-wing Olive, sizes 20, 24
Light Cahill, sizes 16, 18
Dark Hendrickson, sizes 12, 16
Letort Hopper, size 12

Basic Western Dry Flies

Gray Wulff, size 12
Irresistible, size 10
Goofus Bug, size 10
Gray Hackle, yellow, size 12
Red Variant, size 10

Dark Caddis, size 12
Black Quill, size 14
Royal Wulff, size 12
Hairwing Green Drake, size 12

For Spring Creeks

Light Cahill, sizes 16, 18
Olive Blue Dun, size 24
Olive Dun, sizes 16, 18

Olive Quill, sizes 16, 18
Light Hendrickson, size 16
Blue Dun, sizes 16, 18

Basic Western Wet Flies

Carey Special, size 6
Dark Stone, size 4
Rio Grande King, size 12
Mormon Girl, size 12
Black Gnat, size 12
Cowdung, size 12

Royal Coachman, size 12
Gray Hackle, yellow, size 12
Gray Hackle, peacock, size 14
Grizzly King, size 12
Leadwing Coachman, size 10

Basic Western Nymphs

Bitch Creek nymph, size 4
Muskrat, size 10
Yellow Drake, size 12
Granny's shrimp, size 8
Fledermouse, sizes 4, 6 and 8

Gray nymph, size 10
Bailey's Mossback, size 6
Henry's Lake nymph, sizes 6 to 12
Gary Howells' midge nymphs,
　sizes 16, 18 and 20

Basic Western Streamers and Bucktails

Muddler Minnow, sizes 10, 12 and 1/0
White Marabou Muddler, size 4
Light Spruce Fly, size 2
Dark Spruce Fly, size 2

Big Hole Demon, size 4
Black Marabou, size 4
Royal Coachman, size 4
Mickey Finn, size 2

To localize still further, once you reach the area you plan to fish, you should add various local ties to your basic collection. Each area and each river usually has certain preferred patterns, usually developed locally and proven by those who fish the stream constantly. For instance, Dan Bailey, famous fly tyer of Livingston, Montana, recommended the following as a comprehensive selection with which to fish the Yellowstone River:

Best Five Dry Flies

Adams, Light Cahill, Joe's Hopper, Grizzly Wulff, Royal Wulff, all size 12; plus some smaller sizes of the same patterns, to match a hatch.

Basic Eastern Wet Flies, *all sizes 12 to 16*

Black Ant	Gray Hackle, yellow
Leadwing Coachman	Mosquito
Coachman	Quill Gordon
Blue Dun	Black Gnat
Olive Quill	

Basic Eastern Nymphs, *all sizes 12 to 16*

Black May nymph	Yellow May nymph
Light Cahill nymph	Dark Olive nymph
March Brown nymph	

Basic Eastern Streamers and Bucktails, *sizes 8, 10 and 12*

Gray Ghost	Supervisor
Black Ghost	Royal Coachman Streamer
Black-Nosed Dace	Colonel Fuller
Black Prince	Golden Darter
Mickey Finn	Muddler Minnow

Black Marabou streamer, Yellow Marabou streamer, White Marabou streamer, all on hook sizes 4, 6 and 8.

In general, western waters call for bigger flies because the streams are usually larger and hold bigger trout. A good basic selection for Rocky Mountain and West Coast rivers should include:

Best Five Wet Flies

Mormon Girl, Ginger Quill, Gray Hackle, yellow, black and orange, Wooly Worm, yellow Wooly Worm, all in sizes 8, 10, 12 and 14.

Best Five Streamers and Bucktails

Muddler Minnow, Light Spruce Fly, Dark Spruce Fly, White Marabou, White Muddler, sizes 12 to 1/0.

Best Five Nymphs

Bailey's Mossback, size 6, 2X long-shank hook; Gray nymph, size 8; Ed Burke nymph, size 12; Brown Mayfly nymph, size 12; Fuzzyesco, size 10.

Special for the Salmon Fly Hatch

Bird's Salmon Fly, size 6; Bird's Trout Fly, size 8.

Almost everywhere you go, you find one local tie that stands out above all others, and that's why I recommend that you consult the "hometown" anglers. You can be sure that they will know the best producers, proven in everyday fishing of their local waters.

When I fished the Tongariro River in New Zealand's North Island, I tried all my favorite patterns for rainbows in the first pool and came up with a great big zero. Then I turned to my guide, Tony Jensen, of Turangi.

"What do I need, Tony?" I asked.

"The Red Setter is the hottest fly on this river," he said, and handed me one.

I tried it on, threw it out there and watched the Tongariro blow up. I went back over the same water I had fished previously and the results staggered me. I took trout on that Red Setter and I kept taking them throughout my week of fishing on the Tongariro.

Almost everywhere you fish you will find such a pattern, extremely good on local waters, and sometimes almost as good in foreign climes. The Matuka is perhaps the most popular wet fly in Australia and New Zealand, for general use. The name is derived from the New Zealand word for bittern. So popular were the feathers of this bird with the Maoris that the species was in danger of becoming extinct and authorities put it on the protected list. But the fly pattern has persisted, and is equally effective tied with other feathers substituted for the forbidden bittern.

I encountered the Matuka while fishing in Australia with Carl Massy of Severn Park, New South Wales. We worked both lake and stream on the Monaro watershed, and everywhere the Matuka brought hits. Since then I have tried it in North America, and in the far reaches of Argentina, and it has consistently been a good fish taker. Today, in the U.S., the Matuka is understood to be a method of tie, no matter what the feather used. The streamer ribbing is wound through the wing feather resulting in segmentation that gives the streamer the look of a common forage species, the stickleback.

THE MUDDLER MINNOW

Because of the fact that streamers and bucktails are not imitations of insect life, as compared to dry flies, wet flies and nymphs, the ties which appear in several different places under the same name may be quite varied. Each tyer likes to add a little touch of his own, working towards some seen or fancied difference in the performance in his own waters. An outstanding example of this is the now-famous Muddler Minnow fly.

Many years ago at Nipigon, Ontario, I fished the Nipigon River with Don Gapen, who at that time owned a resort there. The river was renowned for its big brook trout, the world record for the species having been taken there in 1916.

"We use the Muddler Minnow fly here," Don told me as we went out to the river. "I first tied it in 1948, and it's been so good that I never use anything else for these brookies."

He told me how the tie came about. One day as he was fishing, he saw an Indian nearby lift a flat rock at the edge of the river and quickly stab down at something with a fork. He came up with a minnow impaled on the tines. The minnow had a flattened head, the body tapered back from the wide head and narrowed towards the caudal fin, and it had very wide pectoral fins. Don recognized it as a member of the numerous and widely distributed sculpin family, also called darter or muddler minnow. The Indian had yet another name for it.

"Cocatouse minnow," he told Don, that day. "Best thing to catch big trout."

"I took that minnow home," Don said, "and set to work to tie a fly which would resemble it in the water."

His original pattern is as follows:

Don Gapen's Muddler Minnow Fly

Head-Hackle	Deer hair, spun on, tied off and clipped to shape the flattened head, and tapered towards the front.
Wing	Gray squirrel wing tied in back of the hackle, about half-inch beyond bend. On either side of squirrel-tail wing, tie in mottled turkey wing fiber.
Body	Flat gold tinsel, not tapered.
Tail	Pieces of mottled turkey-wing fiber, to come out even with the wing.

That original Muddler Minnow proved to be one of the all-time great fly patterns. That same summer I carried a couple of Don's Muddlers west with me to Montana and with them I caught more big trout than with any fly I had ever used. In the water it seemed to come alive, sparkling, somehow managing to resemble all sorts of fish food, grasshoppers, stoneflies, other minnows, as well as the minnow it was designed to represent. And it took all kinds of trout, as well as the brook trout it was first tied to catch.

I showed the fly to Dan Bailey, at Livingston, and he recognized its potential at once and began to tie it commercially; and the wide use of this new fly was responsible for a tremendous increase in the number of big trout that showed up on the Wall of Fame in his shop, the prerequisite for installation there being a trout of four pounds or better, taken on a fly in Montana.

The small Muddlers, sizes 8, 10 and 12, can be fished as a dry fly by greasing the underside and adding fly buoy. I think the trout take it for a small grasshopper, stonefly, or even an alder fly. You can also wet the fly well, and sometimes clip the deer-hair head to make it sink better, and use it as a wet fly. Here the trout probably mistake it for a drowned hopper or stonefly or a nymph.

Float a Muddler in on an eddy, without any added motion, leave it entirely up to the water action to make the Muddler jiggle and dart and wobble, and a trout just can't resist it.

Some years later Dan and his partner, Red Monical, came up with the Marabou Muddler, the regular Muddler tie except for the wing, where they substituted marabou feathers, white, gray, yellow, brown or whatever. It proved a great fish-taker, too, wherever it was used.

Its success was typified by the experience of my friend Gene Anderegg of Ridgewood, New Jersey, who was Sales Manager for E. Leitz, Inc., of Rockleigh, New Jersey, distributors of Leica cameras and accessories. With photographer Bill Browning of Helena, Montana, Gene fished the Missouri River a few miles below the Houser Dam. Gene was using a #2 Gray Marabou Muddler. On his first cast he threw it across the current, let it drift dead for eight feet, then started it back. He had made two strips of the line when there was a big wave in back of the fly and he felt the hard, yanking tug of a heavy fish. He struck and saw his rod tip dip down almost to the surface. The fish hung there, thinking things over, then made a short run towards shore.

"Looks like it's a small one," Bill called to him. "Hurry him in and try for a bigger fish. They're in here."

At that moment the fish jumped and then Bill knew what Gene had already guessed. It was a tremendous brown! Bill changed his tune.

"Take it easy, Gene," he said. "Don't lose that one!"

The fish bolted as soon as he hit the water and raced out into the river 150 feet, swirled, did an oblique turn to the right, headed for the surface, and out he came again, a buster of a brownie. Then he seemed to just lie there, still, figuring the next move. It soon came. He began to swing his massive body from side to side, shaking his head, vibrating from stem to stern. Then he dove and rammed his head against a rock on the bottom. He went on with that kind of infighting until Gene's hands were so tired holding the rod grip that he had to flex them alternately, first one hand, then the other, to keep them supple.

Once he got the big trout within ten feet, but when he saw Gene he turned, throwing a splash of water, and tore away again in a burst of speed that left the angler dazed. He ended that long run with a going-away leap of four feet across the surface, then fell back in with a thud. And so it went on until at long last Gene managed to work that crooked-jawed trout in to about fifteen feet from shore, held his rod high and walked back from the river and skidded him up on the gravel bar. Then he reached down and got some of his aching fingers into the gills and carried the fish well back from the shore.

When he brought the trout into Dan Bailey's Fly Shop at Livingston, to be weighed and for entry on the Wall of Fame, it turned the scale at exactly ten pounds, a massive brownie that just couldn't resist the beckoning call of a Marabou Muddler.

Another famous variation of the Muddler is the Missoulian Spook, invented by Vince Hamlin, creator of "Alley Oop," and named for a character in the comic strip. Vince's tie has the head of white deer hair, clipped, the wing almost white, tied with feather of light turkey wing, underwing or throat, white calf underhair part of wing, barred teal breast feathers (just a streak). The body is white wool ribbed with silver tinsel, red tip; and the tail a small tip of white turkey feather. Because of its light coloring this tie is also known as the White Muddler. In the smaller sizes in particular, from #10 to #4, it proved a deadly fly for rainbows.

Gordie Dean of New York added his touch of color to the Muddler patterns when he came up with the Yellow Muddler, using yellow chicken feathers for the wings, to make a very successful tie.

Always ride a winner—so a few years later Dan Bailey and Red Monical combined the best features of another great western fly, the Spruce Fly, with the Muddler. The Spruce Fly was first made as a regulation wet fly, then became a streamer as tyers tried to produce a fly which would take bigger trout. Tied in two shades—the Light Spruce Fly and the Dark Spruce Fly, it took many fish, especially when used on a sinking line. Dan and Red, in their combination, called the Spuddler, kept the flattened bucktail head of the Muddler, but made the rest of the fly like the Spruce Fly streamer dressing. Like the Spruce Fly, it produced best on a sinking line, and its fame was immediate.

Dave Whitlock ties a whole series of variations on the Muddler, following the body pattern of the original but varying the wings, sometimes using calf tail, dyed, and coyote tail wings.

The Muddler is like the Adams dry fly—everywhere I have taken it in foreign lands, anglers and tyers have been enthusiastic about it. In Argentina, after seeing the American Muddler, José Navas, of the Norysur Club, Lago Melaquina, began tying the pattern and it was a great success. One day he had a visit from an Englishman who had been fishing Lago Futalaufquen in Patagonia with great success, using Muddlers he had purchased in the United States. As he could not remember the name of the fly, he called it after his daughter Maureen. When he saw Navis's Muddlers, he recognized the pattern and indicated his name for it, and Navis began to use that name. The result is that today in Argentina you can buy a fly called the Morin, which is the same original pattern as Don Gapen's Muddler.

In my own travels I have used the Muddler all over the United States and Canada, in England, Ireland, Scotland, Yugoslavia, Norway, Iceland, Germany, Austria, Finland, Chile, Argentina, Tasmania, Australia, New Zealand and South Africa, during the past twenty years, and I class it as the greatest streamer-bucktail fly of all time.

THE CAREY FLY

One of the best-known patterns in the northwestern part of the United States and Canada has also gone through a series of variations and all continue to be great fish takers. This is the Carey fly. Vince Allen of Seattle, Washington, says that according to well-known angler Rex Gerlach, the original Carey Special was tied by Col. Tom Carey and was called the Monkey-faced Louise. It was designed some time between 1925 and 1929, at the urging of Col. Carey's fishing partner, Dr. Lloyd A. Day of Quesnel, British Columbia, to represent the sedge larva rising to the surface, specifically in the Beaver Lake chain in the Kelowna area. Gerlach says he thinks this pattern was once called the Dredge. Credit for the name "Col. Carey Special" goes to Joe Spurrier, now deceased, who operated a sporting goods store in Kelowna.

It is interesting to note that whereas the original representation was that of a sedge, most anglers consider the Carey, particularly the darker hues, as representing the dragonfly and damselfly nymphs.

It is more or less agreed that the original Col. Carey Special was tied on a #6 hook with bunched tail of groundhog hairs, body of groundhog hairs wrapped clockwise around the hook, and ribbed with tying silk wrapped counterclockwise. The hackle has three Chinese pheasant rump feathers wound spider style.

Hank Reynolds, writing in the 1957 Cascade News Letter, of which he was editor at the time, said: "Col. Tom Carey himself was guilty of improved variations as witness the fact that he was constantly changing his own pattern. He tried the Special first with the same sort of pheasant rump feather he used as hackle, then on occasion he would use bucktail or moose mane, and quite often you would find them with bodies made of groundhog hair. The success of the pattern seems to depend on its general rough appearance and insect-like coloration with the no less important action of the rump feather hackle."

"In some areas of Canada the heavy, bushy dressing is still favored," Vince Sellen told me. But it has been my experience, and I think that of most fly fishermen who use the Careys, that the sparsely tied fly is much more effective. The Careys as a family are far from dainty. They look like a man with his hair mussed, but the trout like them, which is all that matters.

BIG BUCKTAILS
—THE BLONDES

When it comes to fishing extra-big water for extra-big fish, it often takes one of the big bucktails to produce the goods. Polly Rosborough, well-known fly tyer of Chiloquin, Oregon, tied a pattern many years ago and named it the Silver Garland. It has white marabou wings, with some blue on top, a silver-tinsel weighted body, and is tied on a 1/0 hook. The wings are about four inches long. The fly is a good match for the big silvery minnows found in the Williamson River in Oregon. I saw Polly take several fish over three pounds on it, then top them with a beautiful 6½-pounder that shook up the entire river with his fight. Polly used a weight-forward line, and he could throw that weighted fly seventy feet. Then he would let it sink and bring it back in fast, foot-long jerks. He told me that he had caught rainbows up to fifteen pounds in the Williamson, on his great Silver Garland.

In my own experience, no bucktail has been more successful than the blonde series of flies. In the late 1930s I used to fish for striped bass, rock, or rockfish, in Maryland and Virginia—in the Susquehanna River near Port Deposit in Maryland, and in the nearby shallows of the Chesapeake Bay. I fished for many years with the late Tom Loving of Baltimore, who caught many fish on a big white four-inch bucktail that he tied. In an effort to get a fly with more action, I tied a white bucktail four inches in overall length, but with two wings, one tied on top of the hook immediately in back of the eye, and another at the beginning of the bend of the hook. The body was wrapped with silver tinsel. This made a good long show of wings and when tied sparsely it looked alive in the water. When you retrieved it the front wing moved down on the shank, then when you hesitated or stopped the retrieve, the wing moved up again, and a continuation of this retrieve had the first wing working overtime. The tail of the second wing stayed in straight position. I tied it on a 1/0 hook, and caught a lot of stripers. Then I used yellow wings and that, too, did very well on stripers. At that time I simply called them white bucktails and yellow bucktails.

It was in Tierra del Fuego, Argentina, that the pattern won its name. Lew Klewer, Outdoor Editor of the *Toledo Blade*, and I were fishing the Rio Grande River for brown and rainbow trout and for the big sea-run brownies that came in there, descendants of a long-ago stocking of the European sea trout. One day when fishing was slow, I pulled out a white bucktail and threw it across current. It drifted a foot and wham! A fish piled into it so hard he startled me and I struck automatically. It was a ten-pound sea trout. Later that day I used both the white and yellow bucktail and had some of the best fishing for big trout I have ever had anywhere.

"What do you call those flies?" Lew asked me at dinner that night.

"Just bucktails," I said. "Yellow bucktail, or white bucktail—or double bucktail, if you like, because each has two wings."

"I have a better name," Lew said. "Why don't you call the white one the Platinum Blonde, and the yellow one the Honey Blonde?"

"Done!" I said.

From that start, a whole series of blondes developed. The Argentina Blonde, with a bit of blue placed on top of the white bucktail wing and tail, shows the colors of the Argentine flag. The Strawberry Blonde has the first wing red, the tail orange; the Black Blonde is all black, wing and tail; the Pink Blonde is pink all over. In all cases the body is wrapped with tinsel, usually silver, but occasionally gold, particularly on the Strawberry and Honey Blondes.

I've fished Argentine waters many times since then and always the blondes make the trout down there go for them hard. My biggest trout on a blonde was a 16½-pounder, a brownie that gave a terrific fight, a deep, long fish that was a past master of all the tricks of the clan.

That day I had worked down the pool without a strike; and then, near the tail, I made a cast. The 1/0 Platinum Blond dropped sixty feet out in the Chimehuin River, just four feet above the tail of the pool. Big browns have a habit of holding right where the water slides out to form the rapids. Many times they are right in front of a protruding rock. My aim was to bring the fly jumping across the nose of such a fish so he'd rush out and have a go at it. I retrieved fast, making foot-long pulls of line, keeping the fly swimming just an inch under the surface. It was a still day and the pool slick and it lulled me into a feeling of relaxation.

Right in the middle of a strip, the river blew up. Flying water blotted out everything, then I saw the crocodile-like jaws of the fish, the massive head, the long, thick body as he cleared the water and smashed down on the fly. I even noticed the big black spots along his sides. His tail looked as wide as a paddle blade. I didn't strike, I was incapable of thinking, let alone doing anything. But the roar of his take, the sight of the fish, the suddenness of it all, made me jump backwards a foot, causing a sort of built-in strike that drove the hook home.

The fish felt the hook, and took off across the pool, traveling a hundred feet like he was in training for the Olympics. He swapped ends out there and ran upstream a bit, then came out again, hidden this time by a wall of water that he put up. Then he went on charging up the pool, 250 feet this time, then across. And back again, towards my bank. That fight went on for forty minutes and through five more jumps. I finally pulled him up on the sloping shore, stuck my fingers under his gill covers, lifted, and carried him back from the river. This 16½-pounder was a powerful big brown trout and he proved the theory that the big ones like a mouthful. And to a fly man, a big mouthful means a streamer or bucktail.

Index